Published by
Black Dog & Leventhal Publishers, Inc.
151 West 19th Street
New York, NY 10011

Distributed by
Workman Publishing Company
225 Varick Street
New York, NY 10014

Manufactured in China

Book and cover design by Kevin Ullrich
Interior layout by Sheila Hart Design, Inc.

Cover photographs, left to right, ©Rick Giase/epa/Corbis;
©Bettmann/Corbis; ©Brian Jenkins/Icon SMI/Corbis

Illustrations and diagrams ©Ken Krug

ISBN-13: 978-1-57912-788-6

h g f e d c b a

Library of Congress Cataloging-in-Publication Data available upon request.

SPLITTERS, SQUEEZES, and STEALS

The Inside Story of Baseball's Greatest Techniques, Strategies, and Plays

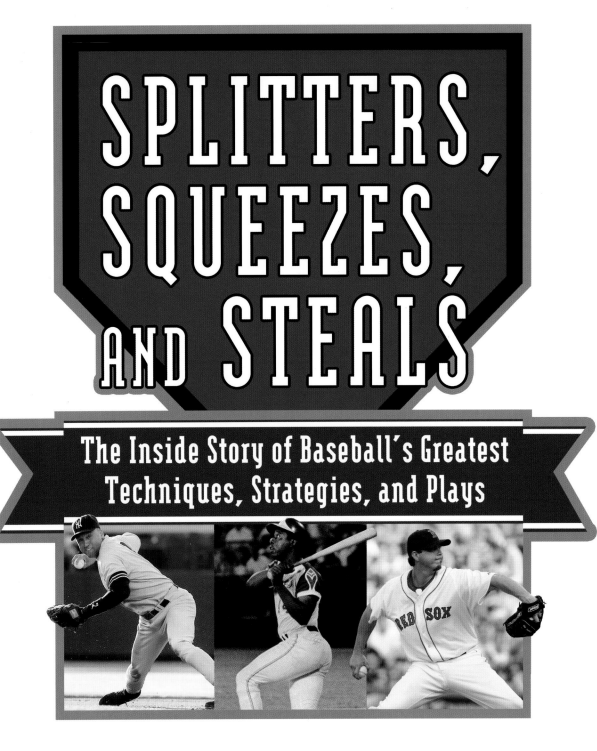

DEREK GENTILE

BLACK DOG
& LEVENTHAL
PUBLISHERS
NEW YORK

Introduction. 6

Part One: Pitching

The Fastball 10

The Curveball 22

The Slider 32

The Changeup 38

The Forkball 44

The Split-Finger Fastball 50

The Knockdown Pitch (aka The Brushback) . . 56

The Knuckleball 64

The Spitball 70

Relief Pitching 80

Part Two: Hitting

Bunting 90

The Hit and Run 98

The Home Run 104

Hitting .400 118

Part Three: Baserunning

Stealing Bases 126

Crashing into Players 136

The Home-Run Trot 140

Part Four: Fielding

The 6-4-3 Double Play 148

The Stretch 154

Catching the Ball in the Outfield 158

Part Five: Tricks of the Trade

The Hidden-Ball Trick 166

Intentionally Getting Hit By a Ball 170

The Corked Bat 180

Steroids and the Steroid Era 186

Part Six: Umpires and Managers

Umpires 196

Leaders and Managers (and Captains) 204

Part Seven: Equipment

Bats 214

Baseballs 218

Gloves 220

Catchers' Equipment 222

Part Eight: Big-League Ballfields and Stadiums

The Evolution of the Ballfield 228

The Home-Field Advantage 236

Hot Dogs and Other Refreshments 242

Bibliography. 247

Index 248

Photography Credits 256

No one can say for sure when the first game of baseball was actually played in the United States. There is a document in Pittsfield, Massachusetts, that goes all the way back to 1791, setting forth an ordinance forbidding the playing of "base ball" too close to the windows of town hall. But, frankly, even the good people of Pittsfield don't believe the game was first played there.

We have other documents that place the first game in central New York, or in New York City itself, but they are equally inconclusive.

It's fair to say, though, that whenever and wherever baseball started, it was a long time ago. And, because of that, it's hard to say exactly how the game evolved. We think that a young man named Candy Cummings, in Ware, Massachusetts (a long, horseless-carriage drive east of Pittsfield), invented the curveball sometime in the 1870s. But there have been other claimants, notably Fred Goldsmith, who insisted until his dying day that he figured out how to make balls swerve before Cummings had.

We've heard that Eddie Cicotte of the Chicago White Sox probably invented the knuckleball when he was toiling in the minor leagues. But there are other players who swear that the pitch was the brainchild of Nap Rucker, a minor league teammate of Cicotte's.

This book is an attempt to brush away a few of the historical cobwebs. The conundrum is that the farther back one goes into history, the more convoluted that history becomes. Sportwriters speculate, ballplayers try to recall and, in a lot of cases, the mists of time seem to get thicker, not thinner.

But it's fun to search. One of the great aspects of baseball is that there is a story behind everything. I've often thought about the tale behind Cummings's alleged innovation. The story has him learning to throw a curve by tossing seashells and watching them twist in the wind. The thing is, the town he grew up in, Ware, is in western Massachusetts. Where did he get the seashells? (The explanation that makes most sense is that the shells were clamshells, which were available at any fish market in Massachusetts.) This legend makes me wish I could have talked to Cummings—really sat down with him in 1896 or so—to get the straight dope, as they say. But I can't.

Anyway, these are some of the tales. I've tried to present the ones that seem most plausible, and in the case (and there were several) where there are one or two or three stories about how a pitch or a technique or a piece of equipment was inaugurated, I went back and did more research. Since I wasn't alive in the 19th century, when a lot of this stuff originated, I referred to books, magazine and news articles and old interviews. I've included a bibliography in this book to give credit where credit is due.

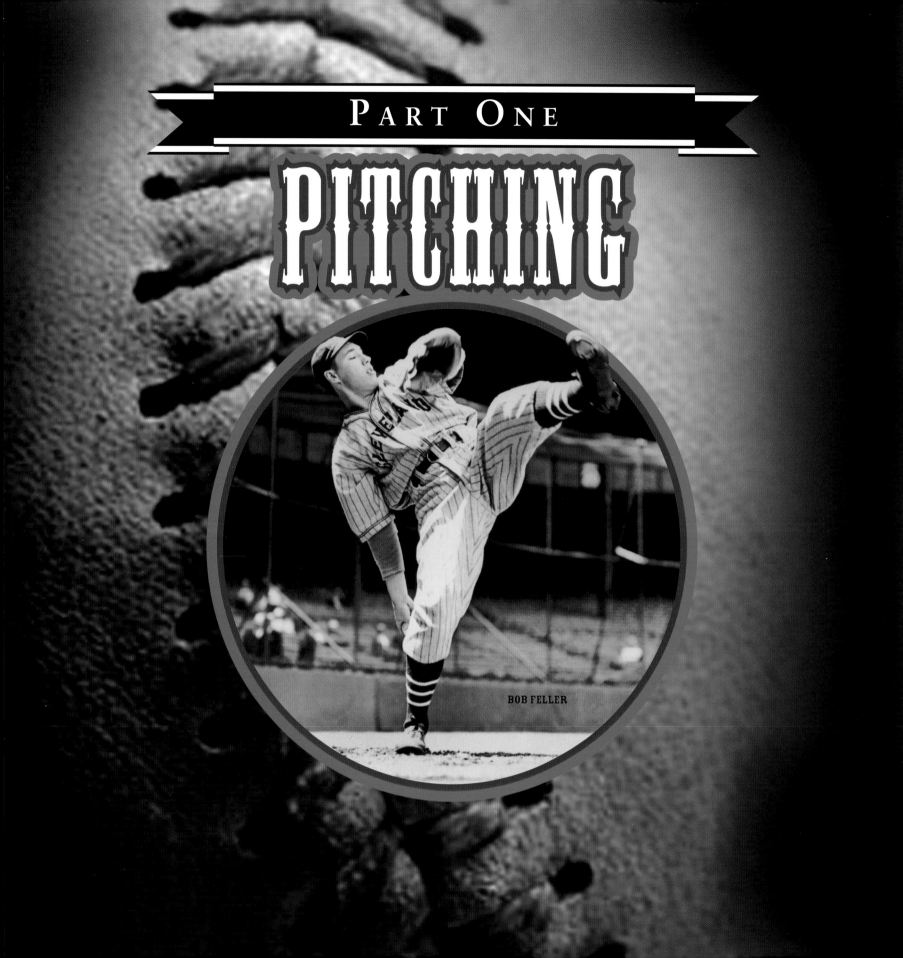

PART ONE

PITCHING

BOB FELLER

JOSH BECKETT

THE FASTBALL

In the early days of baseball, the rules of the game encouraged interaction between the hitter and the fielders. The pitcher was merely the individual who delivered the ball, as best he could, to the batter. In fact, the batter even had the discretion to request low pitches or high pitches. As Bill James and Rob Neyer pointed out in their book *The Neyer/James Guide to Pitchers*, "the pitcher was not supposed to upset the apple cart by striking people out or walking them." Pitches were executed with an underhand motion. The pitcher's elbows and wrists were kept stiff, and his main objective was to allow the batter to hit the ball. James points out that, in fact, there was considerable legislation that discouraged pitchers from throwing hard.

In the first half of the 1880s, the rules gradually began to change, allowing pitchers to throw overhand, which in turn enabled them to throw harder and with more control of the ball.

There is no way to determine who the first fastball pitcher was. When the rules began to relax between 1882 and 1885, a number of pitchers immediately began experimenting with fast pitches. The most successful of that early era was Larry Corcoran of the Chicago White Stockings.

"Larry Corcoran," writes Chicago star Adrian "Cap" Anson in his autobiography, "was at that time in the zenith of his glory as a twirler. He was a very little fellow, with an unusual amount of speed, and the endurance of an Indian pony."

The diminutive (5'4", 120 lbs.) Corcoran pitched for Chicago from 1880 to 1885. He threw three no-hitters in that span and won 175 games for the White Stockings. He was probably the best athlete on the team and was considered, for example, to be a very good boxer. He once knocked out a teammate following a clubhouse dispute, much to Anson's surprise.

But as good as Corcoran was, he burned out his arm after only four years. When pitchers were throwing underhand, the delivery was not particularly hard on a throwing arm; when the new rules came into use, pitchers like Corcoran found that throwing 100 to 130 overhand pitches per game on only two to three days' rest (or less) had a debilitating effect. The situation was exacerbated when throwing fastballs. Many of those early pitch-

CY YOUNG

ers had short careers, as their arms began deteriorating after only a few seasons.

But not everyone suffered. In 1890, a big kid from Ohio debuted with the National League's Cleveland Spiders. At six-feet-two and 210 pounds, Denton True "Cy" Young was probably the biggest pitcher in the majors at that time. His nickname was derived from his early days as a pitcher in Ohio. One of his catchers remarked that Young pitched "like a cyclone," and the name stuck.

Young's best pitch was a fastball, but, more than any other pitcher of his era, he knew how to pace himself. With the game on the line, Young bore down. But if Cleveland had a lead, or was far behind, Young threw more off-speed stuff.

Young was one of several old-timers who began his pitching career throwing underhand from a mound 50 feet from home plate and ended it throwing overhand from a mound 60 feet 6 inches away.

As a result, he mastered a number of deliveries. Young could throw fastballs at varying speeds and had an excellent changeup and a good curve. A batter facing Young might well see a different delivery angle during every one of his at-bats.

Fastball pitchers grew more proficient as the 20th century dawned. Walter "The Big Train" Johnson was perhaps the first pitcher to throw fastballs almost exclusively throughout his long career.

Johnson, according to many of his contemporaries, threw fastballs about 96 percent of the time. He would work in a changeup now and then, and later in his career, he experimented with a curveball. But for Walter it was mostly fastballs.

He was, many players believed, built for the job. He had long, muscular arms, and when he pitched the ball, it came whipping out of his hand in a sharp sidearm motion.

A Johnson fastball seemed to increase in velocity as it neared the plate, and Johnson at his peak was difficult to hit indeed.

Roger "The Rocket" Clemens remains the only pitcher to strike out 20 or more batters in a single game. And, he did it twice. With a fastball that has been clocked in the high 90s, he was one of the most intimidating pitchers of his era.

WALTER JOHNSON

"If the league had scheduled night baseball when The Train was pitching," wrote longtime *Washington Post* columnist Shirley Povich, "he would have had a dozen no-hitters in his career, at least."

As the century moved into its third and fourth decade, pitchers began to experiment more as they came through the minors. It was not enough to be fast, and pitchers began trying to make their speedballs dip or rise. Leroy "Satchel" Paige, who toiled in the Negro Leagues for three decades before playing in the major leagues in the 1950s, had a fastball that bounced around like a Ping-Pong ball in the wind.

Men like Bob Feller and Lefty Grove also threw what began to be called "live" fastballs by gripping the ball either across the seams or with the seams. By the 1960s, pitchers like Larry Dierker and Ferguson Jenkins could move their fastballs up and down the plate, a process that was refined in later decades.

Richard "Goose" Gossage, an overpowering relief pitcher in the late 1970s and early 1980s, had a fastball that seemed to tail away from hitters just

GOOSE GOSSAGE

as it reached the plate. It was around this time that the fastball family began to branch out.

Gossage threw what we now call a "cut fastball"—that's a fastball thrown without snapping the wrist, but which breaks away either right or left as it nears the batter. The speed of the pitch doesn't vary; where it ends up when it gets to the batter is what matters.

Gossage's cut fastball was incredibly effective for him for several seasons. He may not have been the first pitcher to throw it, but again, he was the finest practitioner. A "cutter," as it's called now, is an effective pitch because of the lateness of its break. Since the 1980s, a number of pitchers have thrown the cut fastball.

The most effective cutter for the longest time was probably Roger Clemens's (Red Sox, Blue Jays, Yankees, Astros, 1984–2007). Clemens, after he left the Red Sox in 1996, developed his cutter with the Toronto Blue Jays. He refined it during his years with the Yankees, to the point where he would throw the pitch almost exclusively, perhaps firing a changeup or a curveball when necessary.

STEVE DALKOWSKI'S FAST FASTBALL

The Baltimore Orioles signed Steve Dalkowski in 1957, at age 21. He spent nine years in the Orioles farm system but never made a major-league roster.

His fastball was unofficially timed by a scout at 105 miles per hour, but that number kept inflating until the Orioles tried to settle the matter once and for all. They sent Dalkowski, in the spring of 1958, to a Richmond, Virginia, laboratory to clock his fastball with a special photoelectric calculator. A few years earlier, the same machine had clocked the Indians' Bob Feller at 98.8 miles per hour.

The one disadvantage to the machine was the pitcher could not throw from a mound; he threw from a flat surface, which scientists estimated cost Feller 3 to 5 miles per hour during his test.

Dalkowski's fastest pitch was 93.6 miles per hour, a figure that Orioles officials believe was mitigated by the lack of a mound and the fact that Dalkowski had pitched the night before. In addition, he had to throw 40 pitches before the machine was calibrated. He later told an Orioles coach that following the workout, he was exhausted.

Dalkowski was not physically imposing. He was five-feet-eight and wore thick glasses. His wildness was legendary. He once threw 120 pitches in 2 innings before being taken out of the game. In fact, Nuke LaLoosh, the pitcher in the movie *Bull Durham*, was reportedly based on Dalkowski.

After nine frustrating years, the Orioles released Dalkowski.

This category presents a problem. The pitcher who may have thrown the fastest pitch in baseball history was a fellow named Steve Dalkowski (see page 13) who never pitched in the majors because he couldn't control the pitch. Having a good fastball and throwing fast are, essentially, two different things. So this list is of the best fastball pitchers ever in the big leagues.

Cy
YOUNG

Spiders, Cardinals, Red Sox, Indians, 1890–1911

Young's nickname, "Cy," was conferred on him because his pitches were reportedly as fast as a cyclone. Probably not, but Young threw hard, and he threw hard for many years.

Walter
JOHNSON

Senators, 1907–27

Johnson, nicknamed "The Big Train," had extremely long arms, and his throwing motion reminded some opposing players of a bullwhip.

Bob
FELLER

Indians, 1936–56

Just edging out Lefty Grove, Feller was a 20-game winner 6 times for the Tribe and led the league in strikeouts 7 times.

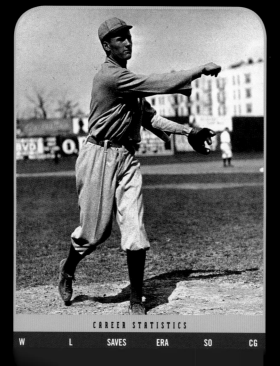

CAREER STATISTICS					
W	L	SAVES	ERA	SO	CG

CAREER STATISTICS					
W	L	SAVES	ERA	SO	CG

CAREER STATISTICS					
W	L	SAVES	ERA	SO	CG

Tom House, a former big-league pitcher who was a pitching coach for the Rangers when Ryan pitched in Texas, conceded that some day there might be a pitcher who throws harder than Ryan. But, he said, "no one will throw harder for longer."

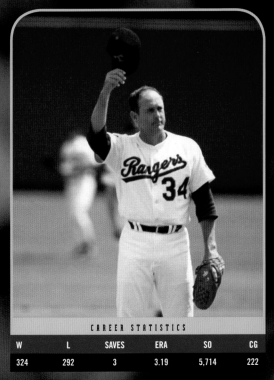

CAREER STATISTICS					
W	L	SAVES	ERA	SO	CG
324	292	3	3.19	5,714	222

By the Numbers Pitching Speed

Since the 2000 season, a total of 15 pitchers have thrown 101 miles per hour or faster. They appear in the chart to the right. The issue is, why in the last several years have so many pitchers cracked 100 miles per hour? Are pitchers in the 21st century so much faster than their 19th- and 20th-century cohorts?

Certainly, today's pitchers have better training habits and a better knowledge of nutrition, and radar guns that measure these players appear to be more accurate. But ESPN analyst and baseball Hall of Famer Joe Morgan believes that modern radar guns, which are now connected to scoreboards in most stadiums, are not particularly accurate.

"I think the readings are inflated, to pump up the crowds," Morgan said a few years ago. "I don't think pitchers are throwing 100-mile-an-hour sliders."

When that magic "100" pops up on the scoreboard, crowds do indeed cheer. But another explanation, alas, is the use of performance-enhancing drugs. Of the 32 pitchers on this list, several have been accused of steroid abuse. At this point, it may be difficult to separate the users from the clean players. So, take this list for what it's worth.

(Note: These numbers, taken from *The Baseball Almanac*, reflect the fastest pitch the player has thrown. He may have thrown more than one pitch at 101-plus miles per hour.)

*Zumaya is tied with Atlanta's Mark Wohlers for the fastest pitch ever thrown in the majors in at least the last 15 years. Wohlers's pitch happened in a 1993 spring-training exhibition game when he was playing for the Braves.

103.0 mph

JOEL ZUMAYA*

Tigers
7/4/2006

102.0

ARMANDO BENITEZ
Marlins
5/24/2002

BOBBY JENKS
White Sox
8/27/2005

RANDY JOHNSON
Mariners
7/9/2004

MATT LINDSTROM
Marlins
5/16/2007

JUSTIN VERLANDER
Tigers
6/12/2007

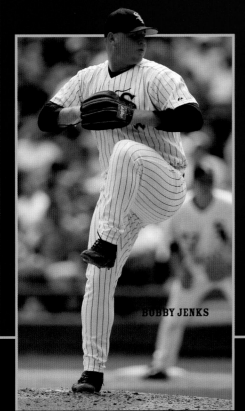

BOBBY JENKS

101.0

A.J. BURNETT
Marlins
5/31/2005

JOBA CHAMBERLAIN
Yankees
8/24/2007

JONATHAN BROXTON
Dodgers
6/26/2007

KYLE FARNSWORTH
Cubs
5/26/2004

ERIC GAGNE
Dodgers
4/16/2004

GUILLERMO MOTA
Dodgers
7/24/2002

BILLY WAGNER
Astros
7/30/2003

SETH MCCLUNG
Brewers
8/21/2007

TONY PENA
Diamondbacks
6/7/2007

ROB DIBBLE
Reds
6/8/92

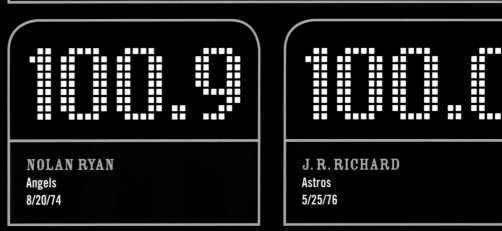

JOBA CHAMBERLAIN

100.9

NOLAN RYAN
Angels
8/20/74

100.0

J.R. RICHARD
Astros
5/25/76

HOW IT'S DONE
The Four-Seam Fastball

It's said that throwing a fastball is not a skill; it's a gift. That may well be true, as most fastball pitchers are generally fastballers from their earliest days of playing baseball. "From the first time I held a ball," recalled Hall of Famer Walter Johnson in a 1925 *Washington Post* story, "it settled in the palm of my right hand as though it belonged there. And when I threw it, ball, hand and wrist, arm and shoulder and back all seemed to work together."

As such, technique is less important than arm strength. One does not, for example, become a fastball pitcher after years of practice. One just *is* a fastball pitcher.

Pitchers grip the ball across the seams (a four-seam fastball) to make the ball rise or with the seams (a two-seam fastball) to make the ball dip.

"The blazer (another term for fastball)," wrote Arthur Daley of the *New York Times* in 1955, "is God-given. A pitcher can be taught curves, sliders and fancy [pitches], but the fastball cannot be acquired."

Maybe. But there is the story Hall of Fame basketball coach Jack Ramsey tells of fastball advice he got during his days as an undergrad at St. Joseph's University in Philadelphia. Ramsey, in addition to playing basketball, fancied himself something of a college baseball player as well. So during his freshman year, he tried out for St. Joe's squad. Ramsey took a turn on the mound, firing what he thought were several pretty hopping fastballs. St. Joe's coach at the time was Lemuel "Pep" Young, the old Pittsburgh second baseman.

"I reared back and threw as hard as I could," recalled Ramsey in David Halberstam's *The Breaks of the Game*. "I mean, I thought I threw smoke. I finished the workout and I thought I did pretty good." Ramsey looked at Young expectantly. "I asked him what he thought, and he stood there looking at me a long time, and he said, 'Put more ass into it, kid.' That was my career as a baseball player."

LEFT: Red Sox pitcher Josh Beckett's fastball is one of the best in the majors. It is the principal reason Beckett is the ace of the Red Sox squad, leading them to the World Championship in 2007. ABOVE: It's actually difficult to determine what aspect of Randy Johnson is more intimidating: his height (6'10"), or his 97-plus-mile-per-hour heater. Even as he enters his 40s, the "Big Unit" is still a force in the majors.

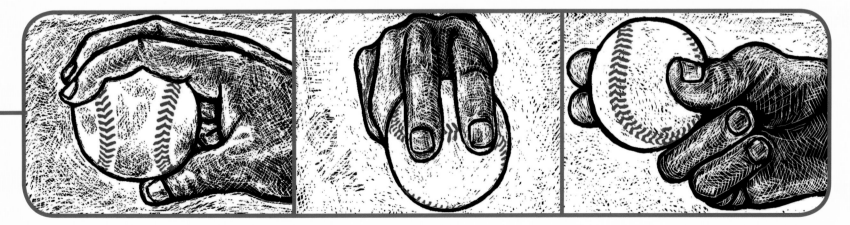

THE SINKER

CHIEN-MING WANG

DEREK LOWE

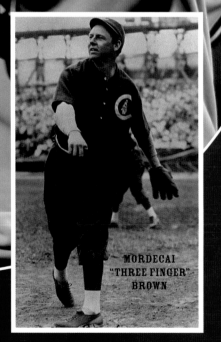
MORDECAI "THREE FINGER" BROWN

There are some managers and pitchers who believe the sinkerball is a pitch in and of itself; there are others who believe it is part of the fastball family, which includes the cut fastball.

The latter seems more reasonable. The sinkerball is thrown by gripping the baseball along the two seams and throwing it like a fastball. This grip causes it to sink.

The principal difference between a two-seam fastball and a sinker is that a sinkerball pitcher has refined the pitch a bit more, making the sink a little more apparent to the batter. He also uses it almost to the exclusion of other pitches.

Sinkerballs tend to drop lower in the strike zone than regular fastballs, and, as such, generate a lot of ground balls. (That is, of course, if a pitcher is throwing it right.)

Mordecai "Three Finger" Brown was probably the first pitcher to throw what is now called a sinkerball, but Curt Simmons (Phillies, Cardinals, Reds, Cubs, Angels, 1947–67) was the first pitcher to be known for his sinkerball.

The players best known for throwing good sinkerballs are the Diamondbacks' Brandon Webb, the Athletics' Tim Hudson, the Dodgers' Derek Lowe and the Yankees' Chien-Ming Wang.

SUBMARINE DELIVERIES

Until 1872, pitchers were required to deliver the ball underhand. When that restriction was removed, many hurlers of that era began working on overhand deliveries, for the most part because they believed they could generate more speed overhand.

Still, by the 1890s, a small number of pitchers emerged who began to throw underhand again.

Al "The Curveless Wonder" Orth (Phillies, Senators, Yankees, 1895–1909) won 202 games without tossing a curveball. What he did throw was a nasty submarine fastball. Orth discovered that, while the submarine fastball did not have as much velocity as regular fastballs, the pitch, which rose up through the strike zone, was tougher for many hitters to find.

The submarine delivery had its best era from the 1900s to the 1920s, when hurlers such as Deacon Phillipe, Jack Warhop and Carl Mays all enjoyed success. In the modern era, Dan Quisenberry (Royals, Cardinals, Giants, 1979–90) and Kent Tekulve (Pirates, Phillies, Reds, 1974–89) have been extremely effective as relief pitchers. Quisenberry saved 244 games over his career, and Tekulve saved 184.

One of the better submariners was Elden Auker (Tigers, Red Sox, Browns, 1933–42), who won 130 games in his 10-year career. In 2000, at the age of 90, Auker wrote *Sleeper Cars and Flannel Uniforms*, a memoir of his career as a Depression-era pitcher. Auker wrote that while some players, like the Yankees' Lou Gehrig, were low-ball hitters and thus feasted on his submarine ball, "I had good success with a guy like [Joe] DiMaggio, who didn't like my style of pitching."

KENT TEKULVE

DAN QUISENBERRY

THE CURVEBALL

The origin of the curveball is one of today's most hotly contested discussions among baseball historians. The man who is most often credited with its invention is a smallish (5'9", 120 lbs.) pitcher named Arthur "Candy" Cummings.

Cummings (Hartford [NA], Baltimore [NA], Philadelphia [NA], Cincinnati [NA] 1872–77) was born in

1848 in Ware, Massachusetts, an industrial town in the western part of the state. According to an interview he gave in 1908, Cummings, who was 15 years old at the time, and a few friends were fooling around with clam shells in his yard. The other boys were watching the shells curve as Cummings threw them.

"In the summer of 1863, a number of boys and myself were amusing ourselves by throwing clam shells and watching them sail along through the air, some to the right, some to the left," wrote Cummings in the September 1908 issue of *Baseball Magazine*. Cummings thought there might be a way to make a baseball take a similar path: "I thought it would be a good joke on the other boys if I could make a baseball sail the same way."

He worked at making a ball curve for about four years before he tried it in a game. "I don't know what made me stick at it," he wrote. "The great wonder to me now is that I did not give up in disgust. My attempts were a standing joke among my friends."

In 1866, Cummings began pitching for the Excelsior Juniors of Brooklyn, and it was with this team that he tried out his curve, finally, in 1867. He pitched 21 games for Excelsior in 1866 and 1867. There is no record of his success or failure, but in the article, Cummings hints that it was mixed, mostly because, as he admitted, "I still couldn't make the ball curve when I wished."

Initially, Cummings was afraid to tell anyone about his discovery, and didn't even clue in his catchers. "I was jealous of it, and did not want anyone to crib it," he told the *Sporting News*. This was the era when catchers stood well back from the plate, and thus Cummings rarely crossed up his teammate when he did throw a curveball.

> ❝THE GREAT WONDER TO ME NOW IS THAT I DID NOT GIVE UP IN DISGUST. MY ATTEMPTS WERE A STANDING JOKE AMONG MY FRIENDS.❞
>
> ARTHUR "CANDY" CUMMINGS

ARTHUR "CANDY" CUMMINGS

THE FADEAWAY

CARL HUBBELL

CHRISTY MATHEWSON

The fadeaway pitch is a curveball that breaks in on a right-handed batter. It is now known as a screwball. By either name, it's a tough pitch to throw, as the pitcher executes it the same way as a curveball but gives the ball a final twist with his wrist to make it curve more sideways than up and down.

These kinds of muscular acrobatics make a screwball very hard on the pitching arm. The pitch itself probably originated in the 19th century, but no one really used it as much or as successfully as Christy Mathewson.

But even Mathewson realized the wear and tear the pitch caused his pitching arm, and he used it sparingly. In his book, *Pitching in a Pinch*, Mathewson conceded that "the threat of the pitch" was almost as effective as the pitch itself.

The other pitcher of note who used the fadeaway to great effect was Giants hurler Carl Hubbell (Giants, 1925–43). Hubbell won 20 or more games five years in a row with New York, from 1933 to 1937, and led the Giants to three World Series. He also won two MVP awards in that span. He is best

known, of course, for striking out American League sluggers Babe Ruth, Lou Gehrig and Jimmie Foxx in the 1934 All-Star Game.

Unlike Mathewson, Hubbell threw mostly screwballs throughout his career. At the end of his career, his arm was twisted almost completely around from throwing the pitch.

The Best of the Best

THE CURVEBALL

There are not a lot of great curveball pitchers whose strength is specifically that one pitch. The curveball is best set up by fastballs or changeups or sliders. Here are a few pitchers that used the curve as their main weapon.

Bert BLYLEVEN

Twins, Rangers, Pirates, Indians, Angels
1970–92

This native of the Netherlands has, by acclaim, the best curveball of the modern era. Blyleven was known for having outstanding control throughout his big-league career, walking fewer than three batters per nine innings.

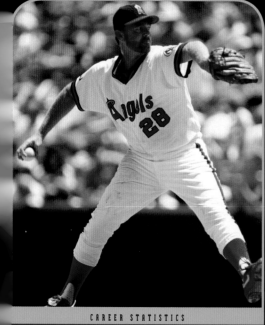

CAREER STATISTICS					
W	L	SAVES	ERA	SO	CG

Virgil "Fire" TRUCKS

Tigers, Cardinals, White Sox, Royals, Yankees
1941–58

Another outstanding control pitcher who tossed two no-hitters in one season in 1952, Trucks also fired four no-hitters in the minor leagues.

CAREER STATISTICS					
W	L	SAVES	ERA	SO	CG

Camilo "Little Potato" PASCUAL

Senators, Twins, Reds, Dodgers, Indians
1954–71

Pascual was recommended to the Senators in 1954 by his big brother, Carlos "Big Potato" Pascual. Camilo was a fastball pitcher who had trouble with his control for several years. But he developed a nasty sidearm curve in 1959, and his career took off. He helped the Twins to the 1965 American League pennant.

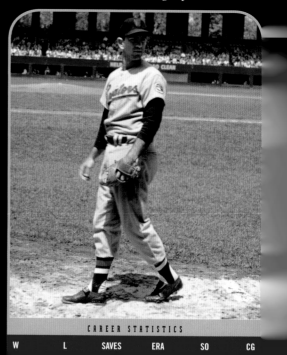

CAREER STATISTICS					
W	L	SAVES	ERA	SO	CG

Sal "The Barber"
MAGLIE

Giants, Indians, Dodgers, Yankees, Browns
1945, 1950–58

Maglie was known as "The Barber" for his practice of throwing close to batters' chins, thus "shaving" them with the baseball. "When I'm pitching," he once said, "that plate is mine."

Dwight "Doc"
GOODEN

Mets, Yankees, Indians, Astros, Marlins
1984–94, 1996–2000

Gooden is best known for his blistering fastball, but early in his major-league career, he developed a sharp curveball that made him almost unhittable in the late 1980s.

CAREER STATISTICS					
W	L	SAVES	ERA	SO	CG
194	112	3	3.51	2,293	68

CAREER STATISTICS					
W	L	SAVES	ERA	SO	CG
119	62	14	3.15	862	93

Here are two guys who had an unfair advantage when it came to throwing the curveball.

Mordecai Centennial "Three Finger" BROWN

Cardinals, Cubs, Whales
1903–16

Brown mangled his right pitching hand in a farming accident as a child. When he was coming up through the minor leagues, most executives figured that, sooner or later, the mangled hand would be a liability. Not so. Brown learned to spin the ball all sorts of ways with his three and a half fingers, and developed a nasty curve that served him well.

CAREER STATISTICS					
W	L	SAVES	ERA	SO	CG
239	130	49	2.06	1,375	271

Urban SHOCKER

Browns, Yankees
1916–28

Born with a permanent crook on the end of his throwing hand's pinkie finger, Shocker used it to his advantage, developing a variety of curveballs by using the crooked finger as a guide for the pitch. He was known mostly for his spitball, but the crooked finger helped him more when he threw the curve.

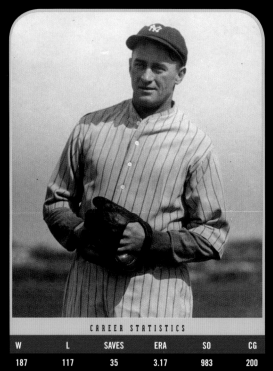

CAREER STATISTICS					
W	L	SAVES	ERA	SO	CG
187	117	35	3.17	983	200

Cummings played for semipro teams for several years, and eventually, in 1868, he began talking about his new pitch.

"Cummings didn't send up there a roundhouse curve," wrote reporter Harold Burr, "but rather a sharp-breaking hook that barely eluded the lashing bats of those grandpas of the game."

Cummings signed on with the Hartford Dark Blues of the National Association in 1871. He started 55 games in 1872, pitching 497 innings and going 33–20. He played in Baltimore in 1873 and Philadelphia in 1874 before returning to Hartford in 1875. Hartford manager Bob Ferguson loved to watch him pitch. "God never gave him any size, but he's the candy," said Ferguson, conferring on Cummings his nickname.

Cummings's claim to being the first curve baller has been disputed by pitcher Fred Goldsmith (Troy [NA], White Stockings, 1879–84). Goldsmith swears he gave a demonstration of the curve in 1872 at the Capitoline Grounds in Brooklyn. The story Goldsmith tells is that he planted three wooden stakes, each about 8 feet tall, along a parallel line 60 feet from a catcher. Goldsmith, who was right-handed, released the ball to the left of the first stake. The ball then carried around to the right of the middle stake and wound up in the catcher's mitt, located to the left of the third stake.

PHONNEY MARTIN

HOW DOES THE CURVEBALL CURVE?

For an awful lot of years, baseball experts argued whether the curveball actually curved or whether it was just an optical illusion. The discussion was finally adjudicated with the advent of slow-motion photography. Photo essays in many magazines showed the balls actually curved as they reached the plate. In 1952, *Look* magazine published a photo essay that showed a ball curving in midair.

Well, great. But how the heck does it work? Here are the basics: when a pitcher throws a fastball, he throws it with backspin, which keeps the ball relatively stable, aerodynamically speaking. The ball travels on a fairly straight line to the plate. But when a pitcher throws a curveball, he grips the baseball in such a way that he throws it with "frontspin," the opposite direction of backspin.

A ball thrown with backspin, according to *The Physics of Baseball*, creates a high-pressure air pocket in front and below it that keeps the ball stable, at least for the distance it must travel to the plate. In addition, the seams of the ball augment the baseball's ability to churn the air in front of it.

A ball thrown with frontspin creates the same kind of air pocket, only the pocket sits atop the baseball. So a pitcher throws the ball slightly up, and the combination of the pressure in the air pocket and gravity will pull it down. (This is called the 12-to-6 curve.) The degree to which the ball drops depends on how much frontspin a pitcher puts on the ball. In the major leagues, the drop can be as much as 20 inches.

The curveball also drops at different parts of its trajectory according to how it is thrown. Thus, all curveball pitchers differ in where exactly their ball will drop on its way home, making each curveball somewhat unique. Which is why, according to Hall of Fame manager Joe McCarthy, "there are no great curveball hitters."

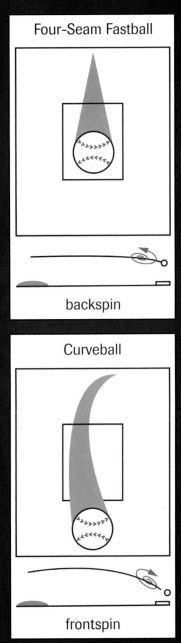

Four-Seam Fastball

backspin

Curveball

frontspin

HERB SCORE

There are apparently no contemporary accounts of such an exhibition, and Bobby Mathews (Keokuk [NA], Baltimore [NA], Hartford [NA], Giants, Reds, Grays, Braves, Athletics, 1871–87), a contemporary of Cummings and Goldsmith and another early curveball expert, gave Cummings the credit for being the first. Still, Goldsmith, on his deathbed, reportedly clutched a newspaper interview he gave years before in which he claimed the curve was his invention.

The earliest curves, thrown by Cummings, Mathews and the wonderfully named Phonney Martin (Troy [NA], Elizabeth [NA], 1872–73), were delivered underhand, as was required by the rules of the time. But by the mid-1880s, these rules were relaxing, and pitchers began experimenting with overhand and sidearm deliveries. In addition to a good fastball, Chicago White Stockings pitcher Larry Corcoran also possessed a sharp-breaking curve that some newsmen called "The Chicago Snake Ball." Will White (Braves, Reds, Detroit Wolverines, Cincinnati Red Stockings, 1877–86) was also said to have mastered the overhand curve by the end of his career.

The curveball soon became a kind of demarcation line for major-league hitters. The great athlete Jim Thorpe played for the New York Giants, Cincinnati Reds and Boston Braves from 1913 to 1919 but was never a regular with any of those squads because he had so much trouble hitting a curveball. The consensus early in the 20th century was that to be a great player, or even a good player, one had to be able to hit the curve with some consistency.

As the 20th century unfolded, curveball pitchers began honing their craft. Bob Feller started his career as a master of the fastball, but as he got older, he worked on his curve. In the last years of his career, the curveball was a better pitch for him than the fastball. Another Cleveland player, Herb Score, broke into the league in 1955 with a good fastball and a great curveball.

The 1950s saw a host of good curveballers, including Camilo Pascual, Sal Maglie and Sandy Koufax. Koufax was better known for his fastball, but was a great curveball ace as well.

A popular nickname for a curve is "the deuce," because it is usually the second pitch in a player's repertoire, behind the fastball. Other nicknames include "the hammer," "the hook," "the bender," "Uncle Charley" and pitcher Dennis Eckersley's famed name for the pitch, "the yakker."

The best curveball pitcher of the modern era was Bert Blyleven, who played for 22 seasons. Blyleven had an effortless motion and excellent control that enabled him to brush the outside of the plate with his curve. Another great curveballer of the latter part of the century was Dwight "Doc" Gooden, whose curve was so sharp that hitters often preferred he throw them his blazing fastball.

SANDY KOUFAX

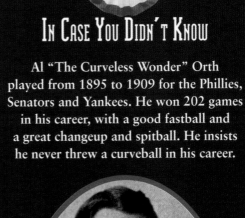

In Case You Didn't Know

Al "The Curveless Wonder" Orth played from 1895 to 1909 for the Phillies, Senators and Yankees. He won 202 games in his career, with a good fastball and a great changeup and spitball. He insists he never threw a curveball in his career.

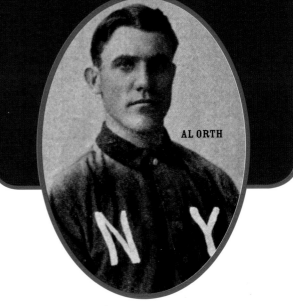

AL ORTH

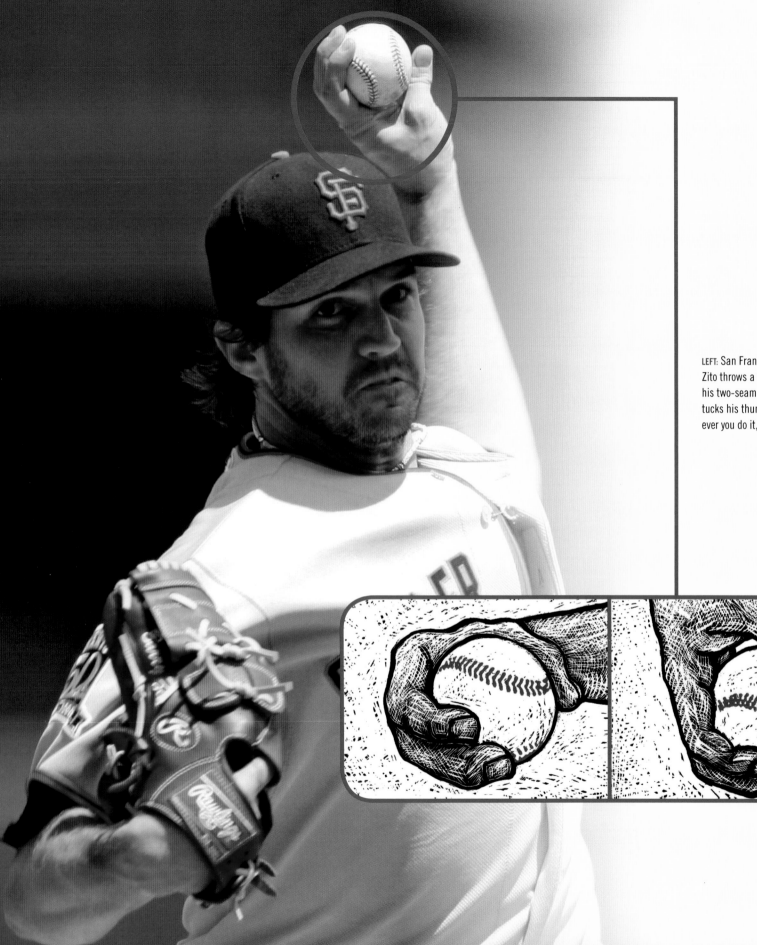

San Francisco pitcher Barry Zito throws a curve like he throws his two-seam fastball, except he tucks his thumb on the seam. However you do it, practice is the key.

HOW IT'S DONE
The Curveball

If the fastball is God-given, the curveball is coach-given. There are several techniques. Grip the ball with your index and middle fingers, with your middle finger on the inside of the ball's seam. Your ring and pinkie fingers should rest under the ball, with only your ring finger touching the ball. The side of your thumb—not the pad—should rest directly on top of the seam. When throwing the ball, your arm motion should be the same as that of pulling down a window shade. For right-handers, your palm should face first base as you release the ball; for lefties, it's third base.

There are variations: for instance, the throwing motion can be more like a karate chop to the ground, except the pitcher releases the ball midway through the "chop."

DWIGHT "DOC" GOODEN

In Case You Didn't Know

One of the nicknames for a curveball is "Uncle Charley." Dwight Gooden's was so good, batters named it "Lord Charles."

THE SLIDER

In 1936, according to ESPN.com, John J. Ward coined the term "slider" when noting that pitcher George Blaeholder (Browns, Phillies, Indians, 1925–36) was best known in his era for throwing the "slide pitch." Pitcher George Uhle (Indians, Tigers, Giants, Yankees, 1919–36) was also given credit for "inventing" the pitch. Maybe Uhle's claim is given more weight because he ended up 200–166. Blaeholder pitched for teams that weren't as good, and ended up 104–125.

Exactly when these two men came across the pitch is difficult to say (although it's interesting to note that both pitched in Cleveland in 1936). *The Ballplay-*

ers, which lists biographies of about 7,000 ballplayers, gives Uhle and Blaeholder pretty much equal credit.

According to Bill James, Uhle taught the pitch to Waite Hoyt in 1930. Hoyt called it "a wonderful pitch." He explained that Uhle's pitch didn't break, exactly, but "skidded [...] like an auto on ice" across the strike zone. Hoyt recalled that sometimes an umpire would be ready to call the pitch a ball, and it would suddenly "slide" back into the strike zone.

What is clear is that the slider changed baseball. Because it was relatively easy to learn, and easy to control, pitchers were eager to learn it. Bob Feller recalled that he learned the pitch just after he came back from World War II and used it with great effectiveness in 1948, the year he struck out 348 batters.

Bill James and Rob Neyer called the slider "the pitch of the '50s," because it had become so popular with pitchers. Many hitters asserted that the slider's break, which came relatively late as it reached the plate, was difficult to pick up. In *My Turn At Bat*, Hall of Famer Ted Williams explained that the pitch gave hurlers a "third option": previously, hitters generally had to deal mostly with opposing pitchers throwing either a curveball or a fastball.

The pitch continued to grow in popularity in the 1960s and 1970s, particularly after Sparky Lyle and Ron Guidry had so much success with it for the Yankees in the latter part of the 1970s. Pitchers like Larry Andersen (Indians, Mariners, Phillies, Astros, Red Sox, Padres, 1975–94) used it almost exclusively. In the 1990s, the Mariners' Randy Johnson became the most intimidating pitcher of his era, in part because he augmented a supercharged fastball with an equally powerful slider.

RANDY JOHNSON

Steve CARLTON

Cardinals, Phillies, Giants, White Sox, Indians, Twins
1965–88

Primarily a fastball pitcher for most of his career, Carlton didn't develop his slider until about 1969— but when he mastered it, the pitch was a devastating addition to his arsenal. The 10-time All-Star won four Cy Young awards during his career.

CAREER STATISTICS

W	L	SAVES	ERA	SO	CG
329	244	2	3.22	4,136	254

Bob FELLER

Indians, 1936–56

Waiddaminit! Feller is listed in this book as one of the best fastball pitchers. Can a pitcher be the best ever at two pitches? Well, if Larry Bird can be the best passing and long-range shooting forward in basketball, Bob Feller can be one of the best fastball and slider pitchers ever.

CAREER STATISTICS

W	L	SAVES	ERA	SO	CG
266	162	21	3.25	2,581	279

Ron "Louisiana Lightning" GUIDRY

Yankees, 1975–89

Guidry, like Bob Gibson, was known mainly for his fastball, but his slider was one of the best ever. A superb athlete who was an outfielder for the Yankees, Guidry's 1978 season was one of the greatest ever turned in by a pitcher: a 25–3 record, 9 shutouts, 248 strikeouts and a 1.74 ERA.

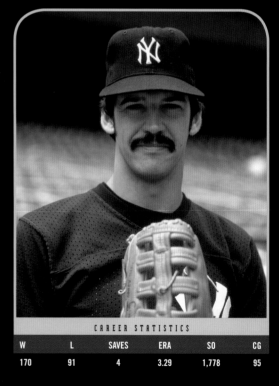

CAREER STATISTICS

W	L	SAVES	ERA	SO	CG
170	91	4	3.29	1,778	95

Albert W. "Sparky"
LYLE

Red Sox, Yankees, Rangers, Phillies, White Sox
1967–82

Lyle was one of the best relievers in baseball for more than a decade, from 1969 to 1979, winning the Cy Young Award in 1977. Lyle almost exclusively relied on his devastating slider, although he also had a very good fastball. He never started a major-league game.

CAREER STATISTICS					
W	L	SAVES	ERA	SO	CG
99	76	238	2.88	873	0

Bob
GIBSON

Cardinals, 1959–75

Another fireballer, Gibson developed his slider early in his career, and it helped make him one of the greatest all-around pitchers ever. A ferocious competitor who was not afraid to pitch inside, "Gibby" won both the MVP and Cy Young awards in 1968.

CAREER STATISTICS					
W	L	SAVES	ERA	SO	CG
251	174	6	2.91	3,117	255

HOW IT'S DONE
The Slider

In his 1948 book, *Pitching to Win*, Bob Feller talks about how to throw the slider: "The delivery is almost identical with that of a fastball until the point of release. I think the release can be best described by comparing it with the passing of a football. The index finger controls the release even as it does a football. [...] Unlike the curve, the snap of the wrist is late, and the arm turns in only half as much as it does for the curve."

To clarify, a pitcher grips the ball slightly off center and throws it like a fastball. The pitcher will let the ball slide along his index finger and will use the ring and pinkie fingers to guide it.

BOB FELLER

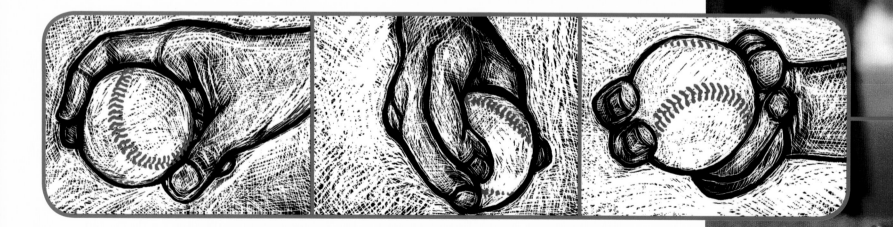

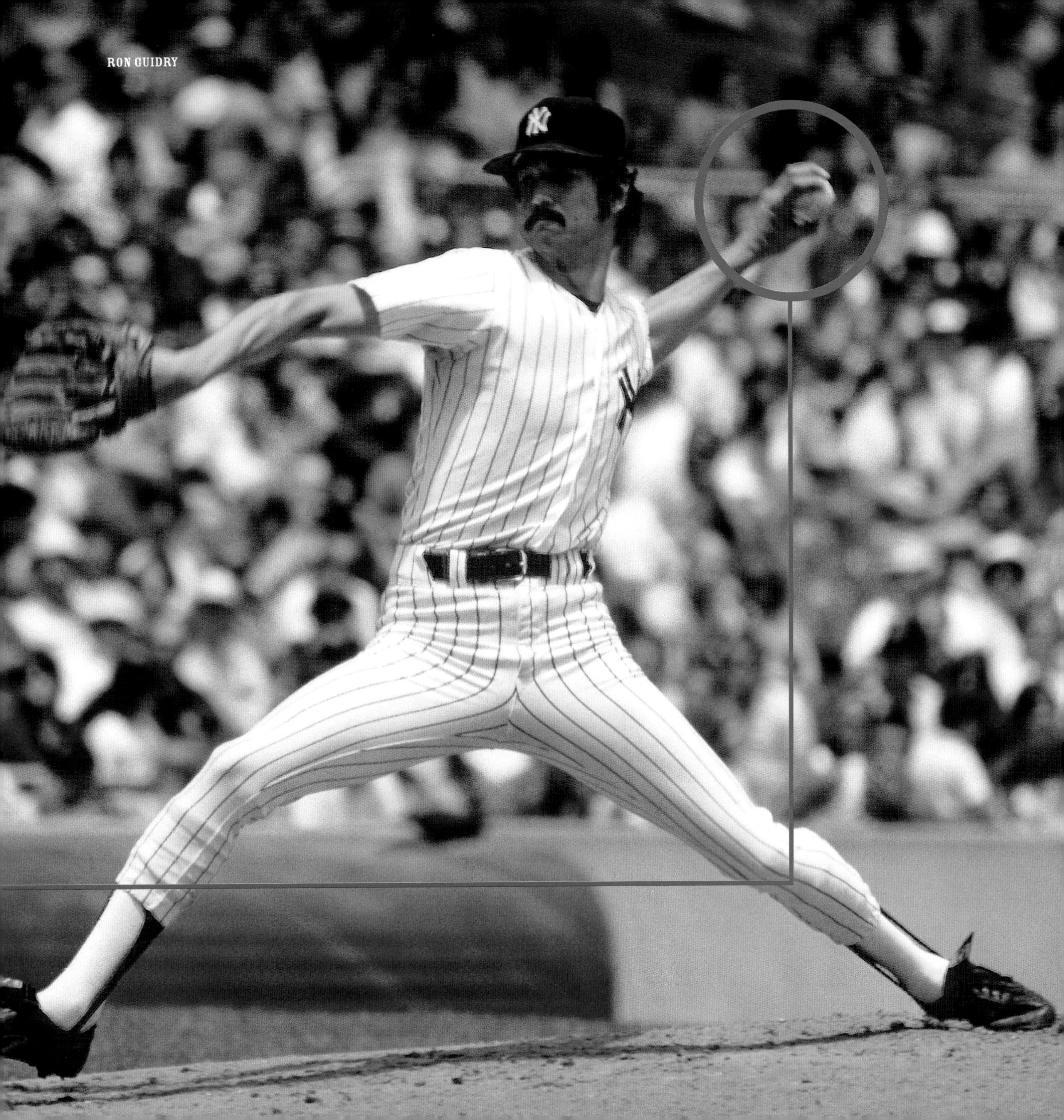

RON GUIDRY

THE CHANGEUP

ABOVE: Harry Wright, of the Boston Red Stockings, is credited as one of the first players to throw a changeup.

Pitchers who were throwing underhand prior to the 1880s had limited options for trying to get batters out (and, as discussed in The Fastball, getting batters out wasn't the job of the pitcher anyway). They had to throw underhand, with wrists and elbows stiff—a motion not unlike modern bowling.

To gain some kind of limited edge, the better pitchers of the early era varied their pitches by changing their delivery speed. In the very early days, this meant merely changing the speed of a pitch from slow to slower to much slower. But this method of changing speeds, or "throwing changeups," was really the first weapon a pitcher had.

Alphonse "Phonney" Martin, who pitched for several club teams before joining the Troy Trojans of the National Association in 1872, was the most accomplished changeup pitcher of his era, though probably not the first.

Martin's pitch was initially called "the slowball," and it was reportedly so slow that batters would swing with nearly all their effort in an attempt to make a solid hit.

In his book, *A Game of Inches*, author Peter Morris points out that calling Martin's pitch a "changeup" or "change of pace" was somewhat misleading, since Martin, like Preacher Roe, didn't really have much of a fastball of which to speak.

Morris's point is that White Stocking pitcher Albert Spalding may have actually been the first, or one of the first, pitchers to throw a changeup because he threw it with the same grip and motion as his fastball.

Harry Wright, the fine player-manager of the Boston Red Stockings of the National Association, was credited as being one of the first pitchers to throw a changeup as well. Wright was mostly a manager in Boston and not a pitcher, so his work was almost entirely in relief.

The concept of the changeup continued through the 20th century, but the way the pitch was thrown began to alter. The "circle change," in which a pitcher curled his thumb and index finger around the side of the ball, came into vogue. Baseball analyst and former catcher Tim McCarver believes former Dodger lefty Johnny Podres (Dodgers, Tigers, Padres, 1953–69) was probably the first pitcher to use the circle change. Warren Spahn (Braves, Mets, Giants, 1942–65) was also known to throw such a pitch in the latter part of his career.

The modern-day pitcher who is, without a doubt, the premier changeup artist in baseball history is Trevor Hoffman, the closer for the San Diego Padres. Hoffman began his career as an infielder in the minor leagues but was converted to a pitcher a few years before his big-league career.

Hoffman became the closer for the Padres in 1994 and has been in that position ever  since. He began his career as a flame-throwing fastball pitcher, but the same year he took over the closer's job for San Diego, he began using the changeup in games. Hoffman credits fellow pitcher Donnie Elliott with showing him the pitch that year.

The key to his changeup, said Hoffman in an interview with *ESPN The Magazine* in 2006, is that he pinches the seam of the baseball with his thumb and forefinger as he releases it.

In 1998, Hoffman had a dominant year, and was one of the keys to the Padres' National League championship. During that 53-saves year, AC/DC's "Hell's Bells" was played over the public-address system as he walked to the mound. This set the trend in major-league baseball for playing "entrance music" over the public-address systems as a dominant closer takes the mound.

TREVOR HOFFMAN

THE EEPHUS PITCH

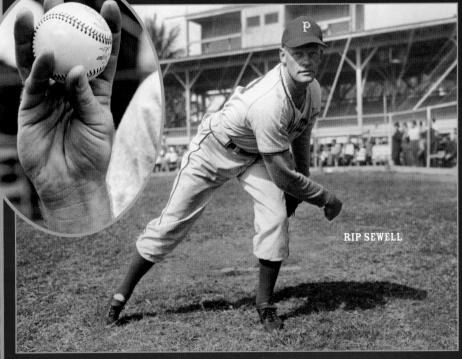

RIP SEWELL

Truett Banks "Rip" Sewell (Tigers, Phillies, Pirates, 1932, 1938–39) is the man credited with inventing the "eephus" pitch, which is thrown in a high arc that comes down over the plate. This is despite the fact that high-arc pitches were being thrown in softball leagues for many years before Sewell's delivery.

Anyway, Sewell was a character, but he was also an effective junkball pitcher who was a three-time All-Star. In 1943, he led the league in wins.

The eephus was a pitch Sewell would throw from time to time in the National League, and the high arc often frustrated batters. ("Eephus" is a term drawn from shooting dice that means gaining nothing from the throw. Maurice Van Robays, Sewell's teammate, actually coined the term for the pitch.)

In the 1946 All-Star Game, Sewell challenged Red Sox slugger Ted Williams by throwing the pitch. Williams blasted the pitch for a home run, and that was the end of the eephus—for a while, anyway.

Williams, according to *The Boston Globe*, had requested a demonstration of the pitch prior to the game. He asked Sewell if he would throw such a pitch in an All-Star Game, and Sewell said he would. He actually threw three eephus balls to Williams before the Sox slugger tagged one. But it shot out of the park like a rocket.

Since then, a few other pitchers have thrown high-arcing pitches, including Red Sox hurler Bill Lee, who called it his "Lee-phus pitch"; Steve Hamilton, with the "folly floater"and Dave LaRoche, with the "LaLob."

THE CHANGEUP

Trevor
HOFFMAN

Padres, Marlins
1993–present

All-time saves leader, with 524, Hoffman basically relies on two pitches: the fastball and the changeup. He throws the changeup anytime in the count—the mark of a very confident pitcher.

Greg
MADDUX

Cubs, Braves, Padres
1986–present

Maddux is the master of the circle change. In fact, he's the master of off-speed pitches overall. No modern pitcher changes speeds as well as he does.

Edwin Charles "Preacher"
ROE

Cardinals, Pirates, Dodgers
1938–54

"I have three pitches," said Roe to author Roger Kahn in 1952. "My changeup, my change off my changeup, and my change off my change off my changeup." In other words, Roe threw slow, slower and slowest. But he varied speeds and had great location.

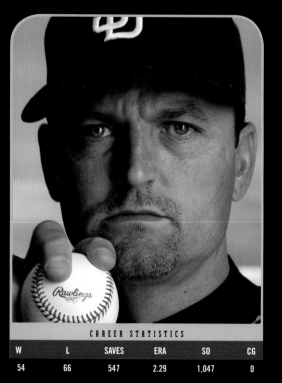

CAREER STATISTICS

W	L	SAVES	ERA	SO	CG
54	66	547	2.29	1,047	0

CAREER STATISTICS

W	L	SAVES	ERA	SO	CG
352	222	0	3.14	3,345	109

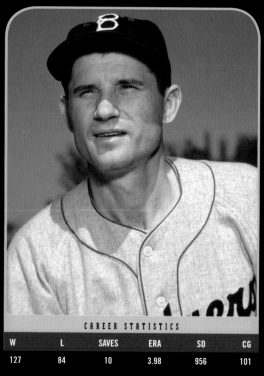

CAREER STATISTICS

W	L	SAVES	ERA	SO	CG
127	84	10	3.98	956	101

Satchel
PAIGE

Negro League, Indians, Browns, Athletics
1926–47, 1948–49, 1950–51, 1965

Paige often named his pitches, and his changeup
was called a "two-hump blooper."

Edward
"Whitey"
FORD

Yankees, 1950–67

Ford had a variety of pitches that he threw at a
variety of speeds. His changeup was probably one
of the better versions of the pitch, especially as
Ford got older and craftier.

CAREER STATISTICS					
W	L	SAVES	ERA	SO	CG
236	106	10	2.75	1,956	156

CAREER STATISTICS		
	W	L
NEGRO LEAGUES	142	92

JAMIE MOYER

HOW IT'S DONE
The Changeup

The changeup is most effective when the pitcher grips the ball and winds up as though he is going to throw a fastball—this alerts the batter to prepare for a hard pitch with great velocity. A pitcher then slows the ball down by gripping it harder than a fastball just before it leaves his hand.

"[A] changeup must be thrown with the same arm speed as a fastball," said Jack Krawczyk, a former pitcher for the University of Southern California from 1995 to 1998, who still holds the all-time Division I college-baseball save record for a season, with 49. "The grip and finger pressure slows the baseball down." In addition, he said, the arm extension for a changeup isn't as much as for a fastball, which is another factor that slows it down.

Krawczyk is currently the pitching coach for Arizona State.

"You are almost having the sensation of pulling backward with [the index and pinkie] fingers" as you throw the ball, he said in a 2005 *Collegiate Baseball* newspaper interview. Ideally, said Krawczyk, a changeup is about 10 to 12 miles per hour slower than a pitcher's fastball. His, he said, was about 8 miles per hour slower.

The circle change, which is more popular these days, is thrown with the thumb and forefinger literally making a circle on the side of the ball. In addition to the pitch coming in more slowly, the pressure of the thumb and forefinger allows a pitcher to put a little sidespin on the ball, which makes it drop slightly.

Jamie Moyer of the Phillies and Johan Santana of the Mets are two peas in a pod when it comes to throwing their changeups. Although Santana will use the fastball to set up his change more than Moyer, both men will throw their changeup at any point in the count, a fearsome conundrum for hitters.

JOHAN SANTANA

THE FORKBALL

The first major leaguer to throw the forkball was probably "Bullet" Joe Bush (Athletics, Red Sox, Yankees, Browns, Senators, Pirates, 1912–28). It was 1921. Bush was pitching for the Boston Red Sox, and his curveball seemed to desert him, so he began experimenting with a forkball.

The forkball was apparently invented, according to Bill James and Rob Neyer, by minor leaguer Bert Hall in 1907, who had a cup of coffee with the Phillies in 1911, the year before Bush signed with the Athletics. Whether there is a connection is unknown, but Bush's forkball helped him win 16 games for Boston in 1921 and, when he was traded to New York the next year, 26 games for the Yankees.

But the pitch was hard to control and, even worse, led to arm problems. Most pitchers eschewed it. But in 1940, Ernest "Tiny" Bonham was a rookie for the Yankees, and his principal pitch was the forkball. Bonham (Yankees, Pirates, 1940–49) had exceptional control of the pitch and threw 6 shutouts and won 21 games for New York in 1942.

In 1958, the Pirates' Elroy Face learned the forkball and revived his career. Face had won just 4 games with 10 saves the year before. But by adding the forkball to his arsenal, Face saved a league-leading 20 games and went 5–2. The next year, he was an amazing 18–1.

Still, as noted before, the forkball was hard to throw. Bonham's career was cut short by injuries, mostly lower-back problems tied to his throwing motion. In 1971, the Reds' Don Gullett had great success with the forkball, winning 16 games, but that year began a cycle of battling arm and shoulder injuries that also curtailed Gullett's career. Even Dave Stewart, who claimed the forkball revived his career in the late 1980s, burned out soon after, winning only 34 games in the last 4 years of his career.

Many Japanese and Chinese pitchers have had success with the pitch, and they appear to have had fewer arm problems. Hideo Nomo, who has now pitched for several teams in the United States, tossed a no-hitter for the Red Sox throwing primarily a forkball. The Yankees' Chien-Ming Wang (2005–present) also has a pretty good forkball in his arsenal of pitches. In 2007, he won 18 games and was a Cy Young Award contender.

CHIEN-MING WANG

"BULLET" JOE BUSH

The Best of the Best

THE FORKBALL

Dave
STEWART

Dodgers, Rangers, Phillies, Athletics, Blue Jays
1978, 1981–94

Stewart struggled for several years with the
Dodgers, Rangers and Phillies before learning the
forkball and reviving his career with the Athletics.
From 1987 to 1990, he won 20 or more games
and became one of the most consistent pitchers in
baseball in that span.

CAREER STATISTICS					
W	L	SAVES	ERA	SO	CG
169	129	19	3.95	1,741	55

Elroy
FACE

Pirates, Tigers, Expos
1953–69

Face revived a sagging career when he learned to throw the forkball before the 1958 season, and led the league in saves.

Don
GULLETT

Reds, Yankees, 1970–78

Gullett learned the forkball just before his second year in the majors, and he went 16–6 with the Reds that year, leading the National League in winning percentage. He claimed in an interview that year that the forkball made him into a winning pitcher.

Hideo
NOMO

Dodgers, Mets, Brewers, Red Sox
1965–present

Nomo is one of several Asian pitchers who throw the forkball. Of those pitchers, Nomo's forkball is probably the best.

CAREER STATISTICS

W	L	SAVES	ERA	SO	CG
104	95	193	3.11	877	6

CAREER STATISTICS

W	L	SAVES	ERA	SO	CG
109	84	11	3.11	921	44

CAREER STATISTICS

W	L	SAVES	ERA	SO	CG
123	109	0	4.13	1,918	16

ELROY FACE

HOW IT'S DONE
The Forkball

The forkball is gripped between the index and middle fingers. The fingers are spread out so that the ball actually fits between them. Pitchers with longer fingers will obviously have more success throwing the pitch. The ball is thrown with a snap of the wrist.

RIGHT: Hideo Nomo's forkball was one of the best pitches in his arsenal, and it served him well. He is one of only a handful of big leaguers to throw a no-hitter in each league.

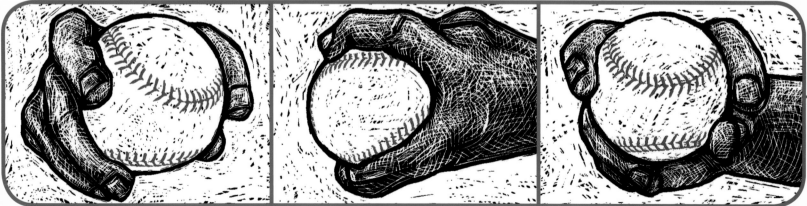

THE SPLIT-FINGER FASTBALL

While Roger Craig is generally accepted as one of the pitchers who popularized the split-finger fastball (also known as the "splitter"), many archivists point to St. Louis right-hander Fred Martin as the originator of the pitch. Martin played for the Cardinals for three years, in 1946 and from 1949 to 1950, with minimal results (a 12–3 record, but an ERA of 5.12 in his last big-league season).

Martin matriculated to the Mexican League, where he began working on a forkball with which he could generate more speed. He eventually moved the baseball closer to the tips of his index and ring fingers and had moderate success.

In 1973, Martin was a roving pitching coach for the Chicago Cubs, and he began working with a pitcher in the Cubs AA Quincy, Illinois, farm team. The pitcher, Bruce Sutter, had already undergone elbow surgery. (Sutter had the surgery the year before and did not tell the Cubs. They found out when, one day, he was pitching in a T-shirt and a Cub official noticed a long scar along his elbow.)

"Today," Sutter recalled in an interview with Peter Golenbock, "teams have a pitching coach at every level. The Cubs had one [pitching] coach for their whole system!"

But that coach was Freddie Martin. He suggested Sutter try the splitter. Martin noted that Sutter had long fingers, which helped him control the pitch.

"Right off the bat, I could make it break," Sutter said. "I had no problem with it. I mean, [sometimes] it bounced a half a foot in front of the plate, and the batter would still swing at it." This makes some sense, as the pitch looks like a fastball (except it's not really as fast), and it usually drops as it gets to the plate.

Sutter was called up by the Cubs in 1976, and almost immediately became the team's closer, pushing aside Darold Knowles and Mike Garman. He led the league in saves twice with Chicago, averaging 30 a year. By his second year, Sutter was the most dominant reliever in the game.

Martin, according to Sutter, showed Craig the pitch, and Craig began teaching other big leaguers, including Mike Scott, Jack Morris, Jeff Robinson (Giants, Pirates, Yankees, Angels, Cubs, 1984–92) and others.

Craig pointed out that the splitter is a faster pitch than a forkball. Ron Darling, for example, also threw a forkball and used the splitter like a changeup.

"Most guys throw it as a [change of pace]," said Darold Knowles. "Bruce threw it hard! I couldn't throw it as well. My hands aren't big enough."

> **"RIGHT OFF THE BAT, I COULD MAKE IT BREAK. I HAD NO PROBLEM WITH IT. I MEAN, [SOMETIMES] IT BOUNCED A HALF A FOOT IN FRONT OF THE PLATE, AND THE BATTER WOULD STILL SWING AT IT."**
>
> BRUCE SUTTER

FRED MARTIN

BRUCE SUTTER

The Best of the Best

Bruce SUTTER

Cubs, Cardinals, Braves
1976–88

Sutter is the acknowledged master of the split-finger fastball. He developed the pitch with the help of Cubs pitching coach Mike Roarke. In 1979, he won the Cy Young Award, going 6–6, but with a league-leading 37 saves.

Roger CRAIG

Dodgers, Mets, Reds, Phillies, 1955–66

Craig was named the "maestro of the split-finger fastball" in 1986 by *Sports Illustrated* magazine. By that year, he had taught the pitch to Morris, Mike Scott and many others. He was such a good teacher that while managing the Giants in San Francisco, he was forbidden to discuss the pitch with hurlers on other teams.

Mike SCOTT

Mets, Astros, 1979–91

Scott is a recognized guru of the splitter. In 1986, Scott won 18 games with five shutouts and 308 strikeouts, stats that can be attributed to his great facility with the pitch.

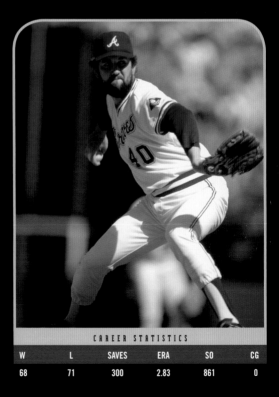

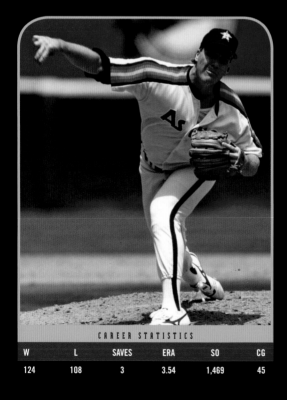

CAREER STATISTICS

W	L	SAVES	ERA	SO	CG
68	71	300	2.83	861	0

CAREER STATISTICS

W	L	SAVES	ERA	SO	CG
74	98	19	3.96	803	58

CAREER STATISTICS

W	L	SAVES	ERA	SO	CG
124	108	3	3.54	1,469	45

Ron
DARLING

Mets, Expos, Athletics
1983–95

Darling, a native of Hawaii, was overshadowed on the Mets by Dwight Gooden. But he was one of the key performers on the Mets' 1986 National League Championship team.

	CAREER STATISTICS				
W	L	SAVES	ERA	SO	CG
136	116	0	3.87	1,590	37

Jack
MORRIS

Tigers, Twins, Blue Jays, Indians
1977–94

Morris was the winningest pitcher in the 1980s for the Tigers. He combined his splitter with a slider and a "regular" fastball to start 33 or more games for Detroit from 1980 to 1988, except during the strike-shortened 1981 season.

	CAREER STATISTICS				
W	L	SAVES	ERA	SO	CG
254	186	0	3.90	2,478	175

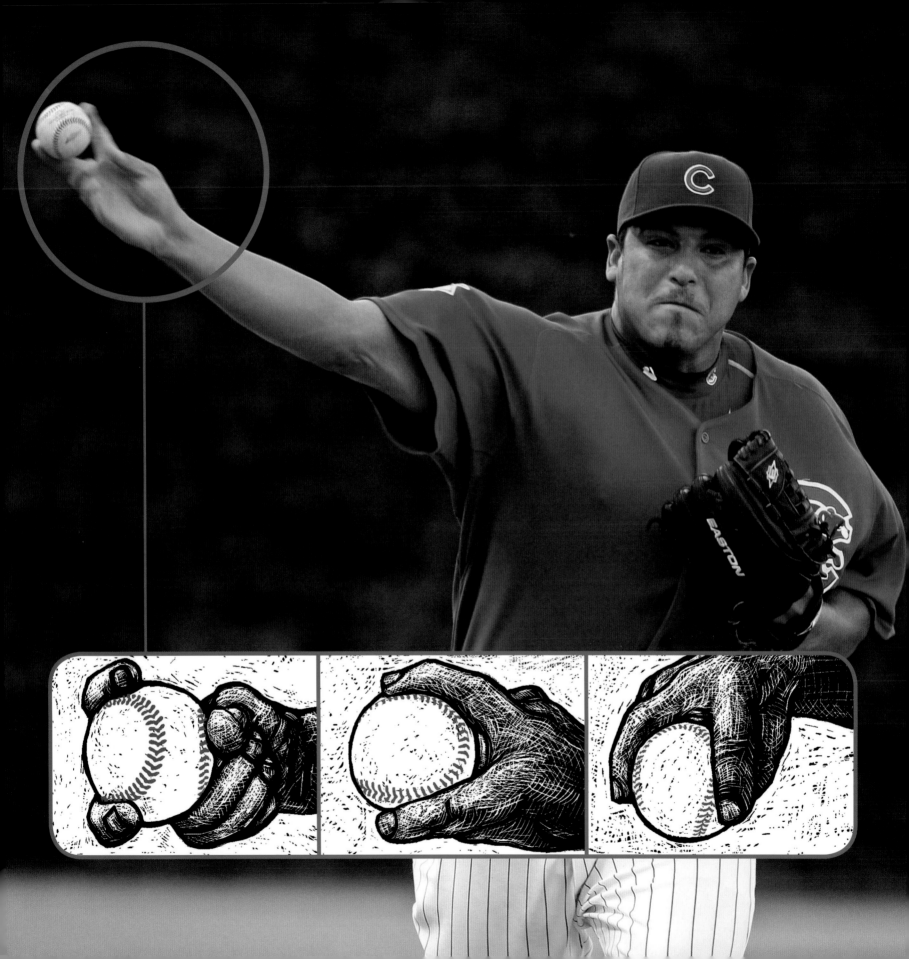

HOW IT'S DONE
The Split-Finger Fastball

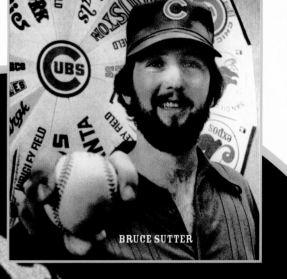

BRUCE SUTTER

The split-finger fastball, or splitter, is thrown almost the same way one throws a forkball. The difference, according to Roger Craig, is one of the positioning of the baseball.

"The forkball," said Craig in a 1988 interview in the *New York Times*, "is a pitch you push deep back in your fingers and you get down on the ball as far as you possibly can. [...] The split-finger is closer to your fingertips and you have your fingers higher on the ball. You can throw it a lot harder."

LEFT: The Cubs' Carlos "The Big Z" Zambrano likes to throw his splitters almost sidearm. The combination of the movement he gets and the speed he can generate with this delivery makes him one of the best pitchers in the league.

ROGER CRAIG

DEREK JETER

in the opinion of an umpire, was intentional. In 1932, the American League authorized umpires to eject pitchers who threw beanballs, and by 1950 both leagues outlawed pitches aimed at a batter's head.

The word "intentionally" was a problem for many umpires. The immortal Jocko Conlan, who officiated ballgames from 1941 to 1965, was one of those so vexed.

"How am I supposed to known what runs through a pitcher's head?" he rhetorically asked in an interview. "How much are [umpires] going to be paid to read minds?"

There are several methods of retaliation for knockdown pitches. Superb bunters like Jackie Robinson or Ty Cobb took care of things in their own way—they would simply bunt down the first-base line, forcing the pitcher to field the ball, then spike them or run them over.

TY COBB

In one famous incident, Robinson was incensed by a pitch from Giant hurler Sal "The Barber" Maglie. On the next pitch, Jackie coolly bunted down the line. But Maglie never bit. Knowing what Robinson intended, he stayed on the mound.

Another way is simply to throw at the other guy. Although modern historians believe the designated hitter rule, enacted in 1970, has limited this type of retaliation, evidence indicates that while a pitcher can't specifically retaliate against an opposing pitcher who has thrown at one of his players, beanball wars have continued.

Pitchers eschewed throwing at the all-time great players, because the all-time great players would respond with a home run, or at least a solid base hit. Red Sox old-timers love to tell the story of the rookie pitcher who buzzed one behind Carl Yastrzemski's head in a game in 1973. Yaz stepped out of the batter's box, calmly adjusting his batting glove, as the fans in Fenway Park booed lustily. Yaz stepped back in and drilled the next pitch past the rookie's cheek for a clean single. For good measure, the next time up, Yastrzemski slapped a double down the line. The rookie got the message.

"They can throw at me all they want," noted Hall of Famer Willie Mays. "When that pitch comes in, I won't be there. But the next pitch, the next strike, I'll be ready for that one."

LEFT: Derek Jeter avoids an inside pitch against the Cleveland Indians during Game One of the American League Divisional Series.
RIGHT: Matt Kemp gets brushed back against the Colorado Rockies.

MATT KEMP

Burleigh
GRIMES

Pirates, Dodgers, Yankees, Braves, Cardinals, Cubs
1916–34

Grimes was called "Ol' Stubblebeard" because he usually didn't shave before a start. An affable man off the field, he was very territorial on it.

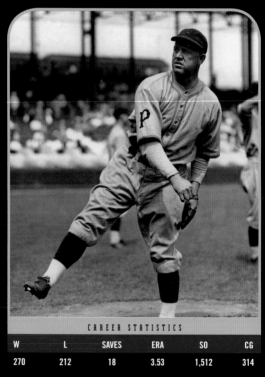

Bob
GIBSON

Cardinals, 1959–75

A ferocious competitor who hated to be shown up by a batter, Gibson would knock down for taking, in his opinion, too long to reach the batter's box to begin an at-bat.

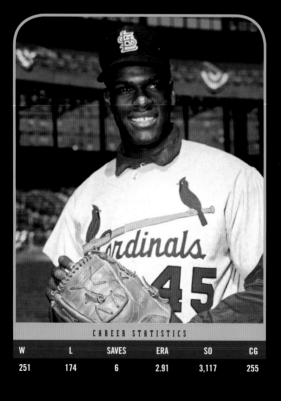

Joe
McGINNITY

Orioles, Dodgers, Giants
1899–1908

The king of the brushback, McGinnity once hit 40 batters in 42 games for Brooklyn in 1900.

CAREER STATISTICS

W	L	SAVES	ERA	SO	CG
270	212	18	3.53	1,512	314

CAREER STATISTICS

W	L	SAVES	ERA	SO	CG
251	174	6	2.91	3,117	255

CAREER STATISTICS

W	L	SAVES	ERA	SO	CG
246	142	24	2.66	1,068	314

Sal "The Barber" MAGLIE

Giants, Indians, Dodgers, Yankees, Cardinals
1945–58

Maglie was another pitcher who often knocked down batters for perceived slights. Once when Dodger Duke Snider was coming to bat against Maglie, he noticed his shoe untied just before he got to the plate. Snider bent down, tied his shoe and took his stance. Maglie knocked him down. "Tie your shoes on your own time!" snarled Maglie to a surprised Duke.

CAREER STATISTICS					
W	L	SAVES	ERA	SO	CG
119	62	14	3.15	862	93

Don DRYSDALE

Dodgers, 1956–69

One of the most affable guys in baseball when he was not pitching, Drysdale had a very nasty streak on the mound. He hit 10 or more batters per year 10 of 11 years.

CAREER STATISTICS					
W	L	SAVES	ERA	SO	CG
209	166	6	2.95	2,486	167

ABOVE: Designated hitter, Gary Sheffield, ducks an inside pitch during a game against the Kansas City Royals. RIGHT: Clint Barnes is upended after a low, inside pitch.

HOW IT'S DONE
The Knockdown Pitch

The knockdown is not a pitch per se. It's more like a strategy. But it has been a very big part of the game, however it is characterized, since the game began.

Throwing inside is actually a little tougher than it sounds. A pitcher needs to understand that throwing inside can result in injury to an opponent. An inside pitch, as many pitchers assert, is a "thought pitch," or a pitch meant to make a batter think about how close to the plate he is, and to think about what might happen if a pitch hits him. For the most part, it is not a pitch meant to injure. It's a fine line; hence most pitchers throw fastball knockdowns, as they are the easiest to control.

"The inside pitch is not a weapon," intoned Dodger great Don Drysdale. "It's a tactic."

ABOVE: Sal Maglie, who toiled for the Giants for many years, advocated throwing inside on a 2–2 count. An inside pitch on two balls and no strikes, he said, is something a batter expects. An inside pitch with the count of two balls and two strikes is a little more surprising, since it would load the count.

THE KNUCKLEBALL

The invention of the knuckleball is credited to either Thomas A. "Toad" Ramsey (Louisville Colonels [AA], Browns [AA], 1885–90) or Eddie Cicotte and George "Nap" Rucker, when both were in the minor leagues together.

Ramsey certainly used a knuckle grip similar to that used for a knuckleball. He had suffered an injury to his fingers early in the 1886 season and was forced to try throwing the ball with his knuckles. He, as well as sportswriters of the day, called it a "drop curve."

Cicotte and Rucker were teammates on the Augusta, Georgia, team in the Southern Atlantic League in 1905. During spring training that year, they were experimenting with various ways to grip the ball (this is now called "goofing around"), and Cicotte came up with a way to throw the ball with his knuckles.

Cicotte appears to have begun throwing the knuckleball in games first, in 1906 with Indianapolis in the Western League, but Rucker clearly used the pitch that year as well, while still in Augusta. When he was signed by the Brooklyn Dodgers (then called the Superbas) in 1907, reports from the day mentioned several times his use of the pitch. By 1908, Cicotte was called up to the White Sox and was also generating headlines with the pitch.

THE KNUCKLE CURVE

This is another of those hybrid pitches that may or may not rate a chapter of its own. The knuckle curve is—surprise!—a knuckleball that curves. It is held using only one finger, usually the middle finger, and thumb to grip the ball, with the rest of the fingers curled behind the ball. This gives the ball a slight drag to the opposite side of the ball, where the fingers are positioned, and causes it to curve.

Pitchers do not often employ the knuckle curve, because it is difficult to control. George Earnshaw (Athletics, White Sox, Dodgers, Cardinals, 1928–36) used it in the latter part of his career. More recently, Burt Hooten (Cubs, Dodgers, Rangers, 1971–85) used it with some success.

BERT HOOTEN

GEORGE EARNSHAW

In 1908, rookie Ed Summers (1908–12) of the Detroit Tigers came into the league throwing a knuckleball, but he was gripping it with his fingers. According to the 1908 *Reach Baseball Guide*, the Summers "fingerball" was as effective as the knuckler. Cicotte and Summers had been teammates in Indianapolis and there, explained Summers, is where he learned the pitch.

Summers added that because his fingers were longer than Cicotte's, he preferred to grip the baseball with his fingertips, which he believed gave him better control.

Summers won 24 games in his rookie year, and the Tigers vaulted into the World Series that year, bringing Summers and his knuckleball into national prominence.

The pitch was easy to throw but difficult to control, and seemed to be petering out in popularity until the spitball was banned in 1922. Edward Rommel (Athletics, 1920–32) was a spitballer for his first two years with the Athletics, but he adopted the knuckleball after the spitball was prohibited. He won a league-leading 27 games that season.

Baseball historian Bill James believes that the knuckleball has enjoyed only sporadic popularity because of its unpredictability and relative velocity, which is generally slower than most pitches. Managers, he noted in his *Baseball Abstract*, would rather have fireballing fastball pitchers on the mound, as opposed to fluttery knuckleball pitchers.

The pitch jumped in popularity (among big-league pitchers anyway) during the World War II years of the 1940s. With many of their frontline pitchers in the service, teams allowed more knuckleball pitchers on their roster. During the 1945 season, the Washington Senators had a pitching lineup that included four knuckleball throwers: Dutch Leonard (17–7 that season), Johnny Niggeling (7–12), Mickey "Itsy Bitsy" Haefner (16–14) and Roger Wolff (20–10). Wolff and Leonard were probably the best one-two pitching punch in the league, and Niggeling, who lost several low-scoring games, was fourth in

Despite a series of injuries to his throwing arm, knuckleballer R.A. Dickey was an effective pitcher for Seattle in 2008.

HOW TO CATCH THE KNUCKLEBALL

There is, according to big-league catchers like Boston's Doug Mirabelli, a definite technique to catching the knuckleball. Here are some tips. (And it goes without saying that a knuckleball catcher should use the largest mitt that is legal.)

1. Be prepared to move. Knuckleballs come in at many different angles and tend to drop abruptly. Catchers have to prepare themselves to be ready for that, because otherwise, it's a long night.

2. Take a stance that's a little wider than normal. This gives a catcher a little more mass to block the plate. And every inch helps.

3. Catch with the mitt closer to your body. This will prevent you from lunging at the pitch. Which brings us to…

4. Don't lunge—let the ball come to you. The more you lunge, the better the chance the ball will get away from you.

5. Tilt the mitt slightly upward—emphasis on "slightly." Knuckleballs tend to drop, and tilting will enable you to guide the ball into your mitt.

Tilt mitt slightly upward.

Hold mitt closer to body.

Wider than normal stance.

opponents' batting average (.240) in the league. The Senators finished second, only two games behind the Tigers, who went on to win the World Series.

Still, when the war was over, knuckleballers began to again fade in popularity. Wolff, for example, only pitched for 7 years and only won 32 more games.

The difficulty of controlling the knuckleball was only part of the problem: catchers also had problems catching it. In his book *Ball Four*, Jim Bouton relates that one of his biggest problems when he pitched for the Seattle Pilots and Houston Astros in 1969 was finding someone to catch him in warm-ups. The problem was not limited to Bouton. Even after catchers began using larger mitts, the knuckleball was a difficult pitch to catch.

Another interesting postwar characteristic of the knuckleball is that most of its practitioners were pitchers who relied on the pitch almost exclusively. Phil Niekro, Wilbur Wood, Tom Candiotti (Brewers, Indians, Blue Jays, Dodgers, Athletics, 1983–99), Charlie Hough (Dodgers, Rangers, White Sox, Marlins, 1970–94) and Tim Wakefield are all players known for throwing the knuckleball a vast majority of the time.

Knuckleball pitchers are, however, a dying breed in the 21st century. Right now, only two pitchers, Wakefield of the Red Sox and Charlie Haeger of the Chicago White Sox, used a knuckleball in 2007. Wakefield has his own catcher on the Red Sox, Doug Mirabelli. (It doesn't hurt that Mirabelli is also a pretty good hitter.)

IN CASE YOU DIDN'T KNOW

It is a myth that pitcher and author Jim Bouton turned to the knuckleball late in his career. Actually, according to his book, *Ball Four*, he learned it as a teenager and used it throughout his high school career. Bouton figures he was probably the only high school pitcher in the country in the 1960s throwing a knuckleball.

HOW IT'S DONE
The Knuckleball

Initially, many knuckleballers threw the pitch by pressing the knuckles of the hand against the seams. (Duh.) But as knowledge of the pitch spread, some pitchers began gripping the seams with the ends of the fingers. An added technique is to dig the fingernail of the thumb right into the baseball.

The aim of the grip, essentially, is to eliminate the rotational spin that is usually generated when a baseball is thrown. In the absence of any spin, the principal factors that affect the movement of the ball are the stitching on the seams and any irregularities on the ball itself. (Hence the action of digging the thumbnail into the ball; that action creates asymmetry.)

The pitch itself is hard to throw, but the strain on the arm is minimal, which is why many big-league pitchers who have some success with it tend to have longer careers than, say, fastball or curveball pitchers.

PHIL "KNUCKSIE" NIEKRO

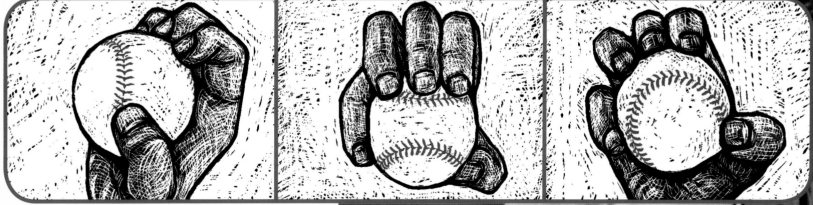

Tim
WAKEFIELD

Pirates, Red Sox, 1992–present

One of the last active knuckleballers in the majors, Wakefield has been successful as both a starter and reliever in Boston.

Jesse "Pop"
HAINES

Reds, Cardinals, 1918, 1920–37

Haines played one game for the Reds in 1918. After that, he played his entire career in St. Louis. An early adherent of the knuckleball, he threw it using the knuckle grip, which he said enabled him to throw it faster.

Wilbur
WOOD

Red Sox, Phillies, White Sox, 1961–78

Wood was a journeyman with the Red Sox and Phillies before learning the knuckleball and becoming an All-Star. In 1973, he started both ends of a doubleheader against the Yankees.

CAREER STATISTICS

W	L	SAVES	ERA	SO	CG
175	154	22	4.30	1,888	30

CAREER STATISTICS

W	L	SAVES	ERA	SO	CG
210	158	10	3.64	981	208

CAREER STATISTICS

W	L	SAVES	ERA	SO	CG
164	156	57	3.74	1,411	114

Phil "Knucksie" NIEKRO

Braves, Yankees, Indians, Blue Jays, 1964–87

Niekro was one of baseball's most durable pitchers, mostly because he relied on the knuckleball for the majority of his career.

Hoyt WILHELM

Giants, Cardinals, Indians, Orioles, White Sox, Angels, Braves, Cubs, Dodgers, 1952–72

Wilhelm read an article about the knuckleball, written by former big leaguer Emil "Dutch" Leonard, and began working on the pitch in high school. Despite the late start in his career, he pitched for 21 years in the big leagues.

CAREER STATISTICS					
W	L	SAVES	ERA	SO	CG
143	122	227	2.52	1,610	20

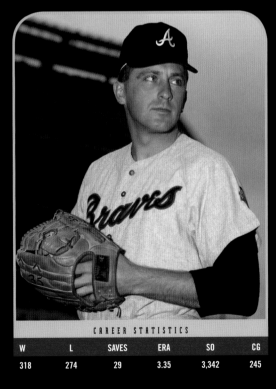

CAREER STATISTICS					
W	L	SAVES	ERA	SO	CG
318	274	29	3.35	3,342	245

THE SPITBALL

JACK CHESBRO

Jack Chesbro, the tough righty who pitched for the Pirates for several years before jumping to the New York Highlanders (who would later be renamed the Yankees), is clearly the pitcher who brought the spitball to prominence. But he never claimed to have originated it.

Chesbro credited a journeyman pitcher, Elmer Stricklett (White Sox, Dodgers, 1904–07) for showing him the pitch in December 1902. Stricklett, in turn, credited another journeyman, Frank Corridon (Cubs, Phillies, Cardinals, 1904–10), with showing him the pitch in the summer of 1902 when both were still in the minor leagues.

Corridon has said in several interviews that he was probably the first pitcher to throw the spitball in a game. The pitch itself apparently came about when one of Corridon's teammates, George Hildebrand, noticed that Corridon had a habit of spitting on his slow curve to give him a better grip.

Hildebrand, an outfielder (and, later, a well-respected umpire), played for only one year in the majors, in 1902 in Brooklyn. But he and Corridon were teammates in 1901 with the old Providence Grays, a minor-league squad.

Hildebrand suggested to Corridon that he try throwing a faster ball after he spat on it. Corridon agreed and practiced with it, and he discovered the ball broke sharply when he did so.

The story comes full circle when we learn that Chesbro was barnstorming in California, where Stricklett lived in the off-season. A team with which Stricklett was pitching beat Chesbro's team 13–1 on December 2, 1902. It was at that game that Chesbro inquired about the pitch and Stricklett showed him how to "load it up."

There are a host of 19th-century pitchers who are also credited with throwing spitballs. Bobby Mathews, a hurler who started pitching for the old National Association in 1871, used to wet his fingers before throwing the ball. In addition, many early sportswriters credited Tim Keefe (Troy [NA], New York [NA], Giants, Phillies, 1880–93) with spitting on the ball before his delivery.

Without splitting too many hairs, there is no doubt that Keefe, Mathews and many other pitchers in the late 19th century wet their fingers or the ball or both before throwing out. That was more to get a firmer hold on the ball than to actually adjust its path to the plate. The true spitballers, at least in the minds of many, didn't really begin practicing their craft until the early 20th century.

Chesbro jumped to the Highlanders in 1902 and won 21 games. The next season, using primarily the spitball, he had what is still regarded as the greatest pitching season in the modern era: 41 wins, 45 complete games, 6 shutouts, 239 strikeouts, 454 2/3 innings pitched.

That season was so well documented because Chesbro and the Highlanders were neck and neck with the powerful Boston Pilgrims (who would become the Red Sox) for the entire summer. Boston eventually won the pennant, but it was not until the last day of the season that they finally accomplished that feat.

Meanwhile, Chesbro was pitching his rear end off. The Highlanders at the time were the ugly stepsons of the far more well-known and admired New York Giants. In fact, according to several sources, Giants manager John McGraw and owner John Brush, who socked away the National League pennant a week before, declared they had no interest in playing the American League champion in what would have been the second-ever World Series.

Boston fans at the time were sure that assertion came about because McGraw and Co. did not want to face defeat at the

GAYLORD PERRY

In Case You Didn't Know

Throughout his career, Gaylord Perry denied he used a spitball, for the simple reason that it was illegal and, if caught, he faced a fine. Perry also counseled his family on the situation. Once, an enterprising (some might say nosy) reporter asked Perry's seven-year-old daughter if Daddy threw a spitter.
"No," she said. "It's a hard slider."

hands of a Boston club, as the Pittsburgh Pirates had in 1903. But the fact was, the Giants powers that be had no interest in a city series with the upstart Highlanders. So even though Boston won out, there was no World Series that year.

But Chesbro's season had intrigued many a hurler. The spitball began growing in popularity—so much so that by 1905, many big-league pitchers threw some form of a spitball.

There is a lot of confusion about why major-league baseball eventually banned the pitch in 1919. Many historians opine the reason was because the pitch was so effective, batting averages were dropping, as was overall scoring in baseball.

FRANK CORRIDON

THE MYTHICAL PITCHES

There is no such thing as a "double curve," but several fictional ballplayers used it to great advantage in literature. The first was a fictional detective-ballplayer called Double-Curve Dan whose adventures were chronicled in pulp magazines of the late 19th century. But the player best known for the double curve, or the S-curve, was Frank Merriwell, the fictional hero of pulp author Gilbert Patten.

Beginning in 1892, Merriwell appeared in more than 900 books and stories, many of them with him pitching or quarterbacking for his dear alma mater, Yale University. In fact, as Stewart Holbrook noted in *American History* magazine, the principal villain in a Merriwell tale was often not a mustachioed Simon Legree, or an evil-hearted gambler type, but students from that Ivy League university in Cambridge that is Yale's chief rival in all things. "You are a cheap cad," said Merriwell to more than one over-dressed Harvard man.

Merriwell's S-curve broke one way early in its delivery and the other way as it crossed the plate. It was unhittable but required considerable muscular control to throw. Problem was, in many of his tales, Merriwell was banged up from some calamity or

another. Thus, he could not always muster up the ginger to throw the S-curve and had to rely on guts and toughness. But he always won the big game.

Merriwell pitched for Yale for about 10 years (eligibility issues apparently were not a problem for the Ivies in those days). He eventually matriculated to more worldly adventures. Still, Patten knew his audience, and several years into Merriwell's career, we met little brother Dick Merriwell, who also attended Yale and also had an amazing pitch: the jump ball.

The jump ball was also a curve, but in complete abandonment of all the rules of physics, the jump ball was thrown at the knees of a batter and curved *up* instead of down. Yikes. It's a wonder Yale ever lost a baseball game.

In at least two separate cartoon episodes in the 1930s, Elzie Crisler Segar's bubble-armed sailor, known to us as Popeye, is shown downing a can of spinach and throwing a "super slowball" to strike out his archenemy Bluto with one pitch. Bluto swings three times at the same pitch. One time, Bluto helplessly screws himself into the ground; another time, Popeye belts him one after striking him out, which would, were they playing today, earn Popeye an automatic ejection and a heavy fine.

Hayden "Sidd" (short for Siddhartha) Finch was a reclusive yogi drafted by the New York Mets who could throw a fastball 168 miles per hour. At least, that was the story written for *Sports Illustrated* by participatory journalist George Plimpton. The story ran in the April 1, 1985, edition of the magazine, complete with photos.

Finch, according to Plimpton's article, grew up in an English orphanage. He was adopted by an English archeologist who later died in a plane crash when Finch was young. After briefly attending Harvard University, Finch moved to Tibet, where he reportedly mastered the secrets of the "yogic mind-body." He returned to the United States, where he was drafted by the Mets. But Finch retired before pitching in a major-league game, ostensibly to play the French horn, his first love.

In the following April 15 issue of *Sports Illustrated*, the story was revealed as an April Fool's Day hoax. It didn't really matter to Mets fans—they had a better pitcher than Finch anyway in Dwight Gooden, who led New York to the World Championship in 1986.

That was certainly part of the reason, but the other issue was the spitball was so, well, unsanitary. Umpires were constantly tossing out balls that were dirty or otherwise defaced, but the minute they tossed one in, the pitcher would step off the mound, load up the ball and begin pitching again.

Another reason was probably Babe Ruth. By 1919, the people in charge were seeing that Ruth's home-run hitting prowess was having a positive effect on baseball attendance. On the theory that low-scoring games weren't pulling in the fans, both the

National and American leagues eventually decided to get rid of factors, such as the spitball, that slowed down run production.

At any rate, the pitch was deemed illegal by the major leagues in 1919. To try to be fair to pitchers who still used it, both leagues allowed those hurlers to continue throwing it.

So, technically, the spitball was not completely illegal until Burleigh Grimes retired in 1934.

But, of course, that didn't stop pitchers from continuing to use the spitball on the sly. The first such

Bobby Mathews, like many 19th-century pitchers, used to wet his fingers before throwing the ball in order to get a better grip.

pitcher to be tossed out of a game for using a spitball was Nelson "Nels" Potter of the St. Louis Browns in 1944. Potter (Cardinals, Athletics, Red Sox, Browns, Braves, 1936–49) had a habit of wetting his fingers before throwing a pitch. When he was ejected by umpire Cal Hubbard in a July 20 game against the Yankees, Potter insisted that he wasn't throwing a spitball, but rather he was trying to get a grip on the ball on a hot, dry day. That ejection may have cost him his only 20-win season. Potter was 19–7 that year for the pennant-winning Browns.

On May 1, 1968, relief pitcher John Boozer (Phillies, 1962–69) got the thumb for tossing a spitter in warm-ups.

The pitcher best known for throwing, or allegedly throwing, a spitball was Gaylord Perry, who pitched in the big leagues for 21 years. Perry's habit of touching his belt buckle, pants leg, cap brim and hair before every pitch was effective and distracting. Often Perry was not accessing any foreign substances; he just wanted the batter and the ump to *think* he was. He was only caught throwing a spitter one time: in 1982, while pitching for the Mariners, he was ejected from the game for using a foreign substance on the ball. Perry said after the game that he didn't know where the slimy, resinlike substance came from, and suggested his opponent might have doctored the ball.

IN CASE YOU DIDN'T KNOW

Leo Durocher, when he was managing the Dodgers, once fined one of his own pitchers, Bobo Newsome, for throwing a spitball—not because Bobo threw the pitch, but "because he lied to me about [not] throwing it." Leo didn't like to be kept in the dark.

THE SPITBALL FAMILY

Pitchers did not use only spit to make their pitches dance. Some used a combination of spit and various other substances. In the 1930s and '40s, pitchers would suck on lozenges during innings to work up a good expectorate. They'd rub the ball with sandpaper, gouge it with belt buckles, fingernails, wedding rings, anything to create a rough surface that might make a ball dip or hop as it came to the plate.

Veteran catchers could also help. Catcher Ted "Double Duty" Radcliffe, a star player in the Negro League from 1928 to 1950, would tape a piece of an emery board to his belt to rough up the ball for his pitchers. As mentioned, the Yankees' Elston Howard would intentionally drop the ball in the dirt or mud to give his pitcher something with which to work.

Sometimes players were caught. In the 1987 season, pitcher Joe Niekro was caught with a nail file in his back pocket. Niekro was spared a fine when he explained that, as a knuckleballer, he needed to file his nails between innings. Well, maybe.

But a week later, Kevin Gross, a pitcher for the Philadelphia Phillies, was caught with a small piece of sandpaper in his glove. He didn't have an excuse and was suspended.

Many pitchers would put foreign substances either on their zippers or inside them, figuring that umpires, being manly men, wouldn't check inside their pants.

The most disgusting foreign substance? In his book *Me and the Spitter*, Gaylord Perry explained that he would sniff chili peppers to make his nose run just before he took the mound, and would use the, uh, result on the baseball. Yuck.

ELSTON HOWARD

Gaylord
PERRY

Giants, Indians, Rangers, Padres, Yankees, Braves, Mariners, Royals, 1962–83

During his career, Perry was constantly accused of throwing a spitball, a charge he denied. The spitball was, of course, outlawed by then. However, after he retired, he wrote a book, *Me and the Spitter*, which pretty much confirmed what everyone believed.

CAREER STATISTICS					
W	L	SAVES	ERA	SO	CG
314	265	11	3.11	3,534	303

Jack
CHESBRO

Pirates, Yankees, Red Sox, 1899–1909

Chesbro also had a good fastball and curve, and in fact led the Pittsburgh Pirates to pennants in 1901 and 1902. He actually picked up a spitball midcareer.

CAREER STATISTICS					
W	L	SAVES	ERA	SO	CG
198	132	5	2.68	1,265	260

Stan
COVELESKI

Athletics, Indians, Senators, Yankees, 1912–28

Coveleski is a pitcher noted for his outstanding control of the spitball. This is probably an exaggeration, but Coveleski reportedly once pitched seven consecutive innings without throwing one ball. It seems odd to try to make the batter swing at a bad pitch, since most pitchers tend to "waste" a pitch when they have an 0–2 count on a batter. And Coveleski, in *The Glory of Their Times*, doesn't mention it. You'd think he would remember something like that.

CAREER STATISTICS					
W	L	SAVES	ERA	SO	CG
215	142	21	2.89	981	224

Urban "Red"
FABER

White Sox, 1914–33

The towering (6'2", 180 lbs.) Faber was having arm trouble in the minors and learned the spitball to save his arm. It also saved his career, as Faber pitched in the big leagues for 20 years and was elected to the Hall of Fame in 1964.

CAREER STATISTICS					
W	L	SAVES	ERA	SO	CG
254	213	28	3.15	1,471	273

Edward "Whitey"
FORD

Yankees, 1950–67

Ford was also called "The Chairman of the Board" for his superb control of a variety of pitches. Like many spitballers of that era, Ford was forced to be somewhat subversive in his approach. Sometimes, catcher Elston Howard would catch a warm-up pitch and "accidentally" lose his balance; he would right himself with his throwing arm, with the ball in his hand, and push the baseball into the dirt, thus giving Ford a nice mudball.

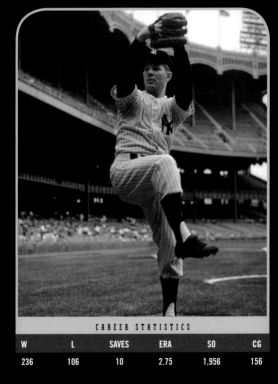

CAREER STATISTICS					
W	L	SAVES	ERA	SO	CG
236	106	10	2.75	1,956	156

HOW IT'S DONE

The Spitball

Typically, a lubricant is placed somewhere on a pitcher's uniform or in his hair. Transferring the "juice" to the ball is relatively easy: the pitcher can step off the mound and rub the fingers of his pitching hand in the lubricant to get some of it on them.

It should be noted that even when the spitball was legal, pitchers who used it tended to hide the lubricant on their bodies somewhere and touch various parts of the uniform so the batter wouldn't know what he was throwing.

A pitcher's grip on the lubricated ball varies. Some pitchers place the spit on one side of the ball and then throw it like a fastball. Such pitches tend to break sideways, toward the "wet" side of the ball.

The same principal is used when pitchers "scuff" the ball, or cut or deface it.

Another way to throw the spitter is to use saliva, or whatever, on one side of the ball and grip that spot with the first two fingers of the throwing hand. Gripping the ball with those two fingers and his thumb, a pitcher sort of pushes the ball out of his hand. This technique tends to make the ball drop more than expected.

LEFT: No, pitcher Burleigh Grimes is not trying to remember the count. He's loading up the ball for the next batter.

Hidden locations for lubricant and other tools for altering the ball

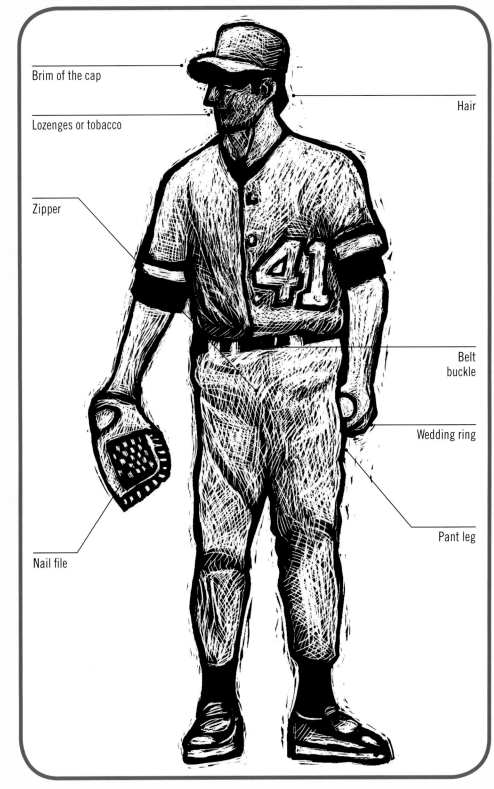

Brim of the cap

Hair

Lozenges or tobacco

Zipper

Belt buckle

Wedding ring

Pant leg

Nail file

RELIEF PITCHING

ABOVE: Cy Young started every fourth day, but also had no problem stepping in as a reliever on his days off.

aseball historian Bill James points out that the first honcho to use relievers was Napoleon Bonaparte, and he's got something of a point. Napoleon, of course, was known for holding back a few of his more elite cavalry units for the latter part of a battle, inserting them at key moments to change the course of a conflict. If he was winning, these units would hasten the outcome; if the outcome was still in question, the reserves could help turn the tide in Napoleon's favor.

Up until the 1880s, the rules of baseball did not allow substitutions. And when this rule was finally abandoned, most substitutions were made due to injury. By the mid-1890s, pitchers were still pitching complete games. The only exception to this rule was if a team was far behind and a manager didn't want to see his top pitcher throwing needlessly in a game that was lost. In such a situation, the least-used pitcher on staff would finish out the game.

But that began to change as the 20th century opened. Managers, particularly the Giants' John McGraw and Boston Red Sox skipper Jimmy Collins, began to see that a late-inning replacement pitcher could sometimes stall an opponent's comeback and help win the game.

Collins, in fact, had an advantage over most other teams:

FREDERICK "FIRPO" MARBERRY

Cy Young—a pitcher who started every fourth day but who had no problem relieving any game in between. Even in his 30s, Young was perhaps the supplest athlete in baseball. He never seemed to pull a muscle or strain a joint, even when he pitched two or three days in a row.

McGraw used a similar tactic, only he spread the relief appearances around, using the entire staff. In 1905, the top four saves leaders in the National League were Giants, led by "Hooks" Wiltse, with six.

Other teams picked this up. The Cubs used Mordecai "Three Finger" Brown in 15 to 20 relief stints a year between 1908 and 1911; and while he was mainly a starter, he led the league in saves all three years. In 1911, Brown was credited with a then-record 13 saves.

By the 1910s, managers began thinking about using a pitcher on the staff principally for relief. If it can be said that one player might be construed as the first "real" relief pitcher, it might well be James Otis "Doc" Crandall for the Giants.

In his book *Pitching in a Pinch*, Christy Mathewson recalled that when Crandall (Giants, Brownies [FL], Browns, Braves, 1908–18) came to the Giants in 1908, the team didn't have enough full uniforms, so Crandall shagged balls in a Giants shirt and the trousers he wore to the tryout.

But Crandall proved to be an excellent utility man, both on the mound and at the plate, and he easily made the cut that year. Crandall started and relieved for most of his career, winning 102 games and saving 25. According to Mathewson, Crandall once told him, "I didn't feel at home out there today until a lot of people got on the bases."

In 1924, Frederick "Firpo" Marberry (Senators, Tigers, Giants, 1923–36), a rookie for the Washington Senators, started 15 games and relieved in 35 more, earning 15 saves. From 1924 to 1926, he led the American League in appearances, averaging 55 annually. He also led the league in saves in all 3 years, averaging 17 a season.

Marberry was the first pitcher in major-league baseball whose main job was to relieve starters. There were games he started, certainly, but that was if the Senators were short on pitchers because of injuries or scheduling. Marberry's principal task was coming in and pitching at the end of games.

He understood his position, and he enjoyed the pressure. Not coincidentally, the Senators won back-to-back American League Championships in 1924 and 1925, and the World Series in 1924.

Marberry's success pushed the role of the reliever into sharper focus. Managers began to look at non-starters at the end of the bench as more than just potential substitutes in case of injury; now they started thinking about keeping pitchers who could come into a game that was close and either hold the lead or continue to keep the game close until the team could catch up. Many of these were cagey veterans who still knew how to pitch—men like Waite Hoyt, or Herbie Pennock of the Yankees, or Jack Quinn of the Athletics.

The next great reliever after Marberry was the Yankees' Johnny Murphy. But again, Murphy also started a handful of games every year. The expectation was that, while some teams have pitchers who

RIGHT: There is no longer any question about who might be the greatest post-season reliever ever. It's the Yankees' Mariano Rivera, here letting fly his famous split-finger fastball.

MARIANO RIVERA

primarily relieved in games, using a pitcher as just a reliever was something of an extravagance. The concept of the pure relief pitcher was still a few years away.

Murphy (Yankees, Red Sox, 1932–47) was a control pitcher who, for the few years of his career, started every once in a while. But as his value as a reliever increased, he started fewer and fewer games every year. He led the league in saves four times and set several records for saving and winning games in relief.

The Yankees continued to be pioneers in the use of relievers. Baseball's next great reliever was Joe Page. Page (Yankees, 1944–50, 1954) had a blistering fastball but had trouble controlling it. Yankee skipper Bucky Harris took him out of the starting rotation and made him a reliever, and Page blossomed, leading the league in saves in 1947 and 1949. In 1949, he saved 27 games, setting a record that stood until 1961.

"In 1947," wrote David Halberstam in his book, *The Summer of '49*, "Page proved he was able to pitch for two or three innings, as he could not for seven or eight. He came in, took charge and simply overwhelmed the hitters."

Page was clearly a huge advantage for the Yankees in the late 1940s. Ted Williams, after one masterful Page performance in 1949, conceded that while the everyday players on his team may have had an advantage over the Yankees that year, Page was such a big factor that he may have been the difference in that year's pennant race, which the Yankees won over Boston by a game.

By the mid-1950s, managers realized they needed a relief specialist to go two or three innings and "save" games. Pitchers like Hoyt Wilhelm and Lindy McDaniel, both of whom began their careers in the 1950s, were among the first pitchers to be career relievers.

Even at that point, though, pitchers (and managers) were still focused on pitching complete games. Relievers were undoubtedly a factor now, but many pitchers still balked at coming out. It wasn't really a part of a manager's strategy to let a starter go five or six innings and turn the game over to a reliever.

By the 1970s, the era of the great career relievers had begun. Managers and starting pitchers still desired to finish games, but the effectiveness of relievers had eroded that concept considerably. It was very obvious that teams

BELOW: Joe Page (center) with Joe DiMaggio (left) and co-owner of the Yankees, Larry McPhail , celebrate winning the 1949 World Series.

JOHNNY MURPHY

with good or great relievers had a considerable edge.

Pitchers like Sparky Lyle, Rich Gossage, Al Hrabosky and Rollie Fingers were now pitching only if their team was ahead or only a run behind. In other words, they were being used more and more in situations where the game was on the line. They never started. They usually pitched two or three innings in a game. Although some managers were experimenting with it, the concept of middle relief had not yet come into vogue.

"Pitchers like Rollie and me did what two or three guys do now," said Gossage, in a 2008 interview with the Associated Press.

The single-inning reliever eased itself into the game. Bruce Sutter was one of the first, because his managers wanted to be able to use him in as many games as possible. Jeff Reardon (Mets, Expos, Twins, Red Sox, Braves, Reds, Yankees, 1979–94) and Dennis Eckersley (Indians, Red Sox, Cubs, Athletics, Cardinals, 1975–98) rarely, if ever, pitched more than two relief innings per game. In New York, closer Mariano Rivera rarely pitched more than one.

Even that concept has expanded. These days, managers, in addition to working out who will relieve the game, also set up their staffs to include a rather extensive middle-relief unit. The Boston Red Sox, who won the World Series in 2007, may not have had the best reliever in baseball in Jonathan Papelbon that year, but manager Terry Francona also had Hideki Okajima, who usually pitched the seventh and eighth innings to "set up" Papelbon. If he felt Okajima could only pitch one inning, Francona inserted Mike Timlin or Javy Rodriguez to "set up" Okajima.

What this meant to Boston was that their starters only needed to pitch five of six innings, after which they could turn the game over to the relief corps. To be honest, the only thing preventing a team from using pitchers to pitch, say, two to three innings and then turning the game over to a three- or four-man relief staff is the limit on the number of pitchers on a roster. A team still has to have four or five guys to start games and go at least five innings. But that may change someday.

FACIAL HAIR

When he temporarily broke the save record in 1990, a reporter asked Boston's Jeff Reardon why it was that all his relief brethren seemed to wear facial hair. Reardon didn't have a real answer, saying, "I don't know. I just like my beard."

But it was a good question. Reardon was known for his beard, Goose Gossage for his Fu Manchu mustache, Rollie Fingers for his Snidely Whiplash mustache and Al Hrabosky for his Fu Manchu and long hair. For some, like Hrabosky and Gossage, it was a form of intimidation. Hrabosky, for one, balked at shaving the mustache when asked to by one of his managers. "How can I intimidate someone with a clean face?" he petulantly asked. For Fingers, it was more of a fashion statement. And for Reardon, well, it just looked good.

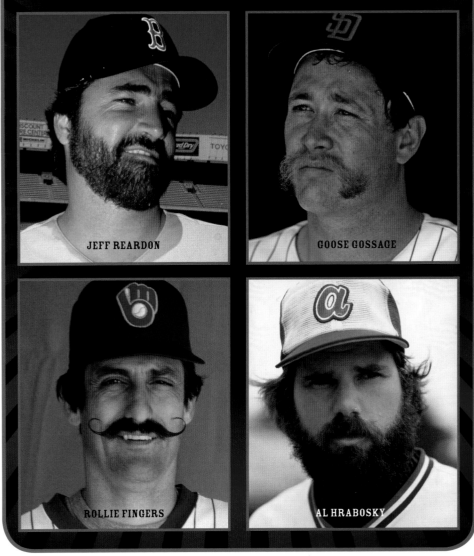

JEFF REARDON

GOOSE GOSSAGE

ROLLIE FINGERS

AL HRABOSKY

The Best of the Best

RELIEF PITCHING

Mariano RIVERA

Yankees, 1995–present

Rivera is one of the greatest postseason closers ever. During the Yankees' run in the late 1990s, he was almost unhittable in the playoffs and World Series.

Rich "Goose" GOSSAGE

White Sox, Pirates, Yankees, Padres, Cubs, Giants, Rangers, Athletics, Mariners, 1972–94

The 6–3 fastballing Gossage was easily the most intimidating reliever of the late 1970s and early 1980s, when he pitched for the Yankees. Yankees teammate Rudy May once said that Gossage threw so hard, opponents feared that if the pitch got away from him, "they'd end up with a tag on their toe."

CAREER STATISTICS

W	L	SAVES	ERA	SO	CG
124	107	310	3.01	1,502	16

CAREER STATISTICS

W	L	SAVES	ERA	SO	CG
66	48	469	2.31	915	0

Trevor
HOFFMAN

Padres, Marlins
1993–present

Hoffman is the all-time saves leader, with 524. Hoffman is underrated as a closer, in part because his teams have not had a lot of postseason success during his career. But 524 saves is a lot of saves any way one looks at it.

CAREER STATISTICS

W	L	SAVES	ERA	SO	CG
54	66	469	2.29	1,047	0

Bruce
SUTTER

Cubs, Cardinals, Braves
1976–88

Consistent and durable, Sutter was overpowering when he pitched for the Cubs and Cardinals.

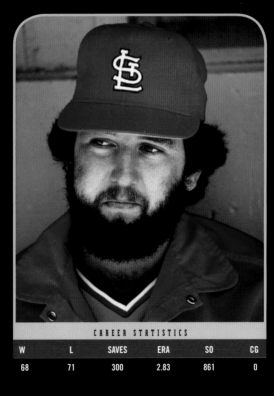

CAREER STATISTICS

W	L	SAVES	ERA	SO	CG
68	71	300	2.83	861	0

Lee
SMITH

Cubs, Red Sox, Cardinals, Yankees, Orioles, Angels, Reds, Expos, 1980–97

Smith, at six-feet-six and 275 pounds, was from the Goose Gossage school of relievers: an intimidating guy who blew fastballs by batters.

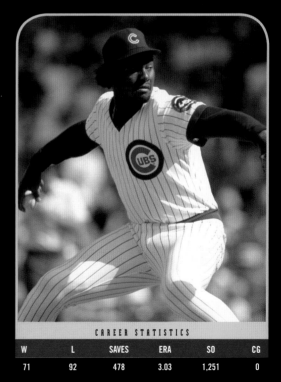

CAREER STATISTICS

W	L	SAVES	ERA	SO	CG
71	92	478	3.03	1,251	0

HOW IT'S DONE
Relief Pitching

If there is one enduring truth or common thread with regard to relievers, it's that they are all impossibly confident. Jonathan Papelbon, Sparky Lyle and Francisco Rodriguez all want the ball in the late innings. Rodriguez was especially spectacular in 2008, becoming the first reliever to record 60 saves in one season.

The strategy of relief pitching has changed considerably over the years. And while most coaches prefer to use fastball pitchers in the role, guys that throw 90-plus miles per hour have not, down the years, been the only option. Red Sox knuckleballer Tim Wakefield was a fine reliever for Boston in 1999, a year Boston won the American League East pennant. Trevor Hoffman, whose principal pitch is his changeup, is now the all-time leader in saves. And former New York Yankee Sparky Lyle won the Cy Young Award as a reliever in 1977 throwing primarily sliders. So pitchers get it done in different ways.

What is needed, according to Lyle and others, is an inherent confidence on the mound. Many times, a reliever comes into a game and there are men on base. There is little room for mistakes.

"With a one-run lead, I attack them and put them away," Angels closer Francisco Rodriguez told *USA Today*.

"You can't be thinking about too many things," said Royals reliever Dan Quisenberry. "Relief pitchers have to get into a zone of their own."

JONATHAN PAPELBON

FRANCISCO RODRIGUEZ

BUNTING

ABOVE: Tom Barlow woodcut. One of the first players to use the bunt consistently. OPPOSITE: The Yankees' Derek Jeter is one of baseball's best all-around hitters: A player who can hit home runs and who can also lay down a bunt as well as anyone in the league.

The bunt is one of those offensive weapons that has its origins in the earliest days of professional baseball. Part of the bunt's very early popularity was due to a rule in the mid-19th century that deemed any struck ball that first hit in fair territory and then traveled into foul ground a fair ball. This generated the "fair-foul" ball, which was a ball struck with sufficient "spin" or "English" that it would bounce fair and then fly off into foul territory. With catchers standing well behind home plate (because, for the most part, they caught pitches bare-handed in those days), this was a not-inconsiderable weapon.

In addition, at the time, foul balls were not counted as strikes. Thus, a batter could stand at the plate, end-lessly attempting to spin a fair ball foul. One of the best ways to generate spin on a ball was for a batter to move one of his hands up the neck of the bat, to the midpoint or farther, for better bat control.

This was not known as a bunt but as a "trick hit" or "tricky hit," which, for many years, was somewhat disparaged.

Some reports indicate that two teammates from the old 1872 Brooklyn Atlantics—shortstop Dickey Pearce (Mutuals [NA], Atlantics [NA], Cardinals, 1871–77) and catcher Tom Barlow (Atlantics [NA], Mutuals [NA], Elm Cities [NA], 1872–75)—were the first play-ers to use the bunt consistently.

Barlow, according to many contemporary accounts, had a two-foot bat he would take to the plate and use to spin a fair hit into foul territory. Some accounts of the day have him trying this as early as the 1860s, when he was a semiprofessional player in New York City.

Other accounts have Pearce as the first to employ the

bunt. Unlike Barlow, Pearce didn't have a miniature bat, and didn't bunt as much, either.

Pearce actually began as a semipro star in Brooklyn in 1856. He was one of the first players ever paid a sal-ary, as opposed to a game-by-game stipend. Pearce may not have bunted balls in the way we recognize today, but rather he tried to hit balls with backspin so they would carry into foul territory.

Regardless of who actually began bunting first, Barlow's minibat drew considerable comment from sportswriters of the day. Since it was a little bit out of the ordinary, most sportswriters spurned the bat, although they appreciated ballplayers who could bunt a fair ball foul with a regular-size bat.

Barlow, whether using the bunt or not, was not a particularly good hitter, and when he retired in 1875, he had few, if any, imitators who used a tiny bat.

Another key chapter in the story of the bunt took place in 1877, when the "fair-foul" rule was abolished and the catcher's mask came into vogue. The mask enabled catchers to play much closer to the plate, and they were therefore better able to field bunts that fell in front of the batter.

In fact, the bunt itself quickly slipped out of vogue after the elimination of the "fair-foul" rule. There is a perception that bunting was a staple of the 19th cen-tury, but this is not so. One finds few, if any, accounts of bunting for almost 10 years after the end of the "fair-foul" rule.

In 1888, a few years after the National League and American Association allowed flattened bats in games, the bunt made a big comeback. Arlie Latham, a star for the St. Louis team, was one of the dominant players in

DEREK JETER

LEFT TO RIGHT: Arlie Latham, Mike "King" Kelly, Tommy Burns

the AA, particularly because his flat bat could lay down some fearsome bunts. In particular, Latham became adept at laying down a bunt to advance a teammate. This eventually became known as a "sacrifice bunt."

The team that became well known during that era for bunting, for both base hits and to move the runner along, was the Chicago White Stockings of the National League. With excellent bat handlers like Mike "King" Kelly and Tommy Burns, the White Stockings (who would become the Cubs in the 20th century) won the National League crown, while St. Louis won the AA championship in 1886.

In fact, the two teams played an early "World Series" that fall, and a Latham bunt in the deciding game clinched the series for St. Louis.

For the next 30 years, the bunt was a huge weapon in professional baseball when a team's basic strategy was to play for one run at a time. One of the reasons most of baseball's all-time best bunters played in the early part of the 20th century was that bunting was an art practiced by nearly everyone at that time. Leadoff men were for the most part expected to be able to lay down a bunt to reach base. Pitchers, even those who were considered good hitting pitchers, were expected to be able to bunt.

That all changed with Babe Ruth. Or at least it started to change. Ruth, a free-swinger with the Yankees beginning in 1920, illustrated dramatically that home runs were more effective than bunts when it came to generating offense. (Babe Ruth, by the way, was an excellent bunter. It was said that on the great 1927 Yankees, only Earle Combs and Mark Koenig were better. Ruth bunted safely 12 times in 1927, the year he socked a then-record 60 home runs.)

Ruth didn't change things overnight. And he was helped greatly by the introduction of livelier baseball in 1920. But, as his biographer Robert Creamer explained, Ruth revolutionized the game. Home runs were in, and bunts and sacrifice bunts were, for the most part, out.

Even the strikeout was not as much of a stigma.

"A strikeout heretofore had been something of a disgrace—reread 'Casey at the Bat,'" observed Creamer. "A batter was supposed to protect the plate [and] get a piece of the ball.

"In Ruth's case, a strikeout was only a momentary, if melodramatic, setback. Protecting the plate declined in importance, along with the sacrifice and the steal. The big hit, the big inning, blossomed."

And teams soon found out that the big hit and the big inning excited the fans. Ruth's home-run hitting was good for the gate, and teams began trying to find their own sluggers.

To be sure, teams still employed the bunt, particularly the sacrifice, because many pitchers were not good hitters. But as a strategy, the bunt declined in the first part of the 20th century.

According to statistics provided by the Society for American Baseball Research, sacrifice bunts for non-pitchers were about 5.5 per 500 plate appearances in the 1940s. By the 1980s, those numbers had dropped to 5.0 per 500 appearances, and by 2004, it was 3.1 per 500 appearances. Coaches and general managers have been shying away from the bunt for the last several decades, decrying it as a "small ball" tactic that no longer works well in an era of home runs and big innings.

THE BALTIMORE CHOP

WEE WILLIE KEELER

The Baltimore chop, the hitting tactic of slapping down at a pitched ball so that it bounces in front of the plate and then high into the air, was not actually invented in Baltimore in the 1890s.

But Ned Hanlon's Orioles were certainly masters of the trick. Hanlon's leadoff man, John McGraw, was a masterful batsman who could foul off ball after ball until he was either walked or got the pitch he wanted. If the infielders were playing too close to him, McGraw would "chop" at the ball and cause it to hit in front of the plate and then over the infielder's head for a single.

McGraw and teammates Hughie Jennings and Wee Willie Keeler were so good at this tactic, sportswriters of the time named it after the team.

However, Ross Barnes, the hitting star for the Chicago White Stockings of the old National Association, was well known for being able to turn the trick in the 1870s. Barnes was a great all-around player and known for his excellent batting skills. He did not necessarily use the "chopping hit" very often, but he probably was one of the first to use it.

The Best of the Best

BUNTING

Earle COMBS

Yankees, 1924–35

Combs was the leadoff man for the great Yankees teams of the 1920s. Blessed with exceptional speed, Combs regularly beat out bunts to reach first base.

	CAREER STATISTICS			
BA	HR	RBI	H	SB
.325	58	632	1,866	96

Arlie "The Freshest Man on Earth" LATHAM

Buffalo [NA], Browns [AA], Chicago [PL], Cardinals, Nationals, Giants, 1880–1909

Latham was a player with one of the greatest nicknames of all time. He was also one of the most accomplished bunters of his era and popularized the sacrifice bunt.

	CAREER STATISTICS			
BA	HR	RBI	H	SB
.268	27	563	1,833	739

Oscar "The Hoosier Comet" CHARLESTON

Negro League, 1915–46

Charleston had otherworldly speed and could hit for power. But when he needed a base hit, he could bunt the ball as well as anyone who's ever played.

	CAREER STATISTICS		
		BA	HR
NEGRO LEAGUE		.330	169

Ty
COBB

Cobb was another player with great speed. He was a master of bat control and almost never fell into a slump because he could bunt his way out of it.

Eddie
COLLINS

Not as fast as Cobb or Combs, Collins still could place bunts with the best of them.

Phil
RIZZUTO

The "Scooter," as he was called, was better known for his defensive abilities, but when he was moved from number eight to the leadoff spot after World War II, Rizzuto's ability to get on base was a huge weapon for the Yankees. One of the best ways for him to get to first was to bunt.

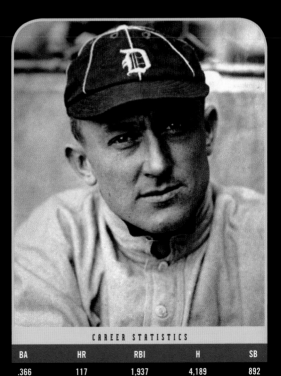

CAREER STATISTICS

BA	HR	RBI	H	SB
.366	117	1,937	4,189	892

CAREER STATISTICS

BA	HR	RBI	H	SB
.333	47	1,300	3.315	744

CAREER STATISTICS

BA	HR	RBI	H	SB
.273	38	563	1,588	149

HOW IT'S DONE
Bunting

The idea of the bunt is to "catch" the ball with one's bat. A good bunter places one hand on the handle of the bat and the other about halfway up. He steps in front of the plate just as the pitcher is delivering the ball. When the pitch comes in, he has to relax his hands and try to soak up as much of the pitch's energy as he can. Thus, a batter tries to "catch" the baseball with his bat, allowing it to bounce away from him as slowly as possible. It's important to remember that good bunters bunt strikes. A good bunter waits for a pitch as much as a good home-run hitter waits for his.

MIKE "KING'" KELLY

Cap Anson's Chicago White Stockings were among the first teams to use the hit and run on a regular basis. It's doubtful that catcher and all-around star Mike "King" Kelly originated the hit and run, but he was well known for it during his career. His teammates Edward "Ned" Williamson and George Gore were also strong batsmen, and all three could work the play as either hitters or baserunners.

Another early team known for the hit and run was the Baltimore Orioles of the National League. Unlike the White Stockings, who had a few heavy hitters, like Anson and Kelly, the Orioles got by on clever hitting, smart baserunning and a little doctoring of the infield.

With solid batsmen like John McGraw, Hughie Jennings and Wee Willie Keeler, the Orioles were a hit-and-run threat in virtually every inning. In addition, according to McGraw's biographer Charles C. Alexander, McGraw and Jennings "hit on the idea of having groundskeeper John Murphy contour the foul lines so that bunted balls would be more likely to stay fair, and pack the dirt hard around home plate to effectuate high-bounce base hits."

A third team, the old Boston Beaneaters (who would later become the Braves) of the National League were also renowned for the hit-and-run play. Historian Bill James believes that Tommy McCarthy

THE PITCHOUT

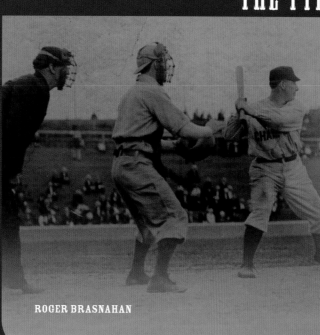

ROGER BRASNAHAN

Pitching out—that is, throwing a ball deliberately outside the strike zone so that a catcher can catch it and gun it to second base to try to nail a baserunner—was not a popular strategy in the 19th century. The conventional wisdom was that "wasting" a pitch to try to catch a baserunner didn't work often enough to make it worthwhile.

But as the hit-and-run play became more popular in the latter part of the 19th and early 20th centuries, the pitchout was one way to defeat the strategy. If the pitcher threw the ball wide, a batter couldn't hit it, and the baserunner was vulnerable to a fast pitch from the catcher. Pitcher Deacon Phillipe (Pirates, 1899–1911) was a fan of the pitchout, and Giants catcher Roger Bresnahan was one of its better practitioners. As the 20th century wore on, baserunners on first would often fake a move to second to draw a pitchout.

RIGHT: Ricky Henderson was part of one of the best-known hit-and-run teams, Billy Martin's Athletics.

of the Best
THE HIT AND RUN

Ray
DANDRIDGE

Negro League, 1933–49

Dandrige had tremendous bat control and was an effective hit-and-run hitter for a variety of teams in his 17-year Negro League career.

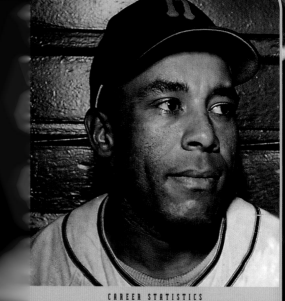

CAREER STATISTICS	
BA	HR

BARRETT

Red Sox, Padres, 1982–91

Barrett is another unsung number-two hitter with exceptional bat control and a great batting eye.

CAREER STATISTICS				
BA	HR	RBI	H	SB
.278	18	314	938	57

Wee Willie
KEELER

Giants, Dodgers, Orioles, Yankees
1892–1920

Keeler was one of the best singles hitters in baseball history. He and teammate John McGraw were masters of executing the hit and run, and helped the Orioles to numerous pennants. Keeler, of course, is the player who, when asked the secret of his success, explained that he would "hit 'em where they ain't."

CAREER STATISTICS				
BA	HR	RBI	H	SB
.341	33	810	2,392	495

Sam
CRAWFORD

Reds, Tigers, 1899–1917

Crawford, for much of his career, batted behind all-time great Ty Cobb. He and Cobb were probably the best hit-and-run combination in the history of the league.

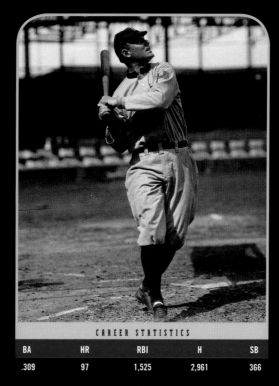

CAREER STATISTICS				
BA	HR	RBI	H	SB
.309	97	1,525	2,961	366

Mike "King"
KELLY

Reds, White Stockings, Braves, Red Stockings [PL], Red Stockings [AA], Reds [AA], Giants, 1878–93

A masterful hitter, Kelly was one of the first players to see the possibilities of the hit and run. He perfected the play with Chicago.

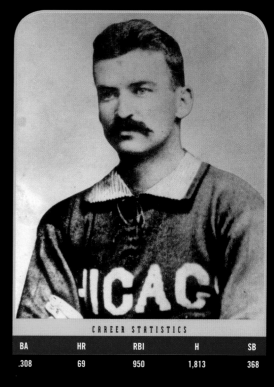

CAREER STATISTICS				
BA	HR	RBI	H	SB
.308	69	950	1,813	368

BOB FERGUSON

SWITCH-HITTING

These days, switch-hitters generally come to bat depending on whether a right- or left-handed pitcher is on the mound. (For the record, if the pitcher is right-handed, a switch-hitter will bat lefty, and vice versa.) But the first known switch-hitter in baseball was infielder Bob Ferguson (Mutuals [NA], Brooklyn [NA], Hartford [NA], Cubs, Troy [NL], Phillies, Pittsburgh [AA], 1871–84). Ferguson, who batted mostly right-handed, was an excellent batsman. He switched to the left side in a game in 1871 against Cincinnati to keep the ball away from the left side of the potent Reds infield. In another game, he batted left-handed for three at-bats, then moved to the other side of the plate and stroked a clean single over the head of the opposing third baseman.

(Reds [UA], Braves, Phillies, St. Louis [AA], Dodgers, 1884–96) was another early user of the hit and run while with Boston in 1892.

The hit-and-run play became a staple of what was called "inside baseball" in the late 19th and early 20th centuries. Initially, players would work out between themselves when the hit-and-run play would be used. But managers like Cap Anson and Connie Mack, of the Philadelphia Athletics, were also key participants.

As with several "small ball" strategies, the hit and run fell out of favor after the Yankees' Babe Ruth began popularizing the concept of playing for the big inning. But the hit and run remained a more viable strategy than, say, the bunt or the Baltimore chop. There were still teams throughout the 20th century that didn't have heavy hitters.

The Chicago Cubs of the late 1960s were managed by future Hall of Fame manager Leo Durocher. Durocher went to Chicago the year after the nightmarish College of Coaches fiasco (see page 207). To some players, it was like night and day. Cub great Glen Beckert, in Peter Golenbock's book *Wrigleyville*, credited Durocher for turning the club around.

"Leo took charge," said Beckert. "He said, 'No more of this bullshit. I'm the manager.'

"Leo helped teach me the hit and run," Beckert continued. "I learned to keep the strikeouts down, put the ball in play and hit behind the runner. Leo would talk to me about it."

Perhaps the best-known hit-and-run teams in most recent years were Billy Martin's Athletics from 1980 to 1982. The overachieving Athletics were aggressive on the basepaths to make up for their lack of power, and Martin's tactics (not much different from Anson's) were called "Billyball."

Today, the hit and run is still a viable play, as some baseball managers realize that the old plays are still useful in some situations.

HOW IT'S DONE
The Hit and Run

During the hit and run, the baserunner or baserunners are in motion before the ball is hit, while the batter attempts to make contact with the pitch. The hit and run is usually employed when a good contact hitter is at the plate. In many cases, the batter will try to hit "behind" the runner—that is, into the gap between first and second base into right field.

If this is successful, the player at first base can advance all the way to third base on even a short hit into right field. If the ball is caught, however, or hit to a fielder, the hit and run often results in a double play, as the baserunner on first base has usually advanced too far along the basepath to return to first base.

DEREK JETER

The hit-and-run is all about placing the ball. Seattle's Ichiro Suzuki and the Yankees' Derek Jeter (right) both have exquisite form when the situation arises.

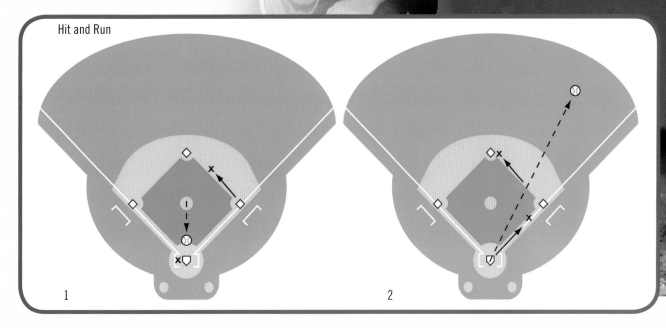

Hit and Run

1

2

THE HOME RUN

In the early days of the game, when baseball was not as lively and strategy was focused more on scoring a single run at a time, home runs were not necessarily a major strategy of the game. In addition, many ballparks at the time had large outfields, and the contemporary thinking in the 19th century was that ballplayers trying to hit a home run would more likely end up flying out.

Some of the league's more aggressive baserunners could sometimes pull off an inside-the-park home run, but the kind of fence-clearing homers that are so prevalent today were rare in the late 19th and early 20th centuries.

"[In 1902], believe it or not, I led the league in home runs," reported Tommy Leach, who played third base for the Pirates from 1900 to 1912. Leach was five-feet-six and 150 pounds. He had six home runs. "None of them," admitted Leach in an interview, "went out of the park."

The next year, Leach had seven inside-the-park home runs. But he finished second in the race, to the Dodgers' Jimmy Sheckard's nine round-trippers. None of Sheckard's made it out of the park, either.

All that changed with the decision by the Boston Red Sox to make a pitcher, Babe Ruth, into at least a part-time outfielder. In 1918, Ruth had experimented with playing the outfield in between pitching starts. The results were good, hitting-wise, but Ruth's pitching had suffered, and frankly, it was Ruth's pitching that enabled the Sox to win the 1918 World Series.

The next season, in 1919, Ruth started the year hitting very well, but he was not the dominant pitcher he had been in previous years, and there was some question as to the effectiveness of using the league's best lefty as an outfielder as well.

That effectively ended in June of that year, when the Red Sox brought up 19-year-old Waite Hoyt, who began pitching superbly. That enabled Ruth to concentrate on hitting—and did he ever, eventually socking a then-record 29 home runs.

The next year, Ruth was traded to the Yankees, and his career as a home-run hitter began in earnest. That year, Ruth hit an unbelievable 54 home runs, more than every other team in the American League and more than all but one team, Philadelphia, in the National League.

It was unprecedented. It was unheard of. And it made Babe Ruth an immensely popular player.

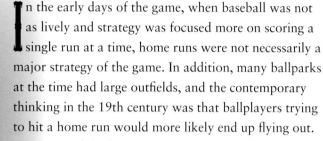

TOMMY LEACH

ROGERS HORNSBY

Exhibiting the superb form that served him well for his entire career, Atlanta's Henry Aaron smashes home run Number 715 against the Reds in 1974. INSET Barry Bonds exults as he hits a dinger in San Francisco.

BARRY BONDS

LOU GEHRIG

The Yankees, who had traditionally drawn between 300,000 and 500,000 in attendance annually, drew more than 1.2 million fans, a record at the time.

There were other factors, of course. The Yankees were in a pennant race—they would ultimately lose to Cleveland—and surely that was exciting. But it was clear that fans came to Yankees games to see Babe Ruth hit a baseball. In fact, one of Ruth's biographers, Robert Creamer, maintained that even Ruth's strikeouts were memorable.

A well-pitched game, a cleverly executed sacrifice play, an unexpected stolen base were all certainly interesting, but it was the home run that brought in more paying customers than ever before.

Consequently, teams began thinking more and more about the "power game" as a way to win baseball contests. Obviously, there was only one Babe Ruth. But other players, including Rogers Hornsby (Cardinals, Giants, Braves, Cubs, Browns, 1915–37), began adjusting. Hornsby was one of the great hitters of all time, three times hitting over .400 during his career. He was an exceptional hitter who switched within two years from being a player who could hit for average to becoming a player who could also hit for power.

Prior to the 1921 season, the most home runs Hornsby had hit in a year was nine. In 1921, he struck 21. The next year, 1922, he hit 42 to lead the National League. From 1922 to 1929, Hornsby would hit 220 homers.

He was not alone. In 1927, a young first baseman for the Yankees, Lou Gehrig, challenged Ruth's supremacy in the American League. Gehrig finished second to Ruth in homers for five consecutive seasons. Hack Wilson, the fireplug-shaped outfielder for the Chicago Cubs, and Hank Greenberg, the towering first baseman for the Tigers, also became home-run-hitting stars.

In fact, the individual outlooks of teams began to change. They began scouting big, physical players to play nonpitching positions. Free-swinging players who could hit home runs were looked at far more closely.

In addition to volume, Ruth was the first player who struck home runs that were noted for their distance. As a rookie in 1915, Ruth crushed a pitch that sailed far over the right-field stands in Sportsman's Park in St. Louis. Estimates at the time were that the ball was hit about 470 feet. It was a long drive, and a number of sportswriters that day began speculating what Ruth the pitcher might do if he were Ruth the everyday player.

The Yankees' Mickey Mantle and Negro League star Josh Gibson were also best known for tape-measure shots. Both men had come close to hitting a ball entirely out of Yankee Stadium, a feat that still has yet to be accomplished.

Ruth hit, as everyone knows, 60 home runs in

HACK WILSON

THE DESIGNATED HITTER

The designated hitter, or DH, was introduced to the American League in 1973 as a way to "spice up" the scoring in the league. It was to have been a three-year program, but proved so popular that it continues in the American League to this day.

Interestingly, baseball's first DH, Ron Blomberg, is less than thrilled with his place in baseball history.

"I screwed up the game of baseball," he admitted in an interview on the 30th anniversary of the DH in 2003. "Baseball needed a jolt of offense for attendance, so they decided on the DH. I never thought it would last this long."

The reason it has lasted this long is due to what some observers call "star power"—that is, players like Al Kaline, Carl Yastrzemski, Tony Oliva and Reggie Jackson were all designated hitters at the end of their careers, and fans enjoyed seeing them hit.

But in the 21st century, most AL teams have taken star power a little further. The best designated hitters are weapons for their teams.

For several years, conventional wisdom had it that former Seattle star Edgar Martinez was the best designated hitter of all time. But it appears that the Red Sox's David "Big Papi" Ortiz has eclipsed him. In 2004, Ortiz had a pair of game-winning hits, including a walk-off home run in extra innings, to help the Sox rebound from an 0–3 deficit and defeat the Yankees 4–3 in the American League Championship Series. For the past few years, he has become a legitimate MVP candidate; something about which Ron Blomberg probably never dreamed.

RON BLOMBERG

SAMMY SOSA

1927. Several players, including Greenberg, Wilson and Jimmie Foxx, came close over the next several years but ultimately fell short.

In 1961, Yankees outfielders Mantle and Roger Maris both made a run at the home-run record. Mantle, who had been a star for several years with the Yankees, was the sentimental favorite to break Ruth's record; but "The Mick," as he was called, was injured late in the season. Maris ultimately broke the record.

It was a tough run for the reticent Maris. As Mantle explained years later in an interview: "Management never really did anything to help Roger. We'd come to a new city and the reporters would be hovering around his locker, asking the same questions over and over again. Roger's hair began to fall out. He couldn't sleep. That he finally broke the record was an amazing thing."

Indeed, conquering the mystique surrounding the passing of Ruth was never easy. As difficult as Maris's feat was, the Atlanta Braves' Henry "Hank" Aaron had an even tougher row to hoe in topping Ruth's lifetime mark of 714.

At least Maris was white. Aaron, a black man who was one of the most consistent ballplayers in major-league history, slowly and methodically closed in on the record. And as he did, he heard about it. At one point, when he was only a few homers away, Aaron was asked if he had heard much from baseball fans about closing in on Ruth. Aaron said, "No, but I've heard from the rednecks."

There were many whites in both the North and the South who didn't want to see Ruth surpassed. Aaron got death threats, and not just on the road. A few days before he was to break the record at home, he received so much hate mail, the Braves hired a security escort to accompany Aaron and his family to the ballpark.

After Aaron finally broke Ruth's record in 1974, he stood at home plate and wept. "Thank God," he sobbed, "it's over." The pressure was finally off.

The home-run race between Mark McGwire and Sammy Sosa to break Maris's single-season mark was, in contrast, much more festive. The two men dueled throughout the 1998 season, with McGwire in the lead for most of the year. On September 8, 1998, McGwire homered off the Cubs' Steve Trachsel for home run number 62. He would go on to hit 8 more, while Sosa, no slouch himself, struck 66 that year to also break the record.

McGwire's quest was an affable one. Maris had died several years before, but his wife and sons were on hand to congratulate McGwire that night; as was Sosa, who came out of the Chicago dugout to hug him. The one dark cloud, which seemed far away at that point, was the specter of steroid use. Both men were under suspicion at that time.

Suspicion of steroid use in the major leagues had expanded greatly by 2001, when Barry Bonds broke McGwire's record by 3, hitting 73 in a season. Bonds was an exceptional all-around player who had displayed some power throughout his career, socking 49 homers in 2000, for example. But he had never hit as many as 50 in a single season in his career, and he won only one home-run crown prior to 2001. So it looked awful funny when he came out of the gate with 11 homers in April and 17 in May. He had 57 by August 21, passed Ruth and Maris on September 9, and topped McGwire on October 4. Almost half of his 153 hits were home runs.

MARK McGWIRE

It was a glorious run in 1998: The Cardinals' Mark McGwire and the Cubs' Sammy Sosa raced to break the home run record set in 1961 by Roger Maris. Both eventually succeeded, but it was McGwire who won the home run crown that year, with 70.

AARON

Mr. Consistency, Aaron hit 20 or more home runs for 20 consecutive years. And this will win you a bar bet: he only hit 40 or more homers twice in his 23-year career.

CAREER STATISTICS				
BA	HR	RBI	H	SB
.305	755	2,297	3,771	240

Willie MAYS

Giants, Mets, 1951–73

The common fan associates Mays with great defense, superb speed on the basepaths and clutch hitting. But the guy belted 660 career homers, won 4 home-run crowns and twice hit more than 50.

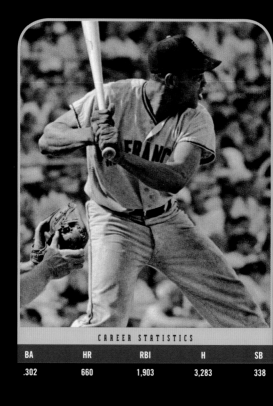

CAREER STATISTICS				
BA	HR	RBI	H	SB
.302	660	1,903	3,283	338

Harry
STOVEY

Worcester [NL], Philadelphia [AA], Boston [PL], Braves, Orioles, Dodgers, 1880–93

Stovey, a 6-time home-run king, was the 19th-century version of Ruth. He won home-run crowns in two different leagues with Worcester and Boston of the National League, and with Philadelphia of the American Association, and was one of the first players to hit 20 or more home runs, doing it 3 times.

George Herman
"Babe"
RUTH

Red Sox, Yankees, Braves, 1914–35

Ruth is a man who needs no introduction. The first player to hit 30 homers in a season, the first to hit 40, the first to hit 50 and the first to hit 60, his approach to hitting and home runs changed baseball from a low-scoring game of bunting and sacrifice hits to a high-scoring game of three-run homers and big innings. There will never be another like him.

Barry Lamar
BONDS

Pirates, Giants, 1986–2007

As Mike Schmidt points out, steroids or not, you still have to swing the bat. But here's another stat that will win you a bar bet: other than the 73-homer season in 2001, Bonds has won only one other league home-run crown—in 1993, when he hit 43.

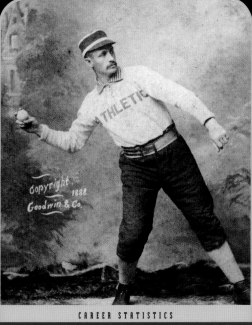

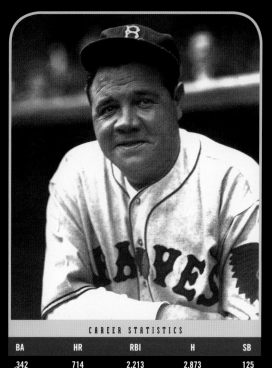

CAREER STATISTICS

BA	HR	RBI	H	SB
.289	122	908	1,771	509

CAREER STATISTICS

BA	HR	RBI	H	SB
.342	714	2,213	2,873	125

CAREER STATISTICS

BA	HR	RBI	H	SB
.298	762	1,996	2,935	514

EVOLUTION OF THE HOME-RUN RECORD

Babe Ruth (left) rewrote the home run record book. Roger Maris's (right) quest to break the Babe's record was carried out under a harsh media spotlight, a spotlight that had softened considerably by the time Mark McGwire (below) overtook Roger. Barry Bonds's (far right) 73-homer season was a statistical wonder, as he hit those 73 in only 155 games.

5
1876
George Hall
Philadelphia [NL]
In a 70-game season, outfielder Hall hit 5 homers, his team hit 7 and the whole league hit 40.

9
1879
Charley Jones
Boston [NL]
The season had expanded to 84 games, and outfielder Jones hit 9 of his team's 20.

14
1883
Harry Stovey
Philadelphia [AA]
Stovey was the game's first slugger, leading his league in homers five times in his career. Stovey hit 14 of Philadelphia's 20 homers that year.

27
1884
Ned Williamson
Chicago [NL]
Williamson was not really a slugger. But in 1884, balls hit over the fence in Chicago's home field of Lake Shore Park were counted as home runs. Previously, they had been doubles. Williamson hit 25 of his homers at home and 2 on the road. That year, the top four home-run hitters in the National League were from Chicago. The next year, the team moved into a new stadium, and Williamson hit three homers.

29
1919
Babe Ruth
Boston Red Sox
Despite pitching part-time, Ruth out-homered 10 of the other 15 major-league teams. The second best individual total was Gavvy Cravath's 12 for the Phillies.

54

★ Babe Ruth
★ New York Yankees
★ Again, Ruth out-homered
★ most of the teams in both
★ leagues. George Sisler's 19
★ was second best. Ruth's
★ slugging percentage of
★ .847 stood for 80 years,
★ until Barry Bonds broke it.

59

★ Babe Ruth
★ New York Yankees
★ Ruth still had more
★ home runs than eight
★ other teams this year,
★ but he was also incred-
★ ibly dominant in other
★ categories in 1921. He led
★ the league in runs scored
★ with 177, 44 more than
★ the Browns' Jack Tobin.
★ His slugging percentage
★ was an unbelievable 240
★ points higher than the
★ Tigers' Harry Heilmann.
★ Many Yankee fans believe
★ this season, not 1927, was
★ Ruth's best.

60

★ Babe Ruth
★ New York Yankees
★ When one looks at the his-
★ torical record this way, it's
★ easy to see how Babe Ruth
★ literally redirected the
★ course of baseball in this
★ six-year span. The results
★ of his home-run hitting
★ were not just notable; they
★ were overwhelming. He
★ rewrote not only the record
★ book but also baseball
★ history.

61

★ Roger Maris
★ New York Yankees
★ Maris actually suffered for
★ breaking Ruth's record.
★ A superb all-around
★ player who won two MVP
★ awards, Maris was tagged
★ forever after for being a
★ one-dimensional slugger,
★ particularly by New York
★ sportswriters who should
★ have known better.

70

★ Mark McGwire
★ St. Louis Cardinals
★ The epic race between
★ McGwire and the Cubs'
★ Sammy Sosa was one of
★ the more exciting stories
★ of the 1998 season. Sosa
★ finished with 66, also
★ breaking Maris's record.

73

★ Barry Bonds
★ San Francisco Giants
★ Bonds got hot early, hitting
★ 28 by May 30, and built
★ upon that foundation for
★ the record. Bonds played
★ in only 155 of the Giants'
★ 162 games.

1920   1921   1927   1961   1998   2001

CAREER

38

WES FERRELL

35

WARREN SPAHN

34

RED RUFFING

33

EARL WILSON

37

BOB LEMON

Who's the best home-run-hitting pitcher of all time? No, it's not Babe Ruth; he only hit 14 homers as a pitcher. The other 700 were as an outfielder.

Here's the list, and it'll probably win a few trivia games.

SEASON

9

WES FERRELL
1931, Indians

7

DON DRYSDALE
Twice
1958, 1965, Dodgers

WES FERRELL
Twice
1933, 1935, Indians, Red Sox

DON NEWCOMBE
1955, Dodgers

EARL WILSON
1968, Tigers

MIKE HAMPTON
2001, Rockies

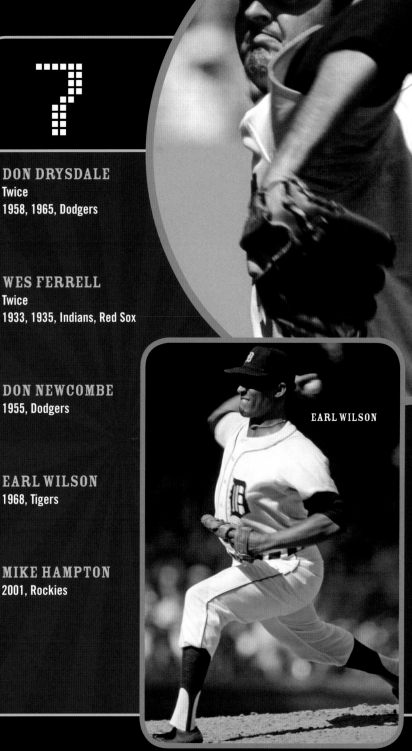

DON DRYSDALE

EARL WILSON

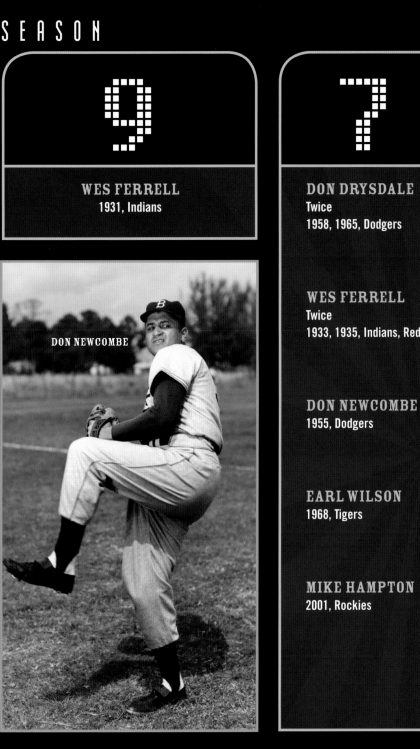

DON NEWCOMBE

BABE RUTH

HOW IT'S DONE
The Home Run

There are different techniques to hitting a home run, but Babe Ruth, in Robert Creamer's best-selling biography *Babe*, perhaps said it best in an interview: "I swing as hard as I can, and I try to swing right through the ball. In boxing, your fist usually stops when you hit a man, but it's possible to hit so hard that your fist doesn't stop. I try to follow through the same way. The harder you grip the bat, the more you can swing it through the ball, and the farther the ball will go. I swing big, with everything I've got. I hit big or I miss big. I like to live as big as I can."

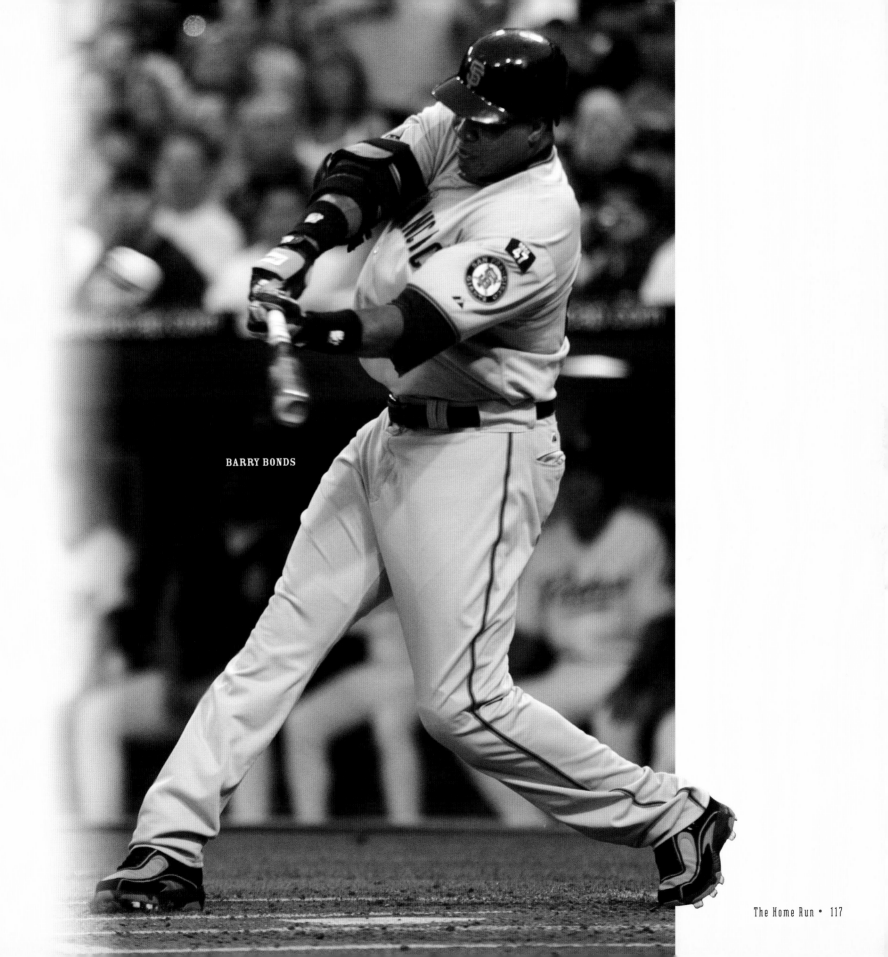

BARRY BONDS

ABOVE: Rogers Hornsby was one of only three players to hit .400 after 1925.

There are a total of 19 players in major-league history who have topped the .400 mark at least once in their careers. Of these 19, only 3—Rogers Hornsby, Bill Terry (Giants, 1923–36) and Ted Williams—hit .400 after 1925. Only Williams did it after 1930.

In the 19th century, .400 hitters were rare but not unheard of. "Big Ed" Delahanty (Phillies, Cleveland [PL], Senators, 1888–1903) did it three times in six years, from 1894 to 1899. Jesse Burkett (Giants, Spiders, Cardinals, Browns, Red Sox, 1890–1905) won back-to-back batting titles in 1895 and 1896, hitting .405 and .410, respectively. These two men were a study in contrasts. Delahanty was, at six-feet-one and 190 pounds, a huge man for his time. He could hit for power and average, and he could run. In 1898, he stole a league-leading 58 bases. Burkett was, at five-feet-eight and 150 pounds, smallish for that era, but he had blazing speed. Burkett was an outfielder; Delahanty a first baseman.

Hugh Duffy was an outfielder for the Boston Braves in 1894 when he hit a record .440. Like Burkett, Duffy was a small player, but unlike Burkett, Duffy wasn't extraordinarily fast. He was a player who was patient, could place hits well and knew how to run the bases.

In the 1800s, that's what made .400 hitters. Relief pitchers were decades in the future.

In fact, pitching rotations were, for many years, one or two hurlers. No one pitched on more than a couple days' rest.

Pitchers had to learn to pace themselves. They rarely came out of the ball game. A smart, patient hitter would get to see two or three good pitches to hit per at-bat, as opposed to seeing maybe two or three good pitches a game in the modern era. The great hitters such

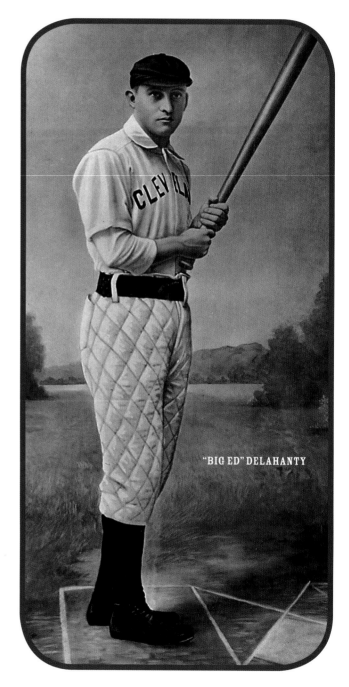

"BIG ED" DELAHANTY

as Duffy, Burkett, Delahanty and Wee Willie Keeler all had excellent hand-eye coordination, great patience and the confidence to wait for the pitch they wanted to hit. The advantage was theirs.

Still, hitting .400 was not easy. A player had to be consistent for more than 150 games, in 8 different cities. In the late 18th and early 19th centuries, there was no air-conditioning in hotel rooms. Ballplayers learned to wet down their sheets in a bathtub and wrap up in them in order to sleep through a hot summer evening. Many players would simply fill a tub and try to sleep there.

"St. Louis, boy did it ever get hot there," recalled Lefty O'Doul (Giants, Yankees, Red Sox, Phillies, Dodgers, 1919–23, 1928–34) in an interview. "You'd roast out on the field and then go back to your hotel room and try to sleep."

Train rides were more leisurely than planes, perhaps, but the constant bumping in the night was often a problem.

"The hotels weren't the best in the world," recalled Sam Crawford in *The Glory of Their Times*, "and the trains had coal-burning engines. You'd wake up in the morning with cinders all over your berth. They had fine little screens on the train windows, but the cinders would still come through."

As the 20th century opened, the great stars such as Ty Cobb, Joe Jackson, Napoleon Lajoie and George Sisler were still overpowering pitchers, but that part of the game was changing. Bigger pitching staffs meant that a hitter would face a certain pitcher only once in a three- or four-game series between two teams. Relievers began to make the game shorter for starting pitchers. They paced themselves less. In 1930, the Giants' Bill Terry hit .401. He was the last National Leaguer to crack .400.

Explaining Ted Williams's .406 in 1941 is harder. Williams hit .406 in an era when league batting averages for both the American and National leagues were declining. Rogers Hornsby's 20th-century record .424 in 1924, for example, was 34 points better than the average of both leagues (.390). Williams hit .406 when the league average was .349, a 57-point difference and by far the widest differential between

TED WILLIAMS

Ted
WILLIAMS

Red Sox, 1939–60

Williams was the last man to do it, hitting .406 in 1941. Will anyone ever do it again? It won't be easy, with platooned relief pitchers and coast-to-coast air travel.

Rogers
HORNSBY

Cardinals, Giants, Braves, Cubs, Browns 1915–37

"The Rajah," as he was called, hit better than .400 three times in his career, including .424 in 1924. The best right-handed hitter ever.

Ty
COBB

Tigers, Athletics, 1905–28

Another three-time .400 hitter, Cobb did not have as much power as Hornsby or Williams but was a terror on the basepaths.

CAREER STATISTICS

BA	HR	RBI	H	SB
.344	521	1,839	2,645	24

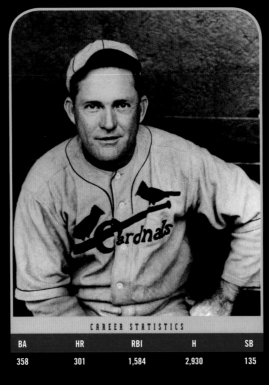

CAREER STATISTICS

BA	HR	RBI	H	SB
358	301	1,584	2,930	135

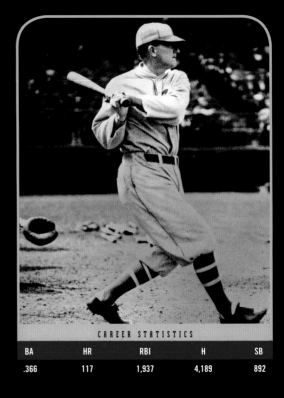

CAREER STATISTICS

BA	HR	RBI	H	SB
.366	117	1,937	4,189	892

"Shoeless" Joe
JACKSON

Athletics, Indians, White Sox, 1908–20

He hit .408 in 1911, and finished second in the batting-average race to Cobb's .409. Still, Cobb believes Jackson was the greatest pure hitter of all time.

CAREER STATISTICS				
BA	HR	RBI	H	SB
.356	54	785	1,772	202

George
SISLER

Browns, Senators, Braves, 1915–30

He twice hit better than .400 in his career, including .420 in 1922. Sisler is often overlooked as one of the better first basemen of all time.

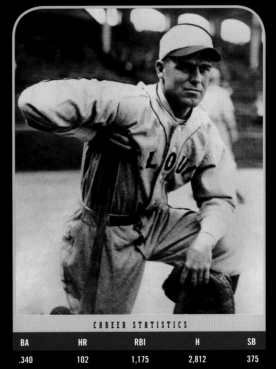

CAREER STATISTICS				
BA	HR	RBI	H	SB
.340	102	1,175	2,812	375

Napoleon
LAJOIE

Phillies, Indians, Athletics, 1896–1916

In 1901, "Nap" hit .426 with 14 homers and 125 RBI to win the Triple Crown. Giants pitching ace Christy Mathewson, a man who feared very few hitters, conceded that he could never figure out how to pitch Lajoie.

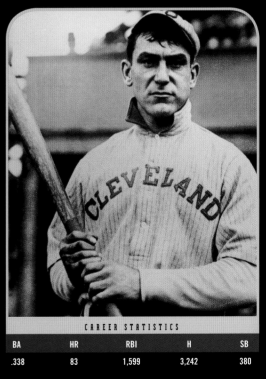

CAREER STATISTICS				
BA	HR	RBI	H	SB
.338	83	1,599	3,242	380

NAP LAJOIE

BILL TERRY

20th-century .400 hitters and the rest of the baseball universe.

Williams started out hitting around .350 in April and May, before he got hot late in the month, going 15–25 (with 12 walks) from May 25 to 30. His average jumped from .383 to .429. Following the All-Star break, an ankle injury threw him into a minislump that saw his average drop to .393. But an extended home stand from July 20 to August 10 pushed his average up to .411, as Williams went 30–64 in that span, roughly a .470 clip.

Williams was at .411 as late as September 14, before going into a relative slump. On September 27, Williams had 179 hits in 448 at-bats, a .400 average, or actually, .39955. It had already been announced that if Williams sat out the final day of the season, a doubleheader against the Athletics, his average would be rounded off to .400.

Williams wanted to play. So much had been made of his hitting that year that Williams did not want to end the year with a .39955 average.

The rest is baseball history. Williams destroyed the Athletics, going 6–8, to push his average to .406, perhaps the greatest hitting feat of all time.

"Excellence is the scarcest and most precious of all human commodities," wrote Harvard professor (and passionate Yankees fan) Stephen Jay Gould in an essay about Williams. "Williams's .406 is a beacon in the history of excellence, a lesson to all who value the best in human possibility."

TY COBB

HOW IT'S DONE
Hitting .400

Be patient. Wait for your pitch. And if you don't get it, don't swing. A walk is as good as a single. And, if one can believe Ted Williams, swing slightly upward, to compensate for the height of the pitcher's mound.

TED WILLIAMS

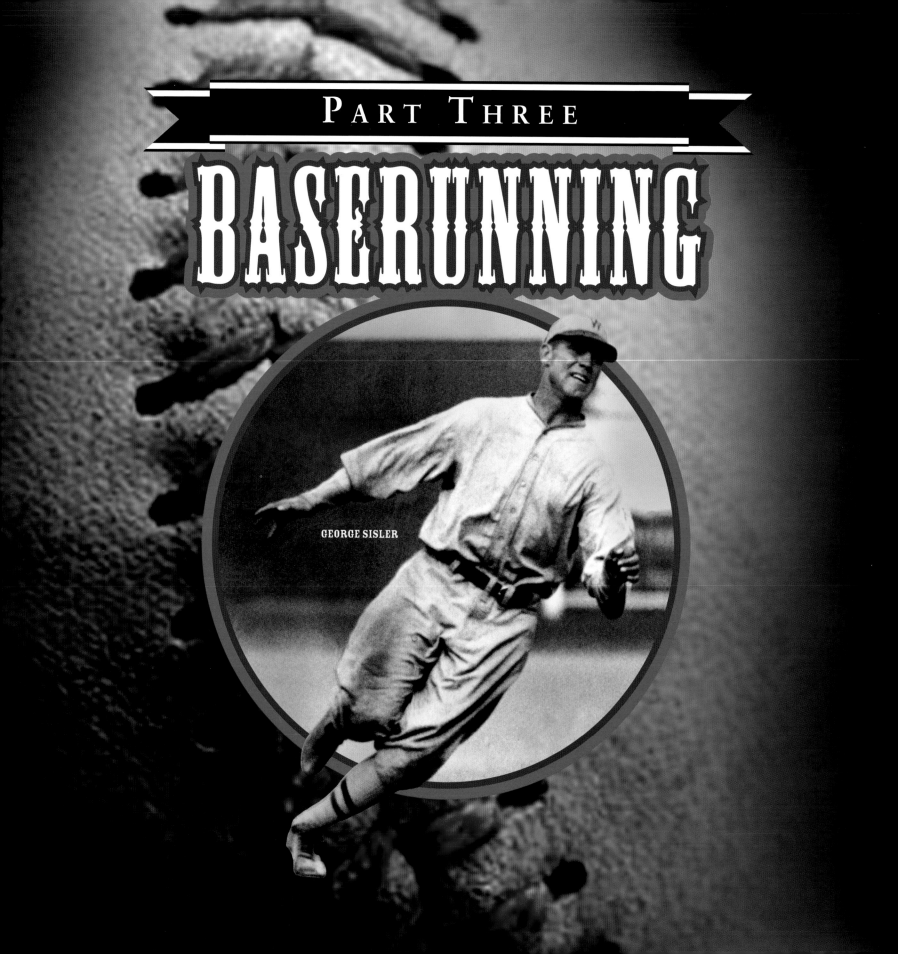

PART THREE

BASERUNNING

GEORGE SISLER

RICKY HENDERSON

STEALING BASES

ABOVE: Ross Barnes is credited as the first player to steal home. **OPPOSITE:** Ty Cobb (left), and Sam Crawford (right), with Joe Jackson. Cobb and Crawford used to work a delayed double steal.

Eddie Cuthbert, a player for the Keystone Club of Philadelphia, is credited with being the first player to attempt to steal a base, in 1865, sliding headfirst to steal second base against the old Brooklyn Atlantics. Stealing bases was, at the time, a relatively rare occurrence. Many baserunners of the era were content with taking an extra base if there was a wild pitch or passed ball.

But as individual players began to see the possibilities of advancing to the next base without the benefit of a base hit, base stealing gradually became more of a weapon into the latter part of the 19th century.

In the mid- to late 1800s, however, stolen bases were tallied differently than they are now. Baserunners were credited with a stolen base if they took an extra base on a hit by a teammate. For example, if a player was on first base, and a teammate made a hit, and the player went from first to third on the hit, he was credited with a stolen base.

Thus, in 1887, Hugh Nicol, an outfielder playing for Cincinnati of the American Association (then considered a major league) swiped 138 bases in 125 games, which is still a major-league record. But according to baseball-reference.com, many of these steals would not be considered stolen bases under today's rules. In 1898, the so-called modern stolen-base rules were implemented, requiring that a baserunner only get credit for a steal if he successfully takes an extra base while the ball is being pitched.

Stolen bases weren't recorded officially until 1886. But the team most famous for taking the extra base in baseball's early years was the St. Louis Browns of the old American Association. From 1885 to 1888, the Browns finished first in the league, were the league

leaders in stolen bases in 1886 and 1887, and finished second in 1888. (Even adjusting for the fact that, obviously, some, or many, of these stolen bases were actually players taking the extra base, the Browns were clearly a hard-running team.)

The Browns featured Arlie Latham, a young Charlie Comiskey and Tip O'Neill, all of whom were smart hitters and good baserunners. Latham and Comiskey became the first teammates to swipe 100 or more bases each.

It was around this time that the "delayed double steal" appeared. Baseball historian Henry Chadwick notes that by 1880, many teams were practicing it. The delayed double steal happens with players on first and third base. It begins when a player on first takes off for second; as soon as he draws a throw from the catcher, the player on third base rushes home. But the player at third must "delay" his attempt until he sees that the catcher has thrown the ball to second base. Again, the delayed double steal became a way for teams to score, or at least try to score, without the benefit of a base hit.

Ross Barnes, a diminutive (5'7", 145 lbs.) second baseman who played in both the old National Association and later in the National League, is credited with the first steal of home, when he played for the Chicago White Stockings in 1876. That year, Barnes was the best baseball player in the league by a long shot. His .429 batting average led the league, as did his 126 runs scored, 138 hits, 21 doubles, 14 triples, .482 on-base percentage, .590 slugging average and .910 fielding average.

Barnes himself wasn't considered fast. But he had begun to "read" pitchers. In other words, Barnes would study a pitcher closely, and if the hurler was not particularly attentive, he would make his move. This strategy was surely not solely the purview of Barnes, but many of his teammates and sportswriters noted it in him.

Once the rules were amended, however, the era of 100 stolen bases per year began to shrink exponentially. By the beginning of the 20th century, Pittsburgh shortstop Honus Wagner, considered one of the smarter baserunners in the league, was averaging about 45 swipes annually. In the American League, Detroit's Ty Cobb was the best on the basepaths. According to Cobb's teammate Sam Crawford, he and Cobb worked a kind of delayed double steal after a base on balls, a strategy few other players appear to have duplicated. Crawford would be at the plate, and Cobb on third base. If Crawford was walked, he would jog casually to first base. Then, just as he reached first, Crawford would sprint for second base. The startled catcher would usually throw the ball to second to nail Crawford, and Cobb would sprint home.

The two men didn't do it every time the situation arose, but Crawford, interviewed in Lawrence S. Ritter's *The Glory of Their Times* recalled, "as I started to go down to first, I'd sort of half glance at Cobb at third. He'd make a slight move that that told me he wanted to keep going—not to stop at first, but to keep on going to second."

Lou Brock was one of the players, along with the Dodgers' Maury Wills, who revived the art of base-stealing in the 1960s. Brock was a threat to score a run every time he reached base, even when he was walked.

THE SKIP PLAY

In the days of only one umpire, who called balls and strikes from behind the pitcher and ruled on all fielding plays from the infield, the skip play was a notorious tactic. (Rules mandated only one umpire until the Players League decreed in 1890 that two umpires would be used [see Umpires].)

In the "skip play," the baserunner on first runs through the infield from first to third base or second base to home plate on certain plays, such as a deep fly ball, which would draw the umpire from his position behind the pitcher into the shallow portion of the outfield.

Although it was said that many players employed the skip play in the 1880s, really only Mike "King" Kelly had the daring to try this maneuver on any consistent basis. Kelly, the biggest star of the 19th century, was fast and tough. According to his biographer, Marty Appel, Kelly used the skip play for years, until more umpires were hired to police games.

Of course, it didn't always work. Detroit outfielder Sam Crawford recalled in an interview, in *The Glory of Their Times*, when teammate Jake Beckley was on first base in 1899, and Crawford socked a double. Umpire Tim Hurst was watching Crawford slide into second from the infield when Beckley, completely skipping third base, slid home behind him. Hurst whirled and thumbed Beckley out.

"What do you mean I'm out?" screamed Beckley. "Nobody even made a play on me."

"You big S.O.B.," said Hurst. "You got there too soon!"

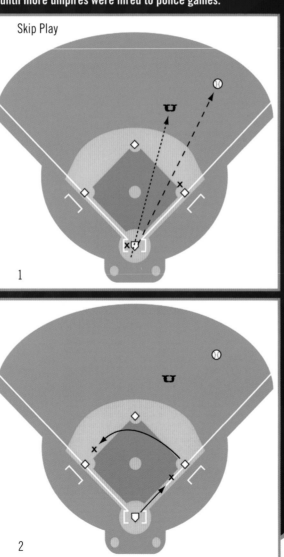

Skip Play

1

2

ARLIE LATHAM

Babe Ruth's ascendancy as a home-run-hitting superstar in the 1920s diminished the steal as a major offensive weapon. The home run, which was more spectacular, pushed the strategy of playing for one run at a time to the sidelines.

During the post-Ruth era, the most aggressive and intelligent baserunner was the Dodgers' Jackie Robinson. Robinson did not rack up huge base-stealing numbers during his 10-year career (although he led the league twice, in 1947 with 29 and in 1949 with 37). But his speed and aggressiveness were such that the threat of a steal was enough to intimidate rivals.

Teams in the mid-20th century that had speedy players, like the St. Louis Cardinals with Lou Brock, or the Los Angeles Dodgers with Maury Wills, certainly took advantage of their speed on the basepaths. Wills, in an essay on base stealing that he wrote in 2003 for the *Sporting News*, noted that, when he came up to the big leagues, in the early 1960s, "[T]he game was much the same as it is now—a lot of sluggers, a lot of home runs. The stolen base was not a big thing."

Wills and others restored an emphasis on the running game, aided by the larger ballparks that began to be built in the late 1960s and early 1970s.

"The Dodgers moved to Dodger Stadium in 1962," said Wills, "and we went from a field [in the Los Angeles Coliseum] that was 250 feet down the line to one that was 350 feet. So we had to change our thinking. The Dodgers wanted to use speed. It's not a coincidence that in 1961 I stole 35 bases, then in 1962, in the new stadium, I stole 104. [...] We made the game into a speed game."

But the home run was clearly here to stay, as was that power-hitting strategy.

"Now stadiums have gone the other way," continued Wills. "They're smaller now. It's easier to hit home runs. Guys are afraid to go for stolen bases. It's easier to wait on home runs."

Wills added that media attention to the recent home-run quests of Barry Bonds and Mark McGwire have not helped to encourage base stealing.

"Young guys in the minors don't think they will get to be millionaires by stealing bases," he admitted.

BELOW: The Dodgers' Jackie Robinson was more than just a pioneering ballplayer who opened up the game to black players, he was a great hitter and a fearless base stealer. Here he steals home against Yogi Berra and the Yankees. RIGHT: The Dodgers' Maury Wills was an explosive runner and a cool-headed performer on the base paths. He sparked the Dodgers' offense in the 1960s.

The Best of the Best

STEALING BASES

Ty COBB

Tigers, Athletics, 1906–28

Cobb led the American League in steals six times, with a high of 98 in 1915.

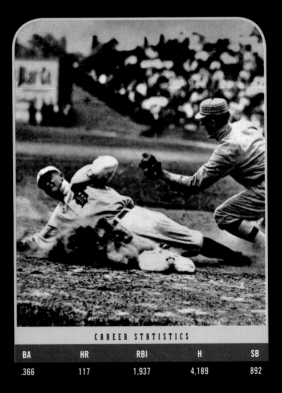

CAREER STATISTICS

BA	HR	RBI	H	SB
.366	117	1,937	4,189	892

Jackie ROBINSON

Dodgers, 1947–56

Top base-stealer in the National League in 1947, his rookie year, with 29, Robinson led the league again two years later with 37. He stole home numerous times, and was considered one of the best ever at that trick.

CAREER STATISTICS

BA	HR	RBI	H	SB
.311	137	734	1,518	197

Lou BROCK

Cubs, Cardinals, 1961–79

Second all-time in steals with 938, Brock stole 118 in 1974. His trade from the Cubs to the more aggressive Cardinals jump-started his career.

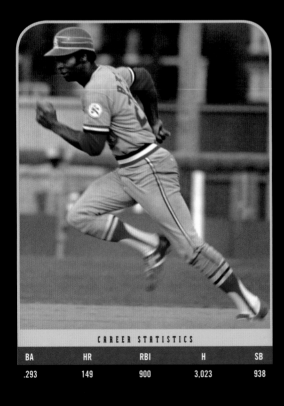

CAREER STATISTICS

BA	HR	RBI	H	SB
.293	149	900	3,023	938

HENDERSON

Athletics, Yankees, Blue Jays, Padres, Angels, Mets, Mariners, Red Sox, Dodgers, 1979–2003

Henderson stole 130 bases in 1982, all-time leader with 1,406. He was probably the greatest leadoff hitter in baseball history.

CAREER STATISTICS				
BA	HR	RBI	H	SB
.279	297	1,115	3,055	1,406

Maury
WILLS

Dodgers, Pirates, Expos, 1959–72

Wills was the first player to steal more than 100 bases in a season in the modern era with 104 in 1962. He was a player who often intimidated pitchers merely by taking a big lead off first base.

CAREER STATISTICS				
BA	HR	RBI	H	SB

SLIDING FEETFIRST

Eddie Cuthbert, in that initial theft of second base, reportedly slid headfirst into the bag. The practice of sliding feetfirst was not as popular and, in fact, was attempted only rarely. But it gained popularity, sadly, in the 1880s, when, according to Negro League historian Sol White, opponents of the Buffalo Bisons of the Eastern League began using the tactic to intimidate the Bisons' star player, Frank Grant, an African American.

Negro League historian Jim Overmyer says that Grant began his pro baseball career as a catcher, but his athleticism enabled him to play virtually anywhere.

Grant signed with the all-white Bisons team in 1887 and played with them until 1888. He was a great hitter, a superior baserunner, an excellent fielder and a popular player who was eventually named to the City of Buffalo's Hall of Fame. But outside Buffalo, Grant was a target. Fans shouted "Kill the nigger!" when he came to bat and, on the field, angry opponents slid into him feetfirst, even when the play was over. The feetfirst slide was used from time to time elsewhere, but outfielder Ned Williamson, himself a former opponent of Grant's, reported in 1898 that the feetfirst slide was almost certainly made popular in the Eastern League. Which is not necessarily something to cheer about. Grant eventually wrapped his shins in wooden shin guards to protect himself; in retaliation, opponents sharpened their spikes.

Eventually, by the end of that decade, all of organized baseball banned African American players. Grant played for almost two decades in the Negro League and was elected to the Hall of Fame in 2006.

Johnny Evers of the Chicago Cubs appears to be the first manager to require that his players actually practice sliding in spring training. In 1913, according to a writer from *The Chicago Tribune*, Evers, in his first year, had a "sliding pit" built for spring training. Later individuals, including Connie Mack of the Philadelphia Athletics and Branch Rickey of the Dodgers, were more noted for that innovation, but Evers seems to be one of the first to make sliding a mandatory spring-training drill.

FRANK GRANT

PINCH RUNNERS

For many years, limitations on substitutions prohibited pinch runners. But in 1890, the rules on replacing players in the field were relaxed. However, the strategy of replacing one player with another on the basepaths was not a popular one for many seasons.

It appears that John McGraw was the first manager to experiment with this tactic. McGraw used Charles "Sandy" Piez as a pinch runner in 1914. Piez came to the plate only 8 times that year, but he appeared in 37 games. He scored nine runs and stole four bases that year, his only one in the majors. Piez was an outfielder and played there in five games, but he was primarily used to run the bases.

Charles O. Finley, the owner of the Oakland Athletics, took this tactic a step further, signing Olympic sprinter Herb Washington in 1974 as the team's designated pinch runner.

In 1972, Finley, like McGraw, had used a player primarily as a pinch runner. Alan Lewis, "The Panamanian Express," played for the Athletics from 1967 to 1973. Lewis was a speedster initially signed by the Athletics as an outfielder, but was used as a pinch hitter from 1967 to 1972. By 1973, he was the Athletics' pinch runner, appearing in 35 games but never batting. He stole 44 bases in his 6-year career.

Washington was another story entirely. When he was signed by Oakland in 1974, he was the world-record holder in the 50- and 60-yard dashes (5.0 and 5.8 seconds, respectively). But he had not played baseball since his junior year in high school.

In two years with the Athletics (1974–75), Washington appeared in 105 games as a pinch runner and never came to bat. He scored 33 runs and stole 31 bases in 48 attempts. Although his stolen-base percentage is not great, it was, according to Finley, "impressive when you realize that as soon as he replaced a runner at first [base], everybody in the ballpark knew he was going to try to steal."

Maybe, but he was not a great baserunner. In the 1974 World Series, he replaced Oakland outfielder Joe Rudi in the ninth inning of Game Two, with the Los Angeles Dodgers leading the game 3–2. He was promptly picked off first base by Dodger reliever Mike Marshall.

HERB WASHINGTON

THE HOOK SLIDE

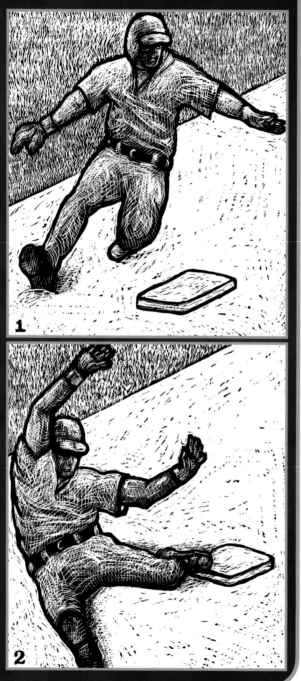

Although the origins of the hook slide have never been documented, the overwhelming consensus is that the versatile and inventive Mike "King" Kelly was the first player to use it consistently. The hook slide happens when a baserunner slides into the bag feetfirst, but angles his body away from the bag as his left foot "hooks" out to touch it.

Kelly, who played for a host of teams from 1878 to 1893, was a well-known innovator (his opponents might use the term "cheater") who starred in the early years of baseball.

According to his teammate Tommy McCarthy, quoted in *The National Game* by Alfred Spink, "[Kelly] never came into a bag twice in the same way. He twisted and turned as he made his famous 'Kelly slide,' and seldom was he caught." In fact, before the maneuver was known as the hook slide, it was known as the "Kelly slide" or "Kelly spread."

The Yankees' Johnny Damon, still speedy in his late 30s, beats the throw at second base against Tampa Bay. INSET: Is there anything Joe DiMaggio wasn't good at? Here, he executes a textbook hook slide to steal home during the 1939 World Series.

HOW IT'S DONE

Stealing Bases

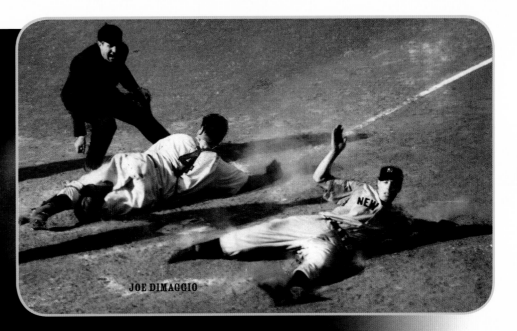

JOE DIMAGGIO

Even if players are not fast, they can be good base stealers. The most important thing about base stealing in general is to be alert. Know the count and the number of outs. Try to stay relaxed, and stay on the balls of your feet. Always be aggressive; always be aware of where the ball is. The best description of good baserunning comes from former Yankee manager Casey Stengel, explaining how Yankee great Joe DiMaggio ran the bases.

"Look at him," said Stengel in 1949. "He's always watching the ball. He isn't watching second base. He isn't watching third base. He knows they haven't been moved. He isn't watching the ground, because he knows they haven't built a canal or a swimming pool since he was last there. He's watching the ball and the outfielder, which is the one thing that's different on every play."

CRASHING INTO PLAYERS

In 1878, the National League introduced a rule that mandated players hold on to the ball after they make a tag. Sportswriters predicted, correctly, that this would result in a baserunner trying to dislodge the ball from the defensive player.

One of the squads that became noted for the practice was the Chicago White Stockings in the late 1870s and early 1880s. There was one very basic reason.

"The White Stockings of the 1880s were a team of large men," wrote Peter Golenbock in *Wrigleyville*. "Seven of the players, including [Mike "King"] Kelly and [Captain Adrian] Anson, were over six feet tall."

Six-feet players in the 19th century were rare. When the White Stockings took the field, they intimidated a lot of teams before the game even started. And with Kelly leading the way, they took no prisoners on the basepaths.

"We had 'em scared ter death," recalled Mike Kelly in an interview a few years later in the *Sporting News*.

Chicago won three consecutive National League crowns, from 1880 to 1882, and two more in 1886 and 1887. They were the dominant team of that decade, more for their pitching and defense than for their baserunning. But, as Mike Kelly showed in 1882, aggressive baserunning didn't hurt either.

That was the year Chicago and the Providence Grays were locked in a tense pennant race. The White Stockings and Grays played a three-game set late in the season in Chicago that, for all intents and purposes, would decide the pennant. Kelly recalled in an interview reprinted in *Wrigleyville* that the first game "was the most hotly contested ball game I have ever played in."

With the score 4–3, and Providence in the lead, Kelly was on first base with one out in the bottom of the ninth inning. Teammate Tommy Burns scorched the ball to Providence shortstop George Wright. Wright ran to second to force Kelly.

Kelly sprinted to the bag, and just before Wright got there, slammed his shoulder into the shortstop. The ball spun away into the grandstand, and both Kelly and Burns scored to win the game. Chicago swept the series and won the pennant.

Providence manager Harry Wright, George's older brother, was furious. After the season, he said that, but for Kelly's "infernal tricks," his team would have won.

Mike Kelly was unrepentant. "I play ball to win," he said. "And if I have to employ a few subterfuges, I cannot help it. I will do everything in the world to win a championship ball game. That's what I am paid for."

Kelly wasn't the only White Stocking who made sure opponents thought hard about trying to impede him. Teammate and captain Adrian Anson, another

load at six-feet-one and 200 pounds, laid out St. Louis catcher George Myers on a play at the plate in 1886. Myers, according to contemporary reports, was knocked several feet backward. But he held on to the ball, thus retiring Anson.

In June 1887, St. Louis outfielder Curt Welch, another big fella at five-feet-ten and 190 pounds, ran over the smaller (5'7", 150 lbs.) Baltimore second baseman Bill Greenwood. Baltimore fans and management were so incensed that Welch was actually arrested; he had to be bailed out after the game.

Eventually, a kind of rough code emerged to deal with the situation (other than having the infielder arrested). Throughout baseball, a majority of shortstops and second basemen turn out to be relatively small men. Generally, it is up to larger teammates to protect them. If a player is thought to have intentionally knocked over an opposing infielder, the unwritten code is that the infielder on the other team is fair game. This, for the most part, has cut down a lot of the potential issues for baserunners who try to take liberties on the basepaths.

RIGHT: Reggie Jackson, like Ty Cobb, would do anything to win. Even "accidentally" deflect a baseball in this World Series game against the Dodgers.

RUNNING INTO BASEBALLS

There may be no real trick to running into ballplayers, but as Reggie Jackson will tell you, there is a trick to running into baseballs. In the 1978 World Series against the Los Angeles Dodgers, Jackson turned things around for the struggling Yankees in Game Four. Jackson was on first base when teammate Lou Piniella hit a single to shortstop Bill Russell. Jackson raced toward second base, but Russell had already fielded the ball and stepped on second to begin a double play. Russell whipped the ball toward first base, and it deflected off Jackson's hip into the infield, eliminating the possibility of the double play. Yankee baserunner Thurman Munson, who had been on first, scored, and the Yankees went on to win the game 4–3 and tie the series. They won that World Series, four games to two.

Reggie, of course, insisted he was trying to get out of the way of the ball (deliberately stepping in the way of a thrown baseball is an automatic out). The Dodgers screamed that he turned his hip and stepped into the ball. Replays were inconclusive.

Pete ROSE

Reds, Phillies, Expos, 1963–86

His nickname was "Charlie Hustle." He even ran to first base when he was walked. Rose only knew one way to play, and that was full speed.

CAREER STATISTICS				
BA	HR	RBI	H	SB
.303	160	1,314	4,256	198

Ty COBB

Tigers, Athletics, 1905–26

Cobb was another fellow who played hard. He generally went after people with his spikes instead of his body. His nasty spiking of Detroit third baseman Frank Baker in August of 1909 put Baker in the hospital.

CAREER STATISTICS				
BA	HR	RBI	H	SB
.366	117	1,937	4,189	892

Frank ROBINSON

Reds, Orioles, Dodgers, Angels, Indians, 1956–76

Robinson was a big (6'1", 195 lbs.), muscular guy who wasn't afraid to knock over people on the basepaths. In 1959, he got into a nasty fight with the Braves' Eddie Mathews after Robinson slid into him hard at third base.

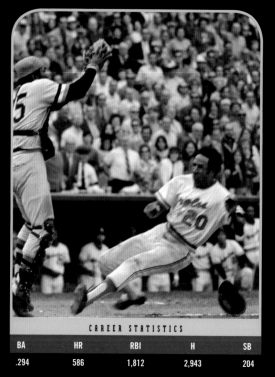

CAREER STATISTICS				
BA	HR	RBI	H	SB
.294	586	1,812	2,943	204

HOW IT'S DONE
Crashing into Players

The most dramatic instance of a player crashing into an opponent and virtually ending his career is the famous—or infamous—play in the 1970 All-Star game, when Cleveland catcher Ray Fosse was bowled over by Cincinnati's Pete Rose. Fosse, who was in his first year as a catcher for the Indians, dealt with an injury-riddled career for years afterward.

But both players later acknowledged that Rose's play was not dirty, and that both men were merely trying to play to win.

Players barreling into infielders is mostly a matter of lowering one's shoulder and diving forward. If there is any real technique, it's essentially this: if you have to hit someone, use your shoulder, not your head.

RIGHT: Pete Rose smashes into Ray Fosse in the 1970 All-Star game.

THE HOME-RUN TROT

For most of the 19th century, very, very few people had to worry about home-run trots, because a vast majority of home runs were inside-the-park jobs. The home-run trot was mostly a sprint.

And, in fact, even when a player did smack a ball out of the park in those days, he usually sprinted at least to first base, because such out-of-the-park home runs were so rare that it was literally a surprise when the ball went out.

Probably because he hit so many, most players copied Babe Ruth's home-run trot for decades. Ruth's usual foray around the basepaths was very low-key: as soon as he hit the ball, Ruth would toss the bat away. Head down, he ambled fairly quickly around the bases, never looking up until it was time to get to home plate. At that point, Ruth would shake the hands of the teammates who were on base when he hit the home run, and then jog into the dugout.

Special home runs, such as the blast in 1932 against the Cubs and his 60th in 1927, got a little more demonstrative: in 1927, after number 60, Ruth stepped on home plate and waved his hat at the Yankee crowd.

Part of the reason his trots were so low-key was because Ruth hit so many home runs, he didn't want to make it seem as though any single homer was anything special. The other reason was that many pitchers of his era would not hesitate to drill the Babe the next time he was up. The message: don't show me up.

Pitchers still don't like to be shown up, so most home-run hitters keep their trots fairly low-key.

There were always exceptions, including Ted Williams's dance around the bases in the 1941 All-Star game, but Ruth's low-key jog was the rule for many, many years.

At some point in the 1930s, the "cap tip" emerged as a way to acknowledge the roar of the fans. The cap tip was usually saved for home games, and players didn't actually take off their caps, but just grabbed the tip of the brim for a second or two.

The Yankees' Joe DiMaggio was said to have an exceptionally smooth cap tip, done a few seconds after he crossed home plate. He would lightly brush the tip of his cap. It sufficiently acknowledged the cheers, but didn't show up the pitcher enough to invite retaliation.

Conversely, Ted Williams's decision not to do the cap tip enraged the sportswriters in Boston. Williams usually traversed the bases quickly and ran into the dugout. As odd as it sounds now, Boston sportswriters wrote reams of copy on how disrespectful this was.

In 1960, Williams hit a home run in his last at-bat in his last game. It was a stunningly dramatic moment, and the relatively small crowd at Fenway Park howled its appreciation. Just this once, it was thought, Williams would tip his cap to the fans. He did not. "Gods," John Updike wrote in his superb *New Yorker* piece on the game, "do not answer letters."

The advent of television, and the replay camera, began to change things. Many people falsely believe that former Yankee Reggie Jackson (Athletics, Orioles, Yankees, Angels, 1967–87) was one of the architects of the "showboat" era. But Jackson, like Ruth, was a low-key homer hitter: he trotted around the bases pretty quickly, head down.

Of course, Jackson, when the moment warranted, would occasionally turn his home-run jog into something a little more. The night in 1977 when he hit three home runs off three different pitchers in Game Six of the World Series, Jackson came out and acknowledged the crowd with a wave.

But as the 1990s wore on, more and more players got more and more demonstrative. Ricky Henderson, for example, would stand in the batter's box for an extra second or two, and then hop out of the box toward first base. Darryl Strawberry (Mets, Dodgers, Yankees, 1983–99) was another guy who liked to watch his homers go out of the park and then take his time circling the bases.

Note: These are the most memorable trots in baseball history, not necessarily the players with the best home-run gait.

Carlton
FISK

Game Six, 1975 World Series

Red Sox fans believe this home run was the most dramatic in the history of the World Series. It's hard to disagree. Fisk was facing Reds' pitcher Pat Darcy in the bottom of the 12th inning at Fenway, with the Sox down in games, 3–2. Fisk turned on a Darcy fastball and sent it whistling toward the left-field foul pole. As the ball headed out to the fences, Fisk was on the first-base line, trying to will the ball fair by waving his arms. You could see him hollering, "Stay fair! Stay fair!" Then, as the ball just slid by the pole, Fisk leaped in triumph, along with the rest of the fans at Fenway Park.

CAREER STATISTICS				
BA	HR	RBI	H	SB
.269	376	1,330	2,356	128

Kirk GIBSON

Game One, 1988 World Series

Kept out of the lineup that day due to a leg injury, Gibson pinch-hit with two out in the bottom of the ninth, with teammate Mike Davis on base. The Dodgers were down, 4–3. Gibson fouled off four pitches before blasting a slider off Athletics' reliever Dennis Eckersley for the game-winning home run. His trot around the basepaths was punctuated by him double-pumping his right arm in joy.

CAREER STATISTICS				
BA	HR	RBI	H	SB
.263	255	870	1,553	284

Babe RUTH

Game Three, 1932 World Series

The Chicago Cubs had been riding Ruth mercilessly throughout the game. The Babe, no shrinking violet, gave as good as he got. Finally, in the fifth inning, against Cub pitcher Charlie Root, Ruth pointed at the dugout and said, "It only takes one to hit it out!" He was right. Ruth drilled Root's pitch into center field. As he circled the bases, chuckling, he clasped his hands over his head and shook them like a heavyweight fighter. The roaring crowd, which had been riding Ruth all game as well, burst into applause.

CAREER STATISTICS				
BA	HR	RBI	H	SB
.342	714	2,213	2,873	125

Ted WILLIAMS

1941 All-Star Game

Williams came to bat in the bottom of the ninth inning with two men on, two out, and the AL All-Stars down, 5–4. Williams blasted a deep drive off Claude Passeau to win the contest, 7–5. Williams, who later said it was the biggest thrill of his career, half jumped, half ran around the bases, clapping his hands and laughing.

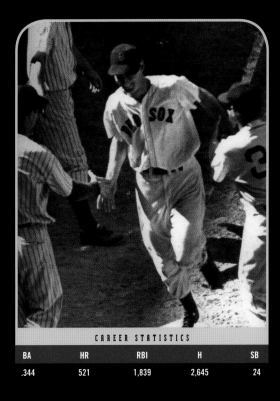

CAREER STATISTICS				
BA	HR	RBI	H	SB
.344	521	1,839	2,645	24

Jeffrey Leonard (Dodgers, Astros, Giants, Brewers, Mariners, 1977–90) told the media during the 1987 National League Championship Series that he had "five different" home-run trots, including the "one flap down," in which he ran around the bases with his right arm at his side, and the "long run," in which he took almost a minute jogging around the diamond. Leonard probably holds the record for most different trots, if there is such a record.

These days, most heavy hitters, like Barry Bonds, David Ortiz (Twins, Red Sox, 1997–present) and Manny Ramirez (Indians, Red Sox, 1993–present), stand at the plate and watch their home runs go out. On Opening Day 2008, Manny drilled a shot to the farthest reaches of the Tokyo Dome in Japan. He stepped out of the box to admire it and suddenly realized it wasn't going to make it out of the park. He sprinted down the first-base line and wound up with a double.

Not to say there aren't some old-school guys. Scott Rolen (Phillies, Cardinals, 1996–present), Jose Reyes (Mets, 2003–present) and Jason Varitek (Red Sox, 1997–present) hit the ball and round the bases in record time. Reyes nearly sprints around the bases.

PIERSALL'S REVERSE TROT

Jimmy Piersall (Red Sox, Indians, Senators, Mets, Angels, 1952–67) was an odd duck. In fact, the self-imposed pressure he placed on himself drove him to a nervous breakdown in 1952. But when he recovered, he decided that since people thought he was nutty, he would act the part. So it was in 1962, when he hit his 100th career home run, that he ran around the bases backward. After the game, Piersall claimed he ran the bases that way in protest for the lack of coverage the media gave Duke Snider (Dodgers, Mets, Giants, 1947–64) when Duke hit his 400th homer.

SAMMY SOSA

HOW IT'S DONE
The Home Run Trot

irst, you have to hit a home run. After that, there are a couple ways to handle it. You can take the humble approach, which is to put your head down and go around the basepath. Or you can stand at first base and admire your handiwork, then trot slowly around the diamond, a move sure to annoy the opposing team, especially the pitcher. Make sure you touch all the bases!

JIMMY PIERSALL

DAVID ORTIZ

ALEX RODRIGUEZ

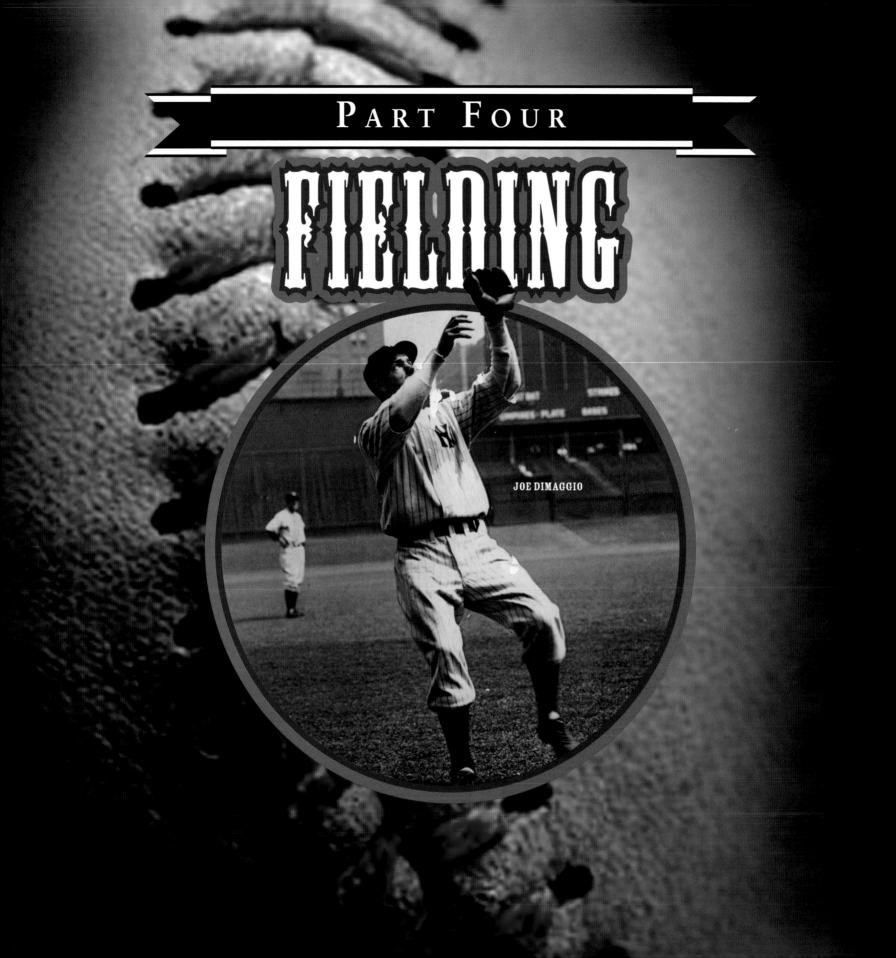

PART FOUR

FIELDING

JOE DIMAGGIO

KEITH HERNANDEZ

THE 6-4-3 DOUBLE PLAY

ABOVE: Fred Tenny is credited with inventing the 3-6-3 double play while playing first base for the New York Giants.

Before the National Association was formed in 1870, barnstorming professional teams were "turning two." By around 1865, teams were routinely making double plays, the most ordinary of which was the shortstop to second baseman to first baseman variety. The second most carried out double play was the first baseman to shortstop and back to first baseman twin killing.

The Chicago White Stockings of the mid-1880s had the first infield to be recognized as a superior defensive unit. Called the "Stonewall Infield," the Chicago squad featured second baseman Fred Pfeffer and shortstop Tommy Burns; third baseman Ned Williamson and first baseman Adrian "Cap" Anson completed the foursome.

Pfeffer played in an era where gloves were non-existent, yet he was considered one of the surest-handed fielders of his era. His nickname was "Dandelion" because he could "pick" ground balls so well.

Anson, in his autobiography, called Pfeffer "a ball-player from the ground up, and as good a second baseman as there ever was in the profession." Burns, Pfeffer and Williamson were also credited by Cub star Johnny Evers with perfecting "the old gag," which is now called a rundown. According to Evers, the three perfected the art of quick-tossing to one another during times when an opposing player was caught off base.

"With the White Stockings," wrote Evers in his autobiography, "no more than three men were ever allowed to participate in the play."

This, said Evers, reduced the confusion during a rundown and allowed a fresh player back into the rundown after every toss. Other teams quickly picked up the concept, which is still used now.

The Stonewall Infield helped the White Stockings win two consecutive National League pennants, in 1885 and 1886. The White Stockings averaged nearly 85 double plays annually during those championship years, the best in the National League.

By the mid-1890s, teams were also practicing the 3-6-3 double play, which is the throw from first base to shortstop back to first base to make two outs. New York Giants first baseman Fred Tenney is credited with this innovation. Tenney may not have been the first player to carry out that play, but by 1896, sportswriters were noticing that he was carrying out this maneuver successfully.

The practice of getting rid of the ball before a fielder actually touches second base is probably as old as the double play itself. Second basemen and shortstops learned very early on that the lead baserunner would try by any means possible to disrupt an attempt to carry out a double play. This included sliding toward second base with baseball spikes aimed at the fielder instead of the bag. Other tactics included sliding head-first, again at the fielder rather than at the bag itself.

Pfeffer, a deft fielder around second base, was often accused of firing the ball toward first base before he had actually touched second. But in the 19th century, when there was often only one umpire, the bang-bang nature of the double play often forced umpires to give the defensive player the benefit of the doubt.

Over the next century, the double play became one of the constants in baseball. If Fred Pfeffer were to sit in Fenway Park this year, watching Sox shortstop Julio Lugo gun the ball to second baseman Dustin Pedroia, who in turn fires the ball to first baseman Kevin Youkilis, to turn two, he would recognize the play instantly.

HOW GOOD WAS TINKER TO EVERS TO CHANCE?

Joe Tinker (left) and Johnny Evers, two parts of the three-man double-play phenomenon of the early 1900s. INSET: Tinker, Evers, and Chance.

Joe Tinker and Johnny Evers, of the Chicago Cubs, played in the same infield from 1903 to 1910. They have been immortalized in one of the best-known poems about baseball players ever written.

That piece of rhyming has led some to imagine that they were the best double-play combination ever and, with third baseman Harry Steinfeldt and first baseman Frank Chance, one of the better defensive outfields of that or any era.

But this crew never led the league in double plays. They never even finished second in any of those years, and Tinker to Evers to Chance twice finished sixth in double plays in an eight-team league.

So where did they get their reputation? Mostly from New York City writer Franklin P. Adams. Adams was a New York Giants fan, and he took it very personally when a Tinker to Evers to Chance double play killed a rally by his beloved Gothamites. He wrote a poem and submitted it to a local newspaper, the *New York Evening Mail*:

These are the saddest of possible words,
"Tinker to Evers to Chance."
Trio of bear cubs fleeter than birds,
Tinker to Evers to Chance.
Ruthlessly pricking our gonfalon bubble,
Making a Giant hit into a double—
Words that are heavy with nothing but trouble,
"Tinker to Evers to Chance."

For those who don't know, a "gonfalon" is a pennant or flag.

Phil RIZZUTO & Joe GORDON

Yankees, 1941-42, 1946

Rizzuto worked with several other second basemen, including Gil MacDougald and, later, Jerry Coleman. All of these combinations were at or near the top in double plays every year.

Mark BELANGER & Bobby GRICH

Orioles, 1973-76

Like Rizzuto, Belanger worked successfully with several second basemen over his career with the Orioles. Grich was a better defensive player than his predecessor, Davy Johnson, although the Orioles' infield of third baseman Brooks Robinson, Belanger, Grich and first baseman Boog Powell, who played from 1970 to 1972, was probably the best defensive infield ever.

Phil Rizzuto (in mid-air) and Joe Gordon putting out Stan Musial at second base, and throwing to first during Game Three of the 1943 World Series.

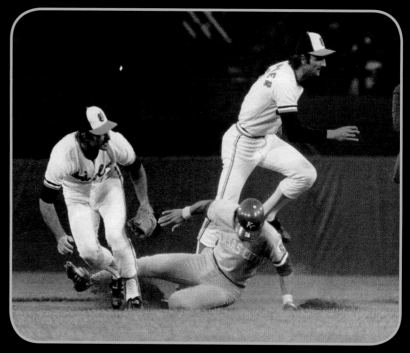

Belanger (right) and Grich turning two.

Billy HERMAN & Billy JURGES

Cubs, 1931-38

These two guys were together a long time and, not coincidentally, represent the last successful decade—the 1930s—in Cub history.

Bill MAZEROSKI & Gene ALLEY

Pirates, 1965-68

This is one of the principal reasons Mazeroski got into the Hall of Fame. He and Alley represented a fearsome double-play combination that was the foundation of those Pirate teams of the 1960s.

Bill Herman throws to first to complete a double-play against the Tigers in the 1935 World Series.

Gene Alley (left) and Bill Mazeroski (center) are pictured here with teammate Roberto Clemente.

PHIL RIZZUTO

HOW IT'S DONE
The 6-4-3 Double Play

For identification purposes, every position on the baseball diamond has a number. They are: 1–pitcher, 2–catcher, 3–first base, 4–second base, 5–third base, 6–shortstop, 7 through 9–outfielders. Thus, a throw from the shortstop to the second baseman to the first baseman is scored as a 6-4-3. Turning the basic 6-4-3 double play is a study in teamwork. Infielders work on it tirelessly in spring training. The fundamental rule is that whichever infield player first fields the ball must get it out of his glove and to the next infielder as quickly as possible. That initial move determines whether or not the double play will work. In the case of the 6-4-3, after the shortstop makes the throw, the second baseman must receive the ball, pivot and make his own throw to the first baseman. The footwork involved in the pivot is what makes the second baseman such a key player in the infield.

Finally, the first baseman has to cleanly field the ball, which, given the speed of the athletes involved, is easier said than done. It's a teamwork thing, and it's why there is no substitute for practice in this case.

Note: There are obviously a host of other double-play combinations out there, but the 6-4-3—shortstop to second base to first base—is by far the most common.

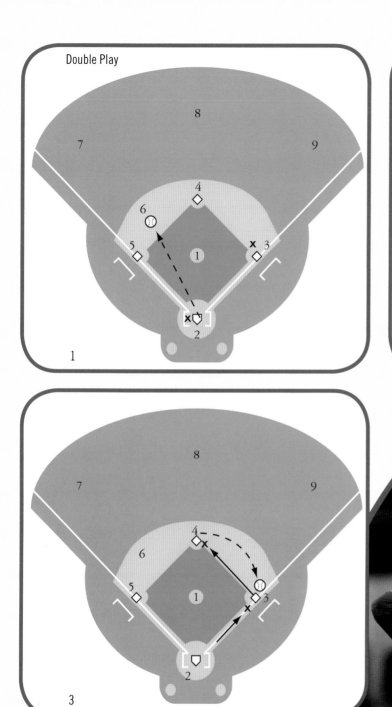

Double Play

1

2

3

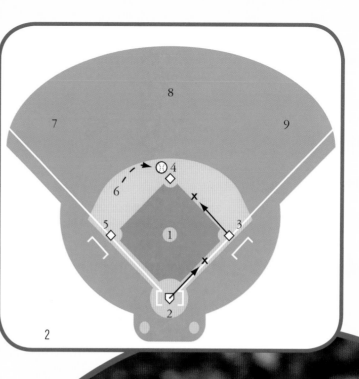

JULIO LUGO

There may be several decades between the careers of Phil "The Scooter" Rizzuto (opposite) and Julio Lugo (right), but as major league shortstops, their challenge is the same: Getting the throw off while avoiding the slide into second base.

THE STRETCH

Two big fellows, Lou Gehrig of the Yankees and Albert Pujols of the Cardinals, show fine form collecting the throw from the infield.

First basemen have been tall drinks of water since the game became popular, but that was merely so they could better field balls hit high. For many years, first basemen took throws from the infield standing up or, at best, crouching only a little, using both hands.

Early first baseman Adrian "Cap" Anson of the Chicago White Stockings was reportedly one of the first players to go into a stretch to catch balls thrown by his infielders. But Fred Tenney of the Boston Beaneaters is regarded as the first player who regularly used a stretch to catch baseballs.

Tenney was not the prototype first baseman. He was by no means a big man at five-feet-nine and 155 pounds. He was a good, but not great, hitter. Tenney's greatest advantage was his work ethic. He would field hundreds of balls almost every day in practice. And that, in fact, enabled him to experiment with various fielding techniques. One of these was the stretch.

Tenney determined that by going into a near split, the baseball would get to him just a tiny bit earlier, which, in turn, could mean the difference between a base hit and an out.

LOU GEHRIG

Tenney's experiments also coincided roughly with the advent of larger fielding gloves. With a larger glove, relatively speaking, Tenney did not have to try to catch the baseball with both hands, which means he could lean out over the basepath to receive the ball.

Another first baseman of that era, Harry Davis (Giants, Pirates, Nationals, Athletics, Indians, 1895–1917), was also known for his stretching style. In fact, more than Tenney, Davis was renowned for picking bad throws out of the dirt and turning them into outs.

As the 20th century progressed, the best first basemen were known for their defensive abilities as well as their prowess with the bat. The Yankees' Lou Gehrig is known for his thunderous home runs, but Gehrig, like Tenney before him, worked endlessly on his footwork around the bag.

Infielders liked throwing to bigger men, like Gehrig, as it gave them a bigger target.

Interestingly, the most agile first baseman of any era was George Scott of the Red Sox and Brewers. Scott was tremendous, when he wasn't overweight. Late in his career, he admitted that he acquired "Dunlop's disease": his belly had done lopped over his waist.

But when he wasn't so afflicted, Scott was one of the best ever. In his autobiography, *The Wrong Stuff*, former Red Sox pitcher Bill Lee recalls a game in which fleet Oakland A's batter Camp Campaneris drilled a ball to Boston shortstop Rico Petrocelli. Petrocelli made a tough catch and rifled the ball to Scott. The

ALBERT PUJOLS

ball bounced wide of first base. Scott stepped across the first-base bag and, according to Lee, actually fielded the ball as it went through Campaneris's legs into foul territory. He caught the ball a split second before Campaneris touched first base.

"Still the greatest fielding play I've ever seen," wrote Lee.

George "The Boomer" SCOTT

Scott was colorful and funny and had an awful weight problem. (One of his Red Sox managers, Dick Williams, noted that Scott sometimes seemed to gain weight between doubleheaders.) But Scott had amazing hands and was masterful at scooping bad throws out of the dirt.

CAREER STATISTICS				
BA	HR	RBI	H	SB
.268	271	1,051	1,992	69

Don MATTINGLY

Yankees, 1982–95

Tremendously sound, Mattingly was not a great fielder when he started out in the big leagues. But his work ethic was relentless, and he eventually became the best defensive first baseman of his era in the American League.

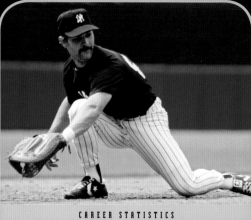

CAREER STATISTICS				
BA	HR	RBI	H	SB
.307	222	1,099	2,153	14

Fred TENNEY

Braves, Giants, 1894–1911

No Gold Gloves were awarded in this era, but Tenney was probably the best defensive infielder of the early 20th century.

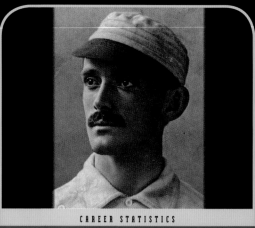

CAREER STATISTICS				
BA	HR	RBI	H	SB
.294	22	688	2,231	285

Keith HERNANDEZ

Cardinals, Mets, Indians, 1974–90

A superb defensive first baseman who set the standard for the National League in the 1980s.

CAREER STATISTICS				
BA	HR	RBI	H	SB
.296	162	1,071	2,182	98

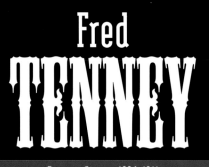

HOW IT'S DONE
The Stretch

The stretch is the almost ballerina-like split that a first baseman adopts when fielding a throw, usually from the infield but sometimes from the outfield. The theory behind the stretch is that by extending himself an extra two or three feet, a first baseman shaves, by a few fractions of a second, the length of time between the moment the baseball leaves a fielder's hand and the moment it settles into the first sacker's glove. That is sometimes the difference between a baserunner being safe or out.

During his 14-year career with the Astros, Jeff Bagwell (above) was known as a very good defensive first baseman. In his career so far, Nick Swisher (left), now of the White Sox, is known as a fair defensive first baseman. But, as can be seen, making plays from the stretch still requires a degree of athleticism and flexibility.

CATCHING THE BALL IN THE OUTFIELD

For most of the 19th century, when outfielders either didn't have gloves or had gloves that were little more than mittens, the fundamentally sound way to catch a ball hit to the outfield was to use two hands. Certainly, there were times when a player had no choice but to try to catch a ball with one hand, but overall, the conventional thinking was that catching a ball with only the glove hand invited disaster.

That began to change as the play of first basemen, who went into a stretch position to catch balls, with glove hand outstretched, became more prevalent. When it became obvious that a good first baseman was able to field throw after throw with only one hand, one-handed catches became more accepted.

But it took a while. Johnny Evers of the Chicago Cubs was the first infielder to make one-handed catches while playing second base, and sportswriters were universally disdainful of his tactics, calling him a "Fancy Dan," a nickname for a ballplayer deemed too flamboyant.

Forty years after Evers practiced it, first baseman Vic Power was still being criticized for making one-handed catches in the infield in the 1950s.

In 1913, shortstop Rabbit Maranville came up with another method of catching balls by cupping his hands at his chest and letting the ball drop into them. Maranville claimed that the technique, called the basket catch, had the advantage of enabling the infielder to use his chest to trap the baseball.

In the 1950s, Giants outfielder Willie Mays began using this technique for routine fly balls. But he was also catching balls with one hand when he had to stretch for a well-hit ball. Mays, because he was so good at it, was one of the players who made the one-handed catch popular, or at least acceptable, to coaches, fans and sportswriters.

JOHNNY EVERS

TRIS SPEAKER'S UNASSISTED DOUBLE PLAYS

Tris Speaker was the fastest outfielder of the early 1900s, of that there is no question. He played a very shallow center field, explaining that he could more easily go back on a ball than come in. Teammates and sportswriters of the era swore he would sometimes play only a few feet behind second base, depending on the circumstance.

Thus, Speaker was involved in a lot of unassisted double plays, which is very, very rare for an outfielder. But Speaker would often be playing shallow and catch a ball hit weakly over the second baseman's head; then, using his speed, he would run into the infield and tag the man running to second base. His 139 double plays in center field (not all unassisted) is still the all-time leader.

LEFT: Roberto Clemente's ability as a defensive player has long been overshadowed by his offensive abilities. But make no mistake. He was a great defensive outfielder.
RIGHT: Willie Mays making his un-forgettable over-the-shoulder catch in the 1954 World Series.

Pirates, 1965–72

Exceptional speed and a cannon arm made Clemente one of the greatest outfielders ever.

Red Sox, Indians, Senators, Athletics 1907–28

One of the fastest men in the history of baseball, Speaker was indisputably the best defensive outfielder of the early 20th century.

Yankees, 1936–42, 1946–51

DiMaggio never seemed to make a tough catch in the outfield. But that was because his knowledge of hitters, speed and athleticism made everything look easy.

CAREER STATISTICS

BA	HR	RBI	H	SB
.317	240	1,305	3,000	83

CAREER STATISTICS

BA	HR	RBI	H	SB
.345	117	1,529	3,514	432

CAREER STATISTICS

BA	HR	RBI	H	SB
.325	361	1,537	2,214	30

Willie
MAYS

Mays was a superior all-around player who routinely made great defensive plays. Ask Vic Wertz, who drilled a sure hit to the deepest part of the Polo Grounds in the 1954 World Series opener, only to see Mays make his famous over-the-shoulder catch to get him out—the most famous catch in baseball history.

CAREER STATISTICS				
BA	HR	RBI	H	SB
.302	660	1,903	3,283	338

One of Mays's contemporaries, Roberto Clemente, also used the basket catch in the outfield. In addition, Clemente's speed and athleticism made him the finest defensive outfielder of his era. Clemente made diving, one-handed grabs almost routine, and his 12 consecutive Gold Gloves in the outfield are still a record. Neither Mays nor Clemente paved the way for the one-handed catch, but being superstars, they made it more acceptable.

In fact, it wasn't really until glove manufacturers began making gloves with deeper "heels"—the part of the glove that covers the palm of the hand—that one-handed catches in the outfield became more common. The deeper heel enabled an outfielder to snag a ball and control it by squeezing it; this was not possible with the smaller, less flexible gloves of the earlier days.

After he retired, Detroit Tiger second baseman Char-lie Gehringer recalled that he never saw an outfielder leap into the stands and catch a baseball in the 1930s, when he played, because it was nearly impossible. The ball, noted Gehringer, just wouldn't stay in the glove. As fielders' gloves became bigger, and their heels became deeper, such catches became more commonplace.

Outfielder Ricky Henderson took the one-handed catch to a greater extreme. Henderson would often make a "snap catch" of a fly ball in the outfield. This consisted of holding his glove by the side of his face and, as the ball came to him, "snapping" his glove sideways and catching the ball like a man brushes away mosquitoes.

Henderson was criticized for this method of catching the ball, as it seemed unnecessarily fancy. But he rarely lost a ball when catching it that way, and he usually only caught balls in that manner when they were relatively easy fly outs.

RICKY HENDERSON

HOW IT'S DONE
Catching in the Outfield

Yankee great Joe DiMaggio once pointed out that if an outfielder tries to catch a ball by going off at the proverbial "crack of the bat," he's already in trouble. A good outfielder knows the offensive tendencies of the batter at the plate, and even more than that, knows the pitching tendencies of his teammate on the mound. He is ever alert to the game situation, including the count on the batter. Speed helps, and anticipation helps more. Athleticism is good to have, but knowing what your pitcher will be throwing in a certain situation, and how the batter will react, is more important.

Ted Sizemore (right) makes a catch at Shea Stadium as he is falling backwards, while Carlos Beltran (above) of the Mets dives to make a snag.

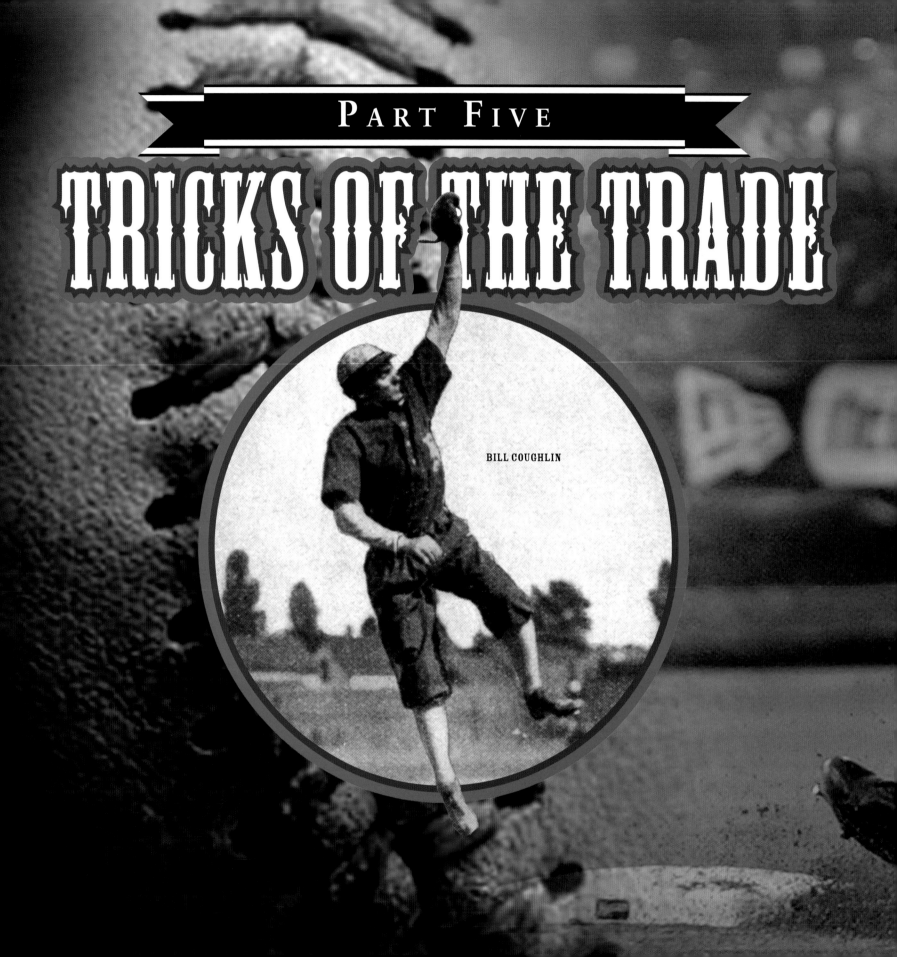

PART FIVE

TRICKS OF THE TRADE

BILL COUGHLIN

MIKE LOWELL

THE HIDDEN-BALL TRICK

ABOVE: Jack Burdock, woodcut.
OPPOSITE: The Red Sox's Mike Lowell looks like a nice guy, but he is as devious as they come and one of the best hidden-ball artists in the league.

The hidden-ball trick goes back to the early days, before there was a National League, and probably even before the old National Association. Players were trying the hidden-ball trick in sandlots in the 19th century. According to the *Sporting News*, Tom Barlow, a shortstop from 1872 to 1875 for the Hartfords and the Brooklyn Atlantics of the old National Association, was notable for it, but it's doubtful he was the originator. Another Brooklyn player, second baseman Jack Burdock, who also played from 1872 to 1875, was notable for the feat.

According to MLB.com, only about 300 hidden-ball plays have been successful in the major leagues since the National League was started in 1875. Still, that's a couple of times a year, on average.

Although most players now hide the ball in their gloves, in the days of small gloves or no gloves, players were wont to hide the ball under their armpits.

The hidden-ball trick was more popular in the early part of the 20th century than it is 100 years later, mostly because veterans could usually get away with fooling rookies more than once. But today the younger guys are savvier, maybe because they've grown up watching baseball on television, where they can see the players from all angles.

With progress comes innovation. The latest twist on the hidden-ball trick has been pulled off at least twice by Matt Williams, who played third base for the Giants, Indians and Diamondbacks from 1987 to 2004. Williams would ask a player to move off the bag so he could brush it off, then he would tag the baserunner out.

Boston Red Sox third baseman Mike Lowell is the present master of the hidden-ball trick, having pulled it off three times in his career, including twice in the past three years, both times when he played for the Florida Marlins. His present Sox teammate, shortstop Julio Lugo, was the only player to successfully pull off the trick in the 2007 season, nabbing Alberto Callaspo of the Diamondbacks.

The all-time champion of the hidden-ball trick is third baseman Bill Coughlin, who played for the Washington Senators and Detroit Tigers from 1899 to 1908. Coughlin, according to *The Baseball Almanac*, reportedly pulled off the hidden-ball trick seven times, including once in the 1907 World Series. In Game Two of that Series, Coughlin caught Chicago Cub Jimmy Slagle with the trick. (It didn't help much; the Cubs swept the Series.)

"IF THE BASERUNNER LOOKS AT YOU AND THEN STEPS OFF THE BASE, YOU'VE GOT HIM: WALK OVER AND TAG HIM."

IN CASE YOU DIDN'T KNOW

The hidden-ball trick is scored as an unassisted put out for the fielder making the play.

INTENTIONALLY GETTING HIT BY A BALL

In the mid-19th century, a batter was not awarded first base if hit by a baseball. However, if a ball did hit a batter, the ball was still live. So there were many instances of batters stepping into pitches to deflect them into the infield to at least advance a runner. It is difficult to say who was the first player to attempt this maneuver.

By 1874, there was a realization that players were trying to get hit deliberately, and the rule was changed: there would be no penalty for a hit batter, and the ball would no longer be in play. This clearly, of course, gave pitchers a major weapon, as they could throw at a batter without worrying about an opposing player advancing. So by 1887, the National League changed the rule again and required that a hit batsman be entitled to a base.

The umpire was allowed to rule on whether the batter had intentionally tried to be hit, and, if so, he would be called out.

Very quickly, one team, the old Baltimore Orioles of the National League, became masters of getting hit by pitches to reach base. Players like Hughie Jennings, Tommy Tucker (Orioles, Braves, Nationals, Dodgers, Cardinals, Spiders, 1887–99) and John McGraw (Orioles, Cardinals, Giants, 1891–1906) would wear shirts with baggy sleeves and extend their arms out over the plate in the hopes that the ball would brush their uniform. They were also unafraid to step into pitches. And if an umpire dared rule that they had allowed themselves to be hit, that umpire was in for major-league griping.

Jennings was declared, in a story in the *New York Times*, the originator of the deliberate hit by pitch, or HBP. But in 1907, Jennings denied that, saying instead that he learned the tactic from Curt Welch. Welch was an outfielder with St. Louis of the old American Associ-ation and, over a 10-year career, was hit by pitches 173 times, leading the league 3 times.

But if Welch was the first, Jennings became the master. He led the league in being hit a total of five times, from 1894 to 1898. Four of those years, the Orioles won the pennant. He was hit 51 times in 1894, and 46 times each in 1897 and 1898, for a total of 287 career bruises. Jennings's teammates were almost as prolific: Tucker's 272 HBP are third all time, and McGraw led the league once and was hit 137 times himself.

Tucker may not always have deliberately maneu-vered himself to be hit at the plate. He was known as "The Foghorn" and "Noisy Tom" in recognition of his tart tongue. Sometimes, as he baited pitchers from the dugout or while on base in the infield, he would earn a retaliatory plunking his next time up.

To be sure, the Orioles of that era developed many weapons besides getting hit by a pitch, but in this, as in many things, they were pioneers.

Baltimore was probably the last team to use the hit batsman as a consistent strategy. But players like Frank Chance (Cubs, Yankees, 1898–1914), Ron Hunt, Don Baylor and Craig Biggio have over the past several decades used the tactic. In Chance's case, it was almost fatal. On May 4, 1904, he was hit 5 times in a double-header, and he was hit 36 times that season. He eventu-ally had to have a special operation to relieve pressure in his brain. Chance was also a boxer in the off-season, which probably did not help.

"But," he proudly told the *Sporting News* years later, "it didn't change the way I played."

Hmm . . .

"To get up there and deliberately attempt to get hit

ABOVE: The Cubs' Frank Chance was called the Peerless Leader, in part, because he was one tough dude. He used to brag about getting hit by a baseball.

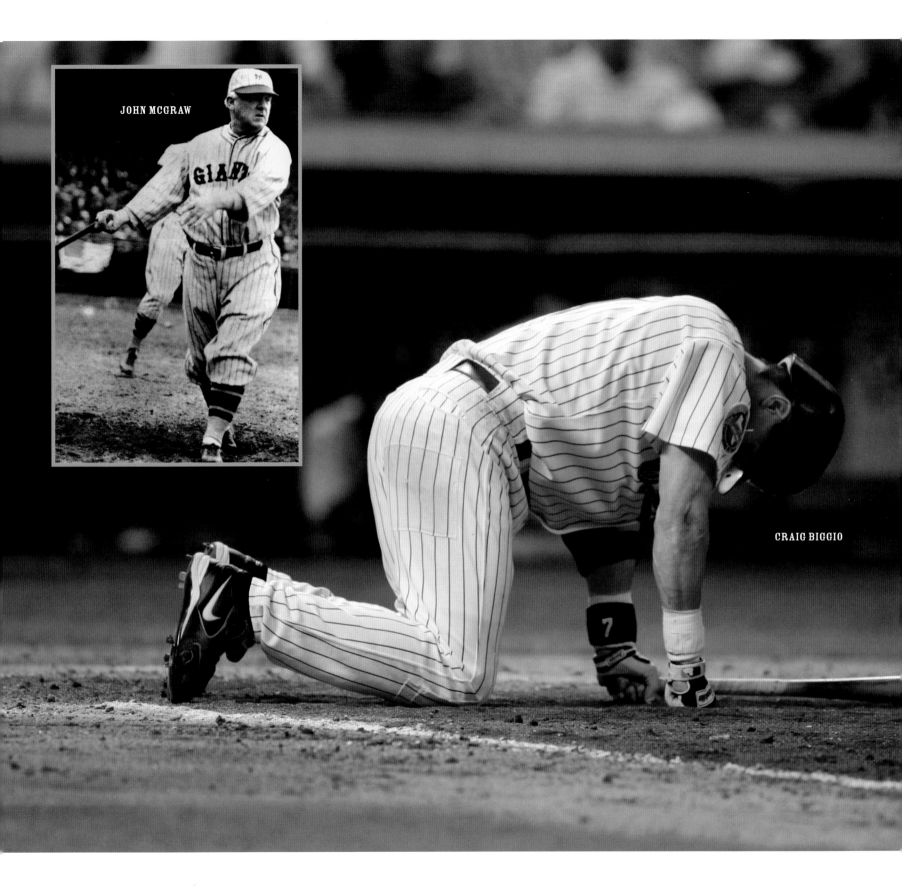

JOHN MCGRAW

CRAIG BIGGIO

by a pitched ball," said former New York Giant Fred Snodgrass (Braves, Giants, 1908–16) in an interview with Lawrence Ritter for his book, *The Glory of Their Times*, "it's a lost art today. Just not done anymore. I had a baggy uniform: baggy shirt, baggy pants. Any ball thrown close inside, why, I turned with it and half the time I wasn't really hit, just my uniform was nicked."

"If it gets me on base, I don't see what's wrong with it," said Hunt in 1971. And in fact, the years he was a regular in San Francisco and Montreal, he never played less than 117 games a season. In 1971, the year he was hit 50 times, he missed only 8 games.

Minnie Minoso (Indians, White Sox, Cardinals, Senators, 1949–1964, 1976, 1980) was hit by a total of 192 pitches and led the league a record 10 times. He admitted in an interview after his retirement that he would do anything to get on base.

And lately, hitters like Boston's David Ortiz and San Francisco's Barry Bonds have taken to wearing what is essentially body armor to protect them from pitches. Bonds, in particular, wears a giant plastic arm shield that protects him. He has been hit about 100 times in his career.

In Case You Didn't Know

Dodger pitcher Don Drysdale used to warn batters that if they didn't back off the plate, they'd get a "kiss." He wasn't talking about a smooch.

By the Numbers

Don Baylor played for six teams in his baseball career. Here are his hit-by-pitch totals for each team.

46
BALTIMORE
1970-1975

59
BOSTON
1986-1987

4
MINNESOTA
1987

32
OAKLAND
1976,1988

66
CALIFORNIA
1977-1982

60
NEW YORK
1983-1985

one as good as O'Neill, a free pass a poor strategy.

Unfortunately, the move backfired for Clarkson, as St. Louis scored with what turned out to be the winning run, when the next batter singled.

Patsy Tebeau, who managed the Cleveland Spiders of the National League from 1890 to 1898, was perhaps the first manager to espouse the intentional walk as a legitimate ploy. But while there were clearly situations in which the intentional walk was well advised, skippers like Clark Griffith, who managed teams in the American League from 1901 to 1920, believed "any pitcher who is afraid of a batter should quit the business."

In 1913 and again in 1920, several club owners proposed banning the intentional walk. But the league's umpires, led by Bill Klem, defeated the proposal both times, explaining that determining what exactly was an intentional walk would be difficult for an umpire. There have been a few other similar proposals over the years, but none have been successful.

There was at least one instance of a "fake" intentional walk. In Game Three of the 1972 World Series, Oakland Athletics relief pitcher Rollie Fingers faced Cincinnati Reds star Johnny Bench with two outs and men on second and third base. The score was 1–0. The count was 3–2 when Oakland manager Dick Williams called time. Williams went out to the mound with A's catcher Gene Tenace. There was a conference. Williams pointed to first base, not once but twice. Williams then pointed to Reds first baseman Tony Perez, who would be up after Bench. Williams went back to the dugout.

Tenace trotted back to the plate and waited for Bench to step back into the box. He dutifully stood up and held up his mitt at arm's length, apparently to take ball four. As Bench relaxed, Fingers wound up.

Alex Grammas, the third-base coach for the Reds, appeared to suddenly glean what was coming, and he opened his mouth to warn Bench.

"I started to holler, but all I got out was, 'Waaah,' " said Grammas, who had seen a similar play in the minors years ago. "By that time, the ball was on its way."

Tenace suddenly dropped back behind home plate. Fingers fired a strike over the dish to strike Bench out. In the long run, it didn't matter: Cincinnati still won the game, 1–0.

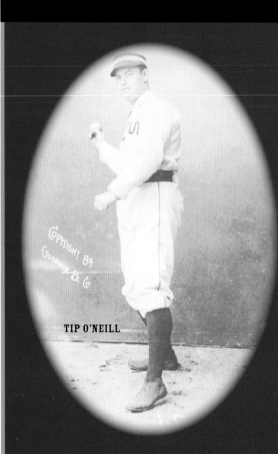

TIP O'NEILL

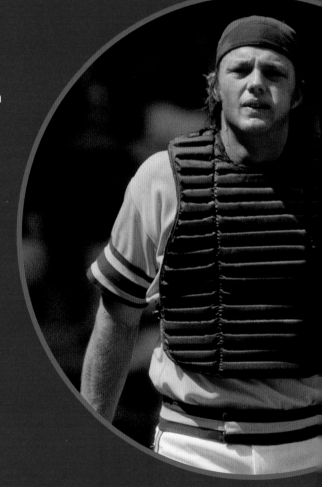

The walk, or base on balls, rule has been part of baseball since the 1860s. The strategy of walking a player intentionally, however, was not a common one, as many pitchers were reluctant to grant a "free" pass to a player.

Still, it was clearly a strategy. According to Peter Golenbock's *Wrigleyville*, during the 1886 "World Series" between the Chicago White Stockings of the National League and the St. Louis Browns of the old American Association, Chicago pitcher John Clarkson intentionally walked St. Louis hitter Tip O'Neill in the ninth inning of Game Four with men on second and third. Chicago player-manager Adrian "Cap" Anson was incensed by the maneuver. Anson, like many old-timers of that era, considered giving a player, even

The most historic "intentional fake walk" in history. Gene Tenace (center) and manager Dick Williams (not pictured) of the Athletics fake out the Reds' Johnny Bench (above and below) in Game Three of the 1972 World Series. The A's, by the way, lost the game but won the World Series.

Don BAYLOR

Orioles, Athletics, Angels, Yankees, Red Sox, Twins
1970–88

Baylor was hit 267 times and led the league 8 times.

CAREER STATISTICS

BA	HR	RBI	H	SB
.260	338	1,276	2,135	285

Ron HUNT

Mets, Dodgers, Giants, Expos, Cardinals
1963–74

Hit 243 times, Hunt led the league 7 times in being hit by a pitch, including a record 6 years in a row. He was hit by 50 pitches in 1971, his career high.

CAREER STATISTICS

BA	HR	RBI	H	SB
.273	39	370	1,429	65

Hughie JENNINGS

Louisville, Orioles, Dodgers, Phillies, Tigers
1891–1918

Hit 287 times, Jennings is the all-time leader. He led the league 5 consecutive years and was hit by 51 pitches in 1896.

CAREER STATISTICS

BA	HR	RBI	H	SB
.311	18	840	1,527	359

Craig
BIGGIO

Houston, 1988–2005

Biggio was hit 282 times and led the league 5 times, the second all-time leader.

CAREER STATISTICS				
BA	HR	RBI	H	SB
.281	291	1,175	3,060	414

DEFENSIVE SHIFTS

Philadelphia Phillies outfielder Roy Thomas (1899–1911) appears to be the first player to consistently face a defensive shift. The speedy Thomas was not a slugger, but instead a masterful left-handed singles hitter who could place balls in the outfield with uncanny skill.

However, Thomas rarely hit to left field, so when Thomas was at bat, teams employed a shift to the right side, whereby the third baseman would move into the shortstop's slot, the shortstop would move behind second base and the second baseman would play midway between first and second base. The opposing outfield would also shift to center and right field. Teams had middling success against Thomas; his career on-base percentage was .416.

The best-known shift came in 1946, when Cleveland manager Lou Boudreau unveiled his "C formation" shift against Boston Red Sox slugger Ted Williams. The C formation essentially placed every infielder on the right-field side of second base. The Indians' right fielder played the right-field line, while the center fielder moved into right field. The left fielder was in left-center field.

This was trumpeted as the first attempt to shackle the pull-hitting Williams. It actually wasn't. According to *Red Sox Century*, probably the best team history ever written about the Sox, several teams prior to 1946 attempted some version of the C formation. In 1941, with Williams scorching the

ball en route to a .406 batting average for the year, Jimmy Dykes, the manager of the Chicago White Sox, tried a similar maneuver. Dykes moved all but his third baseman to the right side on July 23 of that year. It didn't work. Williams hit to left field much more than he was given credit for, and in his first at-bat, dumped a ball into left field for a double as Chicago's left fielder scrambled over from center field to snag the ball. Dykes didn't use it much after that.

In 1978, another Red Sox slugger, Jim Rice, stepped to the plate in a game against the Kansas City Royals and saw four outfielders, as Royal manager Whitey Herzog moved his third baseman back. Rice solved the problem by drilling a long home run in his second at-bat.

"Damn," the affable Herzog told the *Boston Globe* after the game. "I screwed up. I should have put someone in the bleachers."

The Colorado Rockies pulled a similar shift on Sox slugger David Ortiz in Game Three of the 2007 World Series, moving the second baseman midway between first and second base, and the shortstop behind second base. The outfield also shifted to the right.

That was actually marginally successful: Ortiz was 2–7 in Colorado, with two RBI and a run scored in two games. But it didn't prevent the Red Sox from winning both games and the World Series.

IN CASE YOU DIDN'T KNOW

Dave Altizer, a utility man who played for the Senators, Indians, White Sox and Reds from 1906 to 1911, never got hit by pitches more than a few times a year, and in a 6-year career was hit only 33 times. Oddly, 16 of those, or almost half his career total, came in 1909, when he played for the White Sox. He was a backup player that year, appearing in 46 games as a first baseman and 61 games in the outfield. He only hit 233 that season, so maybe he was just trying to get on base to help his team. Or maybe he wanted to lead the league in something, anything.

HOW IT'S DONE
Hit By Pitch

It isn't particularly hard. Most batters accomplish this by crowding the plate—that is, by leaning as close to home plate as possible. Up until the 1990s, there was little protection for a batter, so one had to be a little judicious. But nowadays, many batters wear elbow and shin pads, which makes it easier to get hit. Some, like David Ortiz, wear football-like padding on the forearm that extends out toward the pitcher.

David "Big Papi" Ortiz (left and above) gets thumped by a pitch.

THE CORKED BAT

Corked bats go back to at least the latter half of the 19th century. Hall of Famer George Wright admitted in an 1888 interview in the *Sporting News* that while playing for the Boston Red Stockings of the National Association in 1873, he experimented with hollowing out the top of his bat and inserting a small rubber ball into it. He later added more rubber balls, but was exposed a few years later when the bat broke, scattering balls all over the infield.

Other players of that era were less subtle, hollowing their bats and pouring lead into the holes. These alterations led to the National League passing a rule requiring that bats be made wholly of wood, and that no foreign substances be inserted into them.

This did not by any means stop the practice. When Babe Ruth was on his record home run pace in 1927, he was involved in a minor episode in a game at Cleveland. Apparently, according to the *New York Times*, Ruth drilled a long home run during a game in July. As he was rounding the bases, Indian catcher Luke Sewell picked up his bat and demanded the umpire examine it.

"There's got to be something in there!" Sewell exploded.

Yankee batboy Eddie Bennett burst from the dugout and began try-ing to pull the bat out of Sewell's grasp. The comical tug-of-war ended with the umpire checking the bat and declaring it legal. But Ruth, interestingly, deflected questions about his bats in that game. (Or maybe it was so ludicrous to him to have a corked bat that he disdained those questions.)

In his biography, minor-league ballplayer and later major-league manager Earl Weaver reported that he regularly corked his bats in the 1950s. And Detroit Tiger Norm Cash admitted that in the 1960s he also regularly corked his bats.

Amos Otis, a five-time All-Star with Kansas City who played from 1967 to 1984, and Graig Nettles, a six-time All-Star who played with six teams from 1967 to 1988, were Super Ball guys. Remember Super Balls? They are tightly packed rubber balls that bounce all over the place when you throw them against the wall. They were popular in the 1970s.

So Nettles, Otis and who knows how many other guys would hollow out the tops of their bats and stuff Super Balls inside. Otis shredded the balls before stuffing them in. Nettles just stuffed them in whole, which led to an embarrassing situation in 1974, when he hit a home run to give the Yankees a 1–0 lead over the Tigers. On his next at-bat, he hit a sin-

GEORGE WRIGHT

GRAIG NETTLES

AMOS OTIS

DOES CORKING WORK?

Does corking one's bat gain any advantage? Is being ejected from the game and subjected to media and fan scorn worth the price? In *The Cheaters Guide to Baseball*, Derek Zumsteg notes that studies have shown that corking does makes a bat lighter but it also "dampens" the swing. In other words, because a corked bat is not solid all the way through, the flight of the ball is diminished incrementally when it is struck. Zumsteg also points out that there is no "quality control" when it comes to corking bats. This may sound facetious, but it's true. George Wright or Earl Weaver or Sammy Sosa all had to doctor their bats differently because there was no manual on how to do it. So what might have worked for one player probably didn't work for another.

gle, and the bat cracked open. Five Super Balls popped out onto the infield. Nettles was called out and ejected, but his earlier home run stood, and New York won, 1–0. Asked about the bat, Nettles explained that he had been given it by a fan who wanted him to have it as a good-luck charm. Right.

The latest and most infamous corked bat incident was Cub Sammy Sosa's ejection on June 3, 2003. After his bat split during a game against the Tampa Bay Devil Rays, umpires found that cork was inside.

Sosa, who was already catching heat because of his possible steroid use, actually had a decent explanation: the bat was a special bat he used during batting practice to hit long home runs for the fans. (Ah yes, always the fans.) Although this theory didn't get a lot of support from sportswriters, some of Sosa's teammates backed up his statements. But of course, there was a lot of speculation about just how many of his home runs were aided by cork.

ABOVE AND RIGHT: June 3, 2003: Sosa swings, the bat breaks, and the cork is exposed. Sosa swore he grabbed the wrong bat. LEFT: June 5, 2003: Cubs fans show their loyalty.

The Best of the Best

THE CORKED BAT

Sammy
SOSA

Cubs, Orioles, 1988–2006

Reportedly Sosa's technique of choice was to stuff cork in a bat and carefully cap it with a wooden peg. He admitted to having a special corked bat that he would use in batting practice to hit tape-measure homers to thrill the fans.

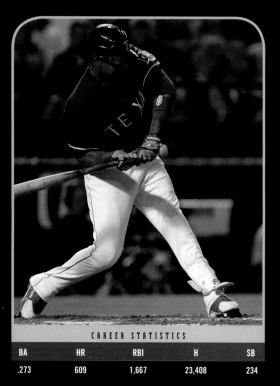

CAREER STATISTICS

BA	HR	RBI	H	SB
.273	609	1,667	23,408	234

Norm
CASH

White Sox, Tigers, 1958–74

Cash was a heck of a hitter for the Tigers in the 1960s, winning the batting title in 1961 with a .361 average. In his autobiography, Cash admitted to corking his bat throughout most of his career.

CAREER STATISTICS

BA	HR	RBI	H	SB
.271	377	1,103	1,820	43

Graig
NETTLES

Twins, Indians, Yankees, Padres, Braves, Expos
1967–88

Nettles used to drill a large hole in his bat and stuff anywhere from five to seven Super Balls in the hole. In 1971, he broke his bat in a game and five balls popped out. Nettles said that must have been the bat given to him by a fan. Okay.

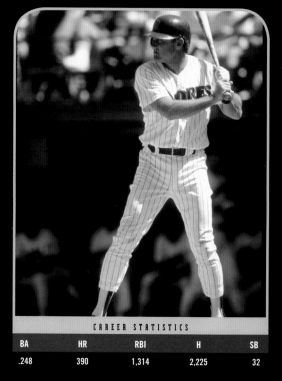

CAREER STATISTICS

BA	HR	RBI	H	SB
.248	390	1,314	2,225	32

HOW IT'S DONE
The Corked Bat

The myth of the corked bat is that one needs to add cork to the entire length of the bat. Not so!

Generally, a small hole is drilled in the top of the bat, down five or six inches, and stuffed with either cork, rubber, Super Balls, or whatever works for the particular batter. The key is to make the bat lighter, and thus give the batter a little more speed on his swing. Bats lightened with cork are easier to swing, as the corked head moves the center of gravity closer to the middle of the bat. The thing to remember is to make sure your batboy collects the bat as soon as you're done using it, so the other team doesn't get a chance to examine it.

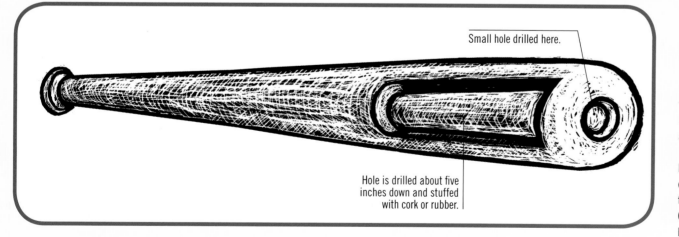

Small hole drilled here.

Hole is drilled about five inches down and stuffed with cork or rubber.

ABOVE: Los Angeles Dodgers manager Bill Russell and home plate umpire Thomas Rippley (second from right) examine the bat broken by Wilton Guerrero in a game against the Cardinals on June 1, 1997, while third base ump Bruce Froemming and another Dodgers coach look on. It was found that the bat had been corked and Guerrero later admitted that it had been doctored.

STEROIDS AND THE STEROID ERA

It's important to note that baseball's so-called Steroid Era began more than a decade after allegations of steroid use began surfacing in the National Football League, and more than 35 years after it first surfaced during the 1954 Olympic Games.

Testosterone-based steroids were invented 18 years before that, in 1936. In 1938, German doctors, funded by the Nazi Party, experimented with giving test subjects anabolic steroids to increase endurance. There is no basis to the story that soldiers were given steroids in the field, but that urban legend consistently surfaces when the steroid story is told.

By 1954, weightlifters from several countries, including the United States, began experimenting with steroids. Over the next three decades, Olympic athletes in every sport except women's synchronized swimming and women's field hockey would test positive for their use.

As steroid use spread among pro athletes, the perception of most baseball players (and writers and coaches, for that matter) was that because steroids increased strength and mass, ballplayers would not necessarily benefit from their use.

But as weight training among baseball players increased, the use of that family of drugs finally crept into the major leagues. Former Oakland Athletics players Jose Canseco and Mark McGwire, who were known in the late 1980s as the "Bash Brothers" for their tendency to stroke long

KEN CAMINITI

home runs, may or may not have been the first players to use steroids in the major leagues. They were, at least, the first players who drew attention to the practice. In 1988, they led the A's to the American League West Championship. Canseco led the league with 42 home runs, while McGwire was third with 32.

In the American League Championship Series against Boston, Sox fans taunted Canseco with the chant, "Steroids! Steroids!" Canseco laughed it off and, in fact, flexed his muscles for Sox fans while in the on-deck circle. He also got the last laugh, leading the A's to a four-game sweep with three home runs.

But it's not surprising that Canseco's success began to attract more interest. In 2000, in an interview with *ESPN The Magazine*, Jeff Bradley, the brother of Scott Bradley, a catcher for the Yankees, White Sox, Reds and Mariners from 1984 to 1992, told how an unnamed major-league player approached his brother in 1991. The player suggested Scott Bradley try steroids. Bradley reportedly turned him down and was out of baseball the next year.

In 1998, fans everywhere were celebrating the feats of McGwire and Cubs outfielder Sammy Sosa, who were racing to beat the home-run record of Roger Maris. But amid the excitement, there were many national columnists who were speculating that the two men were using steroids.

In 2002, in an interview with *Sports Illustrated*, Houston third baseman Ken Caminiti revealed that he used steroids during the 1996 season, the year he won the National League's Most Valuable Player award.

"It's still a hand-eye coordination game," Caminiti was quoted as saying, "but the difference [with steroids] is the ball is going to go a little farther. Some of the balls that would go to the warning track will go out. That's the difference."

In the story, former outfielder Chad Curtis estimated that between 40 to 50 percent of baseball players used some kind of performance-enhancing drug—including amphetamines as well as steroids or human growth hormones—in the 1990s. Caminiti, plagued by depression and drug use after his retirement, died of a heart attack in 2004 at age 41.

But it was clearly Canseco's book *Juiced*, published in 2005, that blew the controversy wide open. In his book, Canseco explains that he personally injected McGwire with steroids when the two were teammates, and similarly helped (and injected) Rafael Palmeiro, Ivan Rodriguez and Juan Gonzalez.

He reiterated these claims in testimony before a Congressional hearing later in 2005, and again in an interview on *60 Minutes*. In his book, Canseco extols the benefits of steroid use, particularly in assisting athletes in recovering faster from injuries. He also predicts that, within a relatively short time, steroids will be legal.

In 2006, it was Barry Bonds's turn to go under the microscope, when two San Francisco–area sportswriters, Lance Williams and Mark Fainaru-Wade, published *Game of Shadows*, which detailed Bonds's involvement with BALCO, a local "health food" laboratory. The book explained how the lab dispensed steroids to track-and-field athletes, football players and baseball players, including Bonds, Gary Sheffield and Jason Giambi. It also detailed Bonds's reasoning for his steroid use: he had been jealous of McGwire's pursuit of the home-run record in 1998 and wished to set a home-run record of his own.

It worked, somewhat. Bonds's pursuit in 2007 of Hall of Famer Henry Aarons's home-run record was probably one of the most joyless news stories of the baseball season. Sportswriters outside of San Francisco had difficulty working out exactly how to couch the feat, and most were critical of Bonds.

JOSE CANSECO

Jose CANSECO

Ken CAMINITI

Astros, Padres, 1987–2001

An extraordinarily tragic tale, as Caminiti, only 41, was found dead in his apartment in the Bronx in 2004. The talented third baseman for the Astros admitted using steroids during his MVP season in 1996. But a battle with depression and drug use did him in.

Athletics, Rangers, Red Sox, Devil Rays, Yankees, White Sox, 1985–2001

Canseco has not only admitted to being a steroid user, he wrote two books in which he detailed that use and celebrated it. Canseco believes proper steroid use will one day lead to longer life and better health. That may be true, but many steroid users that are pro athletes have suffered poor health following their careers.

CAREER STATISTICS				
BA	HR	RBI	H	SB
.266	462	1,407	1,877	200

CAREER STATISTICS				
BA	HR	RBI	H	SB
.272	239	983	1,710	88

Barry
BONDS

Pirates, Giants, 1986–present

The all-time home run king continues to maintain that he has not knowlingly used steroids in the latter part of his career. He has been the subject of several books and a grand jury probe into his steroid issues.

CAREER STATISTICS				
BA	HR	RBI	H	SB
.298	762	1,996	2,935	514

Gary
SHEFFIELD

Brewers, Padres, Marlins, Dodgers, Braves, Yankees, Tigers, 1988–present

Sheffield was named in the Mitchell Report, an extensive exploration of steroid use among major league ballplayers, as being a steroid user in 2001. He has strenuously denied the allegation.

CAREER STATISTICS				
BA	HR	RBI	H	SB
.293	489	1,608	2,581	249

Raphael
PALMEIRO *

Cubs, Rangers, Orioles, 1986–2004

Palmiero appeared before a Congressional committee in 2002 to publicly deny his steroid use. He was subsequently suspended from the Baltimore Orioles for testing positive for a steroid. Although he is not technically retired, he hasn't played major league baseball since 2005.

CAREER STATISTICS				
BA	HR	RBI	H	SB
.288	585	1,835	3,020	97

* Tested positive after testifying under oath that he "never, ever, ever used steroids."

The Best of the Best

STEROIDS AND THE STEROID ERA

Mark McGWIRE

Athletics, Cardinals, 1986–2001

McGwire was named by Jose Canseco in his tell-all steroids book as one of the players who explored steroid use in the 1990s. McGwire has denied the allegations.

Juan GONZALEZ

Rangers, Tigers, Indians, Royals, 1989–2004

Gonzalez was named, along with Palmiero, by Canseco as one of the players who used steroids while all three were playing for Texas.

Ivan RODRIGUEZ

Rangers, Marlins, Tigers, 1991–present

One of the players citied in the Mitchell Report as a steroid user, Rodriguez has denied the allegations, and continues to play for the Yankees.

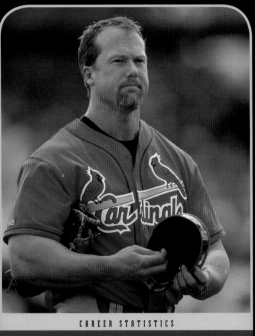

CAREER STATISTICS

BA	HR	RBI	H	SB
.263	583	1,414	1,626	12

CAREER STATISTICS

BA	HR	RBI	H	SB
.295	434	1,404	1,936	26

CAREER STATISTICS

BA	HR	RBI	H	SB
.302	294	1,215	2,587	120

Miguel TEJADA

Athletics, Orioles, 1997–present

Named in the Mitchell Report, Tejada has denied the allegations, and continues to play for the Orioles.

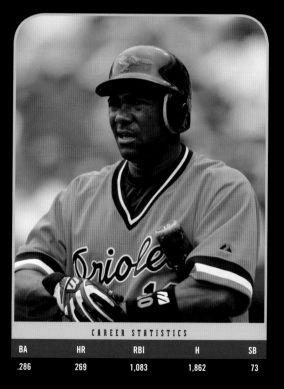

	CAREER STATISTICS			
BA	HR	RBI	H	SB
.286	269	1,083	1,862	73

Roger CLEMENS

Red Sox, Blue Jays, Yankees, Astros, 1984–2007

Named in the Mitchell Report, Clemens is probably the most vocal of the prominent athletes named in the Mitchell Report and has denied his use of steroids. In 2007, he appeared on the television show "60 Minutes" to issue his rebuttal of the report.

	CAREER STATISTICS				
W	L	SV	ERA	SO	CG
354	184	0	3.12	4,672	118

Andy PETTITTE

Yankees, Astros, 1995–present

Maybe honesty is the best policy. Pettitte, also named in the Mitchell Report, admitted to using Human Growth Hormone in 2004 to recover faster from an injury. The admission moved many baseball writers to forgive him, and in fact, enabled Pettitte to move on after the controversy subsided.

	CAREER STATISTICS				
W	L	SV	ERA	SO	CG
213	122	0	3.86	1,960	25

JUAN GONZALEZ

ROGER CLEMENS

In November 2007, Bonds was indicted by a federal grand jury for allegedly lying to a previous jury about his steroid use. His trial is expected to begin in 2009.

Meanwhile, on December 14, 2007, a total of 85 current and former major-league players were named as users of steroids and of human growth hormone in the so-called Mitchell Report, named after former United States senator George Mitchell. These included Bonds, Palmeiro, Canseco, Juan Gonzalez and many others, including likely Hall of Fame pitcher Roger Clemens, his teammate Andy Pettitte and ace Boston reliever Eric Gagne, who had just won a World Championship with the Boston Red Sox.

This report, alas, may have created more questions than it answered. Mitchell completed it without the cooperation of all but one member (Canseco) of the Major League Baseball Players Association. In addition, Mitchell did not have subpoena power, and thus had to rely on the sworn testimony of team employees and trainers. His critics believe that the report did little more than outline what was already evident: that major-league baseball had a substance-abuse problem.

Mitchell believes that not naming the players whose names he has gathered would have blown the credibility of the report. "If I had not named names in the report, if I had said, 'We have the names, but we're not going to release them,' then the report would have had no credibility. No one would have cared," he said in an interview with the Associated Press the next day.

The Mitchell Report rocked many in the baseball world. Clemens emphatically denied his involvement, while Pettitte, a few days after the report came out, admitted to using HGH in 2002 to recover from an injury more quickly.

But Clemens, who, according to a timeline set forth by the report, won four of his seven Cy Young awards after he began dabbling in steroids, has taken the biggest hit. A first-ballot Hall of Famer before the report, he may wait a long time before baseball writers forgive him. Bill Madden of the *New York Daily News*, one of the top baseball columnists in the sport, asserted that he would not be able to vote for Clemens's induction.

Despite a highly publicized report, steroid use has by no means ended, although it may be curtailed somewhat. In a survey among 12th-grade students interviewed in 2000, a total of 2.5 percent reported using steroids at least once. Four years later, according to the United States Bureau of Statistics, that figure was 3.9 percent.

In addition, steroids are still being used in a variety of positive medical ways: to treat AIDS patients, to speed the recovery of burn victims, to fight breast cancer and to fight off osteoporosis, for example.

In the end, there is some comfort and logic in the words of Washington, D.C., columnist George Will. Will posted to the Web site townhall.com about the Bonds controversy in 2006, but his observations are relevant to the rest of the steroids nation: "[Barry] Bonds's records must remain part of baseball's history. His hits happened. Erase them and there will be discrepancies in baseball's bookkeeping about the records of the pitchers who gave them up. George Orwell said that in totalitarian societies, yesterday's weather could be changed by decree. Baseball, indeed America, is not like that. Besides, the people who care most about the record book—serious fans—will know how to read it. That may be Bonds's biggest worry."

HOW IT'S DONE
Steroids

Different steroids are applied in different ways. Certain steroids must be injected, while others are ingested. "The Clear," which is a steroid-based cream, can be applied to the skin.

It's pretty easy, which is why it's so widespread.

BARRY BONDS

JASON GIAMBI

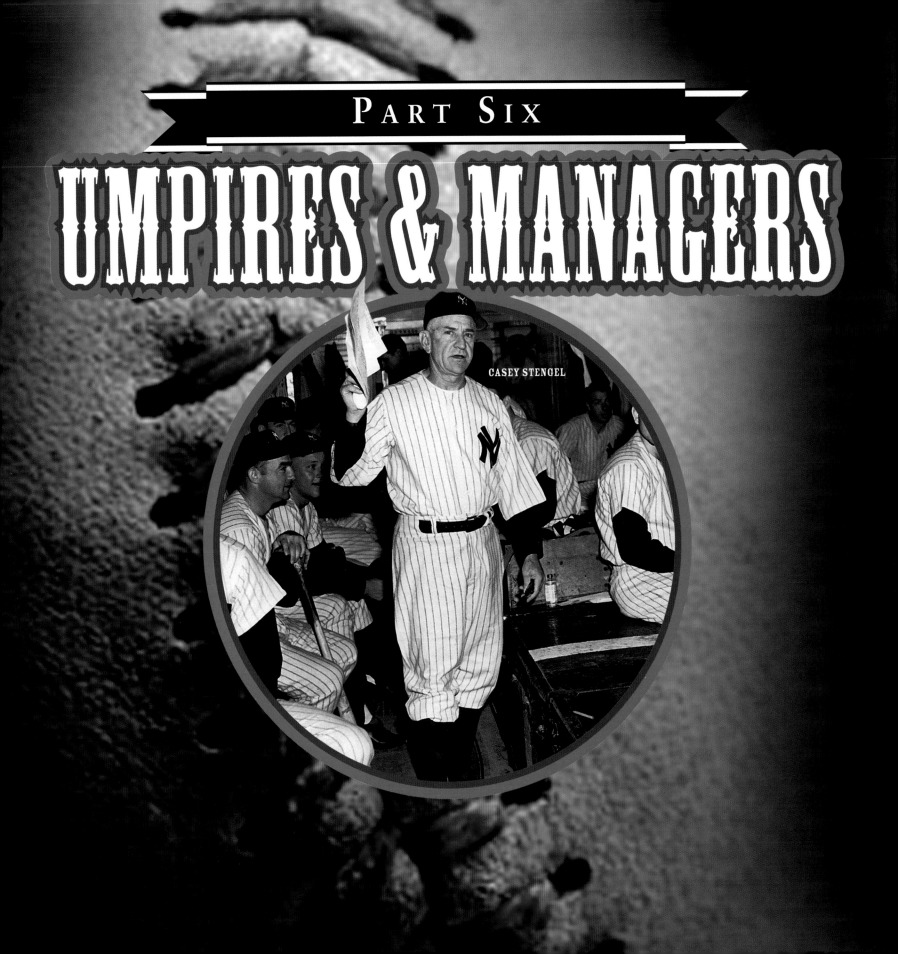

PART SIX

UMPIRES & MANAGERS

CASEY STENGEL

BRUCE FROEMMING

UMPIRES

The first umpires of the mid-1800s were amateurs, often chosen by the home team to officiate a game. Initially, they were unpaid, in part because the job was supposed to go to an unbiased observer.

But umping was a lot of work for no recompense. So in the 1870s, teams began hiring umpires and paying them a stipend. But the concept of paying umpires brought forward a big problem: no matter which team paid the umpire, the perception, obviously, would be that the ump favored that team. (Although at one point, several leagues adopted the policy that an umpire's pay would be split fifty-fifty by the home and away teams.)

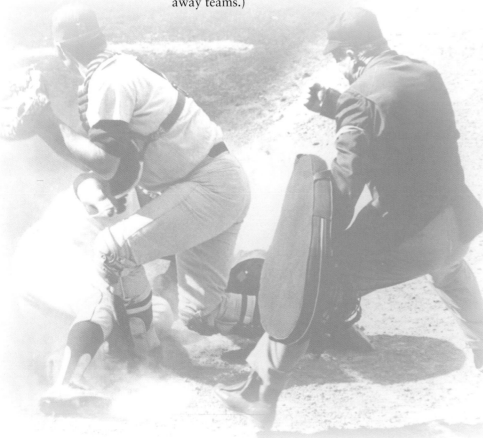

BELOW: Nestor Chylak calling a play at the plate.

As baseball became more competitive, and fans and players alike became more invested in the outcome, the one factor that came in for abuse from both on a consistent basis was the officiating of a game.

Initially, many team owners weren't so reluctant to see umpires vilified. They realized that fans who were incensed by umpires' calls would pay to see the umpire officiate the next day, or the next week, so they could yell at him again. This, however, was somewhat self-defeating, since the umpires themselves weren't eager to return to a hostile venue.

These issues finally forced the various baseball leagues into realizing that to obtain any form of integrity, umpires simply would have to be paid by the leagues themselves, not by individual teams.

There were probably a number of umpires who worked professionally in the early 1870s, but in 1878, Billy McLean was the National League's first umpire to make a living as an arbiter. McLean was paid $5 a game, plus his traveling and lodging expenses.

McLean was a decent baseball player. More important, he was a big fellow and a darn good boxer, and that was apparently the deciding factor for the league in hiring McLean.

But McLean was basically just a step up from the concept of using local umpires. At the time, most umpires were still local hires in the sense that they lived in the area of the home team—even in the National League, considered to be the one major league at the time. This fact made it nearly impossible to quell the ongoing charges and countercharges on the part of teams, fans, players and sportswriters about the fairness of a particular contest or the bias of a particular ump,

EJECTIONS

As early as 1867, the baseball "rule book" allowed a player to be ejected if he was verbally or physically abusing an umpire. Whoever that first player was is lost to history.

But in 1933, Heinie Manush (Tigers, Cardinals, Senators, Red Sox, Dodgers, Pirates, 1923–39) was the first player to be ejected from a World Series game.

This was a big deal. Manush, after home-plate umpire Charley Moran called him out, walked up to Moran, pulled his bow tie, held in place with an elastic band, and let it snap back, according to the *New York Times*.

Manush, playing for the Senators, was one of the key players on the team. The Senators were trailing in games, 2–1 to the New York Giants. Following Manush's ejection in the fifth inning, they lost that contest, 2–1 in 11 innings. The Giants would eventually win the World Series in five games.

Many thought Manush's ejection was a potential turning point in the Series. But more important, many writers and fans believed that such an important contest should have been decided with both teams' best players available. No one seemed to seek out Moran's opinion.

In the wake of that World Series, then commissioner Kenesaw Mountain Landis decreed that, from then on, only the commissioner would be allowed to eject players during the World Series, an edict that evaporated when Landis retired.

Judge Kenesaw Mountain Landis was a harsh guy, as this photo shows (He couldn't even enjoy himself throwing out the first ball of the World Series). He supported the ejection of Heinie Manush (inset) in the 1933 World Series but decreed that, from then on, only the Commissioner would be able to rule on the ejection of a player during the Fall Classic. This decree ended with Landis' retirement.

despite the fact that they were now league hires. And when two teams met for a championship contest, or even for a key game in season, the umpires came in for a fair amount of abuse, no matter how professionally they worked.

It was actually the old American Association, a second major league formed in 1882 and run until 1891, that first came up with the idea of doing away with local umpires and hiring an umpiring staff to travel to games. This was in 1883, and it proved to be so successful that the National League followed suit a year later.

But as the 1880s waned, it became clear that more than one umpire was needed. Players routinely skipped bases while umpires were concentrating on plays at the plate (Hall of Famer Mike "King" Kelly was a master at this); and there was always a problem of trying to rule on two plays at once, say, two different players sliding into second base and home plate on a double steal.

In 1887, the National League and American Association hired two umpires to work their "World Series." The umpires, John Gaffney and John Kelly (both known, by the way, as "Honest John") did an excellent job, and the experiment was deemed a tremendous success.

The problem was, the team owners in both leagues were still loath to spend money to essentially double their umpiring corps. But in 1890, the outlaw Player's League mandated a two-umpire system for all its games. If nothing else, umpiring in that league was likely better than in the National League and American Association because of that innovation. But the Player's League had other problems and folded after a year.

Still, it became clear that two umpires, one behind home plate and one in the field, was a preferred option. But it wasn't until 1911 that the National and American leagues' rule books actually mandated a second umpire during the regular season. Prior to that, leagues would often assign two umpires only to a key contest.

BILLY EVANS

The move to three-man crews, according to the book *The Ballplayers*, wasn't an official rule until 1944. Until that time, both the American and National leagues only used the three-man crew for a big in-season series; for relatively minor contests, the two-man crews sufficed.

In contrast, four-man crews became a regular World Series staple by 1909, when Pittsburgh defeated Detroit. According to author James Kahn, the initial plan was to alternate two two-man crews from each league. This was carried out in the first two contests, played in Pittsburgh.

UMPIRES' UNIFORMS

There was no dress code in the 19th century for umpires, but a typical umpire's uniform was a far cry from what we see today. Umpires in the early days dressed not unlike a gentleman on his way to church: top hat, stylish topcoat, spats and a cane. The effect was to deliver a message to the players on the field that the umpire was a gentleman, who expected the ballplayers to act in a civil way as well. Alas, the message was not always received.

The umpire in those days would stand, kneel or sit on a stool in foul territory along the first-base line. Umpires would also sometimes stand well behind the catcher, and at an angle, usually on the first-base side. Some umpires chose to judge pitches opposite the pitchers' throwing arm—that is, if a pitcher was right-handed, the umpire would stand to the left of the catcher, and vice versa.

It was Billy Evans, who umpired in the American League from 1906 to 1927, who pioneered the dark, somber uniform that umpires wear today. Evans started out as a sportswriter, but his umpiring career began when he substituted for an absent arbiter in a minor-league game. He was so good, several players encouraged him to continue. At 22, he became the youngest umpire in the majors.

Evans's conservative sartorial style was soon picked up by other umpires, and by 1910, almost all were wearing dark suits with white shirts.

STRIKE ZONES

Initially, the strike zone was whatever the batter wanted it to be. In fact, according to *The Baseball Almanac*, after 1871, a batter had to notify the umpire if he wanted a "high," "fair" or "low" strike zone. The umpire would then notify the pitcher, who was then obliged to deliver the ball where the batter wished.

A high strike zone required pitches to be over the plate between a batter's waist and shoulders. A low strike zone required the pitcher to deliver the ball between the batter's waist and at least a foot from the ground. The fair strike zone combined these two zones, requiring a pitcher to deliver the ball between the batter's shoulders and at least a foot from the ground.

Few batters requested the fair strike zone in the 19th century. Batters could not change their strike zone in a single at-bat, but they were allowed to change their strike zones from at-bat to at-bat.

By 1887, the rule had changed. Umpires in particular complained that the varying strike zones were simply too difficult to call. Strike zones, although defined, were even then very difficult to actually police. So umpires around the country began to put their collective feet down: there had to be one strike zone for all batters.

Thus the rule makers all agreed that a "strike" was defined as a pitch that came over the plate, not lower than a batter's knees or higher than his shoulders.

In 1901, the National League ruled that a foul tip not caught on the fly would be a strike, unless there were already two strikes on a batter. In 1903, the American League adopted the rule.

Although these have been the basic rules since that time, Major League Baseball from time to time, and for various reasons, monkeys with the strike zone. In 1950, the powers that be tightened up the strike zone, dropping strikes from a batter's shoulder to his armpits and raising it from a batter's knees to, specifically, the top of his knees.

But in 1963, in part because some umpires were adhering to the new strike zone and some were still calling balls and strikes in accordance with the old strike zone, Major League Baseball returned to the old definition of top of the shoulders to the knees. But a caveat was added to give an umpire more leeway: in the final analysis, the umpire was to be the judge of the strike zone.

This did not stay static. In 1969, the strike zone shrank back to the armpits and top of the knees. In 1988, it went back to the top of the shoulders but stayed at the top of the knees. The most recent change was in 1996, when the strike zone expanded from the top of the knees to the bottom of the knees.

Of course, none of this guaranteed a consistent strike zone. Freddie Patek (Royals, Angels, 1968–81), at five-feet-five, had a much smaller strike zone than six-feet-seven Frank Howard (Dodgers, Senators, Rangers, Tigers, 1958–73). (This did not give Patek any particular advantage in drawing walks. Howard has about 200 more career walks than Patek, in part, of course, because he was a better hitter.)

In addition, many players tried to squeeze the strike zone. Ricky Henderson used to almost squat and lean far back into the batter's box. That shrank his strike zone and, in theory, forced pitchers to make better, more accurate pitches. Yankees Hall of Famer Earle Combs (Yankees, 1924–35) had a similar stance.

But in the end, as Red Sox great Ted Williams explained, there are really three strike zones for every batter: his own, the umpire's and the pitcher's. The best a hitter can hope for is that the strike zone of the umpire behind the plate is consistent throughout the game, and that he can eventually determine what the pitcher's strike zone is. The closer they are to a batter's strike zone, the more success a batter will have.

The Best of the Best

UMPIRES

#1 Bill KLEM

National League, 1905–41, Hall of Fame, 1953

Klem is regarded as the best umpire of all time. He spent the first 16 years of his term almost exclusively behind the plate. His official nickname was "The Old Arbitrator"; unofficially, because of his prominent lips, he was called "Catfish." All a player had to do to earn an ejection, according to most old-timers who played in Klem's era, was call him "Catfish," or even mention the word "catfish" within Klem's hearing.

#2 Doug HARVEY

National League, 1962–92

Harvey's authoritative way of making calls earned him the nickname "God." Harvey was one of the first umpires to make "delayed" calls. That is, he would sometimes hesitate for a split second before making the call. This, early on, infuriated managers and players, as they thought Harvey was hesitating because he was unsure of the call. But he was usually right.

#3 Tommy CONNOLLY

National League, 1898–1900, American League, 1901–31, Hall of Fame, 1953

Connolly was a short, dapper man with an Irish brogue, which was surprising since he was born in England; his family moved to Natick, Massachusetts, when he was young. Connolly was absolutely fearless as an umpire, and his first year in the National League he ejected 10 players. That cemented his reputation as a bad man to cross. Ty Cobb once said that when Connolly's neck got red, he knew to back off.

#4 John "Jocko" CONLAN

National League, 1941–65
Hall of Fame, 1974

The affable Conlan was known for his accuracy and his polka-dot tie. But he also had a temper, and his battles with managerial firebrands like Leo Durocher and Frankie Frisch were legendary. Conlan actually got his start in 1935, during a Browns–White Sox game. One of the umpires in the contest, Red Ormsby, was overcome by heatstroke, and Conlan, then a substitute outfielder for Chicago, offered to fill in. He enjoyed it so much, he retired from baseball the next year to begin a career as an umpire.

#5 Nestor CHYLAK

American League, 1954–78
Hall of Fame, 1999

During his career, Chylak was considered the best umpire of his era. A fine technician who knew the rules inside out, Chylak worked a quick, confident game. Known for his willingness to listen to both sides of an argument, Chylak had few enemies among players or managers, which was a ringing endorsement in itself. He was notable for being the lead umpire in Cleveland during the infamous "Ten-Cent Beer Night" in 1974, which climaxed with fans storming the field in the ninth inning with the score tied 5–5. Chylak eventually declared the game a forfeit, giving the win to the visiting Texas Rangers.

Honorable Mention Bruce FROEMMING

National League, 1971–99,
Major League Baseball, 2000–present

In a 1986 poll of players and managers, Froemming was declared the best ump in the big leagues. He is still working today and is still considered one of the best. Froemming is best known for working a 1972 game in which Cubs pitcher Milt Pappas was working on a perfect game. With two outs in the bottom of the ninth, Pappas had a 3–2 count on the 27th batter. Froemming called the next pitch a ball, and Pappas lost his perfect game, although he got the next batter out and was credited with a no-hitter. Pappas felt he got a bad call and was critical of Froemming. Froemming, for his part, shrugged and pointed out that the integrity of the game was more important than Pappas's chance at a perfect game.

But by the third game, the four men, Jim Johnstone and Bill Klem of the National League, and "Silk" O'Laughlin and Billy Evans of the American League, agreed just before game time that all four would take the field. After that, four-man crews were a World Series tradition for many years. In 1952, both leagues agreed to hire four-man crews for regular-season games as well.

This relatively rapid increase in the need for umpires at both the major-league and minor-league level led to the emergence of umpiring schools. Veteran National League umpire George Barr opened the first umpiring school in 1935, and in 1939, Bill McGowan of the American League opened a second school.

Five-man crews came about, in part, because of expansion. In 1961, with more teams coming into the National League the next season, an extra umpire was added along the basepaths. These extra umps were younger umpires the league was grooming to be part of the regular four-man rotations in 1962.

The six-man crews seen throughout the postseason started in the World Series in 1947. In the 1930s, Major League Baseball began assigning six umpires to a World Series, using two umps as reserves in case of injury or illness to a regular official. But in 1947, it was reasoned, apparently by the Baseball Commissioner's Office, that if the leagues were going to pay for six umpires, they might as well use them.

If there was one area in which umpires lagged behind in major-league baseball, it was in integrating minorities into its crews. It wasn't until 1966, when Emmett Ashford joined the American League, that big-league baseball had its first African American umpire. In 1973, Art Williams integrated the National League. In 1974, Armando Rodriguez became the first Hispanic umpire.

DOUG HARVEY

In Case You Didn't Know

There has never been a female umpire in the major leagues, but Pam Postema's quest to be the first ended when she was released, in 1989, from the Triple-A Alliance after 13 years in the minors.

HOW IT'S DONE

Umpires

According to the American Federation of Umpires, here are the five most important attributes of a good arbitrator:

1. Know the rules. Read the rule book often to make sure you have everything covered.
2. Allow the play to come to an *end* before making the call.
3. Be crisp when making a call; hustle all the time.
4. It's *your* game to run. Stay calm and in control at all times.
5. Earn the players' respect, and dress well.

UMPIRE HAND SIGNALS

As early as 1880, there were umpires signaling balls and strikes, although usually under unusual circumstances. The popular story is that umpires began using hand signals to assist the deaf ballplayer William E. "Dummy" Hoy (Nationals, Buffalo Brotherhood, Browns, Reds, Louisville Colonels, White Sox, 1888–1902) during his at-bats.

This story has become a little muddled over the years. Umpires did indeed use hand signals when Hoy played, but that was when Hoy played for the Ohio School for the Deaf as a high schooler. Because all the players on his team were deaf, umpires in that league would use hand signals to communicate with the players.

When Hoy began playing professionally, during both his minor- and major-league careers, his third-base coach would relay ball and strike signals. At that time, umpires believed they simply had too many other things with which to deal to add giving the balls and strikes by hand signals.

But late in the 19th century, as stadiums —and, by extension, crowds—grew larger, sentiment for some kind of hand signals began to grow. By 1905, three years after Hoy's retirement, Cy Rigler, an umpire in the Central League, began using hand signals regularly. By 1907, most major-league umpires had adopted the practice of signaling strikes, and by 1909, virtually all umps were doing it.

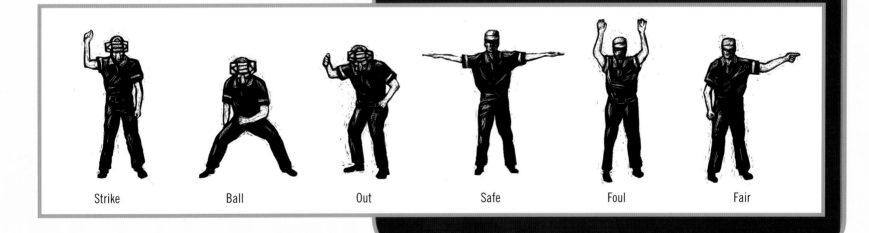

Strike   Ball   Out   Safe   Foul   Fair

LEADERS AND MANAGERS (AND CAPTAINS)

Before there were managers, there were captains who performed many of the duties that a manager does today. Initially, captains were required almost exclusively to determine lineups and figure out who batted where. In the early to mid-1800s, captains weren't permanent either and were generally rotated.

But the role of a captain got a little more complicated as baseball evolved. Someone had to arrange schedules, determine where the game might be played and, when teams began to charge admission, collect the money.

Enter Harry Wright. In 1868, Wright managed and played for the Cincinnati Red Stockings, a team that can be construed as being the first true professional team.

Wright, according to baseball historian Henry Chadwick, managed virtually every aspect of the Red Stockings, including making sure the team uniforms were clean, collecting money, making travel arrangements, scheduling games with other teams and arranging for publicity for his games.

Wright also made out the lineup, decided who would and wouldn't start and sometimes played himself. He was an excellent outfielder and a decent relief pitcher.

Wright oversaw the Red Stockings as a player-manager from 1869 to 1870. When he moved to Boston, he largely eschewed playing to concentrate on managing.

Most teams in the latter half of the 19th century had a manager who dealt with the business side of the operation, and a captain who dealt with the playing side of things. Wright did both, and did them well, for more than 20 years. The Red Stockings won four consecutive National Association championships and two more National League pennants as the Boston Braves.

In 1889, the National League adopted a rule allowing a team one free substitution per game. Formerly, teams could not take a player out unless there were special circumstances, such as injury. In 1890, two substitutions were allowed, and personnel strategy began to take a larger role in the game.

By the end of the 19th century, teams had more than one starting pitcher and several substitute players. The era of managers molding teams to their specifications began.

"With the development of baseball," wrote Christy Mathewson in his book, *Pitching in a Pinch*, published in 1912, "coaching has advanced until it is now an exact science."

Mathewson pointed to a game in 1908, when one of his teammates hit a deep fly ball and raced to third, but held up, when it was obvious, according to Mathewson, he could have scored.

When the inning was over (the player had not scored), manager John McGraw asked the player why he had not advanced. The sun, noted the player, was

CONNIE MACK

in his eyes and he was not wearing his smoked glasses. After that, wrote Mathewson, McGraw resolved to be on top of these types of managerial situations.

This is a nice story, which may have been true in some aspects but not as far as McGraw's attention to detail. McGraw began managing in 1899, and he was a master of the smallest detail even then.

McGraw had a reputation for meanness, which was well deserved, in connection to his relationships with other teams. But among his players, he was well known for being fair and being an excellent teacher. These characteristics were similar for many managers in the early part of the 20th century, such as Connie Mack, Frank Selee (Braves, Cubs, 1890–1905) and Ned Hanlon (Pirates, Orioles, Dodgers, Reds, 1889–1907).

Mack, for example, was as low-key as McGraw was volatile. But Mack was also firm, and an excellent communicator and teacher.

By the 1910s, managers were clearly required to know more strategy. Relief pitching, the hit-and-run play and late-inning substitutions were all coming into vogue, and managers had to actually oversee the flow of the game. Mathewson and others called it "the inside game," which was a reference to a good manager having "inside knowledge" that enabled his team to win championships.

"The brain of McGraw is behind each game the Giants make," asserted Mathewson in his book, and he was probably right.

The "power era" of Babe Ruth, Lou Gehrig and similar players curtailed managers' options somewhat. Teams with big sticks like the Ruth and Gehrig duo tended to wait for the so-called big inning and play for runs in bunches. Waiting for the big inning meant, essentially, waiting for Ruth and Gehrig

TONY LARUSSA

Two managers with a low-key style: Connie Mack (left) of the Athletics and Tony LaRussa (right) of the Cardinals. Both men rarely raised their voices, but were successful in getting their point across to players.

JOE MCCARTHY

to come to bat, which didn't require a heck of a lot of strategy.

But the biggest change came in the 1930s, when player salaries began to rise beyond those of the managers. No longer were skippers among the highest-paid employees on the team. For managers whose authority rested wholly or partially on this factor, things got tougher. Field generals like Joe McCarthy found they had to be more sensitive in the 1940s than they were in the 1930s. McCarthy clearly accomplished this: he had many supporters on the old Yankees teams of that era and was the most successful coach of that span.

"He always protected us from the front office," said Charlie Keller of McCarthy in David Halberstam's superb book *Summer of '49*. Keller added that McCarthy "always protected us from the press. He never said anything bad about us to the writers."

That kind of support generated loyalty. And with loyalty usually came productivity.

In addition, every club now had a front office that made personnel decisions, which were formerly a part of a manager's job. This sometimes unilateral decision making did not make things easier for managers. (The most egregious example of an owner overruling a coach on player matters was, of course, in 1918, when Red Sox owner Harry Frazee sold Babe Ruth to the Yankees. Frazee reportedly went into manager Eddie Barrow's office and cried, "I'm selling Ruth, Eddie!" "I was afraid you would," said Barrow, and quit within a year.)

When Casey Stengel took over from McCarthy as the manager of the Yankees in 1949, he was a different kind of manager with different methods—methods that were not always very popular. Stengel was the first manager to make liberal use of his bench. Some of his players, of course, hated it, because it meant they wouldn't play every day. But, since Stengel was clearly the most successful manager of his era, it was difficult to argue with his methods, which led to 10 American League pennants and 8 World Championships.

In fact, with the success Stengel enjoyed, many managers adopted platooning, and specialization in baseball became even more widespread.

As the 20th century wound down, coaches like Sparky Anderson in Cincinnati, Billy Martin in New York and Oakland and others expanded on Stengel's philosophies. Anderson became known as "Captain Hook" for his tendency to remove his starting pitchers at the least sign of trouble. Martin's brand of hustling, cerebral baseball, became known as "Billyball," although it was certainly not a heck of a lot different from the style of John McGraw or Johnny Evers, two men who had been successful 60 years earlier.

To be sure, the Stengel way was not the only way. Earl Weaver, the so-called Earl of Baltimore, won several American League titles and a World Championship in 1970 with his philosophy, which, as he termed it, was "pitching and three-run homers." This "strategy" was leavened with a solid dose of fundamental baseball; but as one of his outfielders, Paul Blair, once said, "You laugh at Earl, but I can't tell you how many games we won on a three-run homer. It seemed like quite a few."

TERRY FRACONA

With the age of the computer upon us, today's managers like Tony LaRussa in St. Louis and Oakland, and Terry Francona in Boston win, in great part, by taking advantage of technology.

Francona, in an interview with the *Boston Globe* after he had won his second World Championship with the Red Sox in 2007, pointed out that his day started seven to eight hours before a game, with him studying on his laptop an opponent's tendencies. This included study of both team and individual tendencies, a practice also followed by LaRussa.

The Red Sox, as do many clubs, have DVDs that show every pitcher in the American League in action, to enable a hitting coach to review a pitcher his team might face in an upcoming game. In the same way, pitching coaches are able to help their pitchers to determine a hitter's weaknesses. It is a far cry from the 1918 World Series, when, according to teammate Herb Pennock, Sox star left-hander George Herman "Babe" Ruth announced his strategy for pitching against every Chicago Cubs player he faced: pitch 'em low and away.

Francona became the winningest manager in Boston postseason history in 2007, after leading the Red Sox to a four-game sweep over the Colorado Rockies. His World Series record is 8–0, the best winning percentage of any manager who has skippered two or more Series teams.

But there are other tools for today's managers besides technology. Joe Torre, who managed the New York Yankees for 12 years and now skippers the Los Angeles Dodgers, has been very successful in running a team by consensus and communication.

Certainly, the Yankees use modern technology as well as anyone, but Torre generally delegates that job to his coaches. Torre helped the Yankees to 4 World Championships and 6 World Series in that 12-year span. The same can be said for Atlanta's Bobby Cox, whose teams dominated the National League East for more than a decade.

Admittedly, it helps that both Atlanta and New York were blessed with solid players. But having a guy at the helm who knows his stuff is always an advantage.

THE COLLEGE OF COACHES

In the history of bad ideas in baseball, it's difficult to find one as bad as the College of Coaches, which lasted but two years, from 1961 to 1962.

In theory, it made some sense: Cubs owner Philip K. Wrigley, frustrated by his team's poor play, opted to hire nine coaches and rotate them throughout the Cubs' major- and minor-league system. The coaches would impart their wisdom at every level of the organization. Thus, every player would understand what the "Cubs system" was all about.

The problem was, the nine coaches Wrigley tapped to be the "College of Coaches" didn't talk to one another much. So these coaches would rotate up and down the Cubs organization every five or six weeks and coach without really discussing what they were doing. The idea was basically implemented with no real plan of how it would work.

The players all hated the College of Coaches, and for good reason: it didn't work a lick.

"Basically, the [coaches] just waited their turn [to manage the Cubs]," explained former Cubs player Don Elston in Peter Golenbock's *Wrigleyville*. "Continuity was definitely not there. The guy who played third base didn't know on the day they changed one manager to the other if he was on the new guy's good side. And I have absolutely no idea what the criteria was for changing coaches. And who made the decision when to change? I have no idea."

The Cubs were not a great team in either 1961 or 1962, but in interviews since that "experiment," many Cubs players believe that they would have been a better team in that span of years had they one manager and not a rotating crew. The College of Coaches was discontinued in 1963.

"We were just glad it was over," said Elston.

P.K. WRIGLEY

Harry WRIGHT

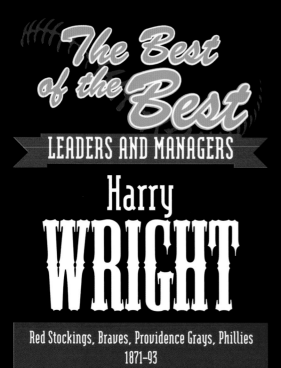

Red Stockings, Braves, Providence Grays, Phillies 1871–93

Wright was the best-known of the old-time player-managers. An excellent athlete as well as a tactician, Wright managed Boston to five pennants in this dual role. He won six pennants overall.

CAREER STATISTICS			
W	1,225	L	885

John McGRAW

Orioles, Giants, 1899–1932

The crusty, feisty McGraw was despised by opponents and, for the most part, loved by his players. Four of his New York Giants teams won 100 or more games in a season.

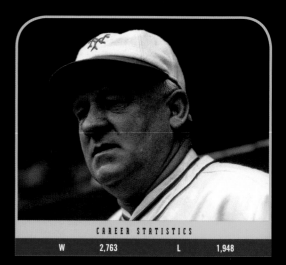

CAREER STATISTICS			
W	2,763	L	1,948

Connie MACK

Athletics, 1894–1950

Cornelius MacGillicuddy (his real name) managed for 53 years, including 50 with the Philadelphia Athletics. He lost more baseball games (3,948) than any other manager in baseball history even managed.

CAREER STATISTICS			
W	3,731	L	3,948

Joe McCARTHY

Cubs, Yankees, Red Sox, 1926–56

With seven World Series champions and a .615 record, "Marse Joe" was one of the best ever.

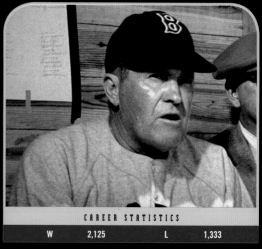

CAREER STATISTICS			
W	2,125	L	1,333

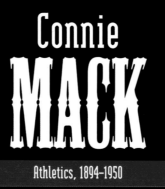
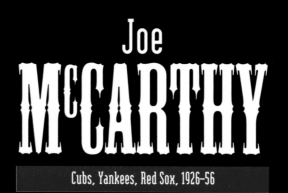

Walter ALSTON

Low-key and laconic, Alston managed the Dodgers for 23 years, winning more than 1,600 games and four World Series.

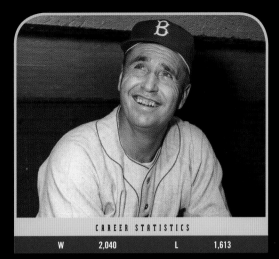

CAREER STATISTICS			
W	2,040	L	1,613

Joe TORRE

Mets, Braves, Cardinals, Yankees, Dodgers 1977–present

In 1995, when he was fired by the St. Louis Cardinals, it looked as if Joe Torre was at the end of his managerial career. Now, 13 years later, he is an almost certain Hall-Of-Famer and part of the discussion of the best managers ever. An amazing turnaround for a true gentleman.

CAREER STATISTICS			
W	2,151	L	1,848

Casey STENGEL

Dodgers, Yankees, Mets, 1934–65

The worldly and wordy Stengel was one of the most successful managers ever, in terms of winning championships. The "Old Professor" won seven World Series with the Yankees, including an unprecedented five in a row (1949-53).

CAREER STATISTICS			
W	1,905	L	1,842

THE BOX SCORE

One newspaper executive recently estimated that only about 10 to 15 percent of his sports readers actually peruse box scores. But those who do are fanatics. Box scores are the condensed story of a game, and even a reasonably savvy baseball fan can construct the flow of a game from a modern box score.

The first box score, according to the *New York Times*, was printed by the *New York Morning News* on October 22, 1845. The box score had its roots in cricket, so the first box scores merely listed when a batter succeeded, by scoring a run, or failed, by making an out. These early box scores were only nine lines long, because there were no substitutions and no relief pitchers.

By the 1850s, box scores expanded to list fielding and baserunning feats. For example, many box scores listed the ground balls and fly balls fielded by individual players, and which bases a runner eventually reached in a particular at-bat. But there were many different leagues in this span before the National Association in 1871, and there was no set way to construct a box score.

Around 1880, many newspapers began adding line scores under the box scores themselves. Line scores are the notations explaining in what inning runs were scored. (For example, "000 012 000 _ 3" means that a team scored three runs: a run in the fifth and two in the sixth.) Sometime after 1880, newspapers began adding the number of hits and errors behind the number of runs scored (in other words, "000 012 000 _ 3 5 1" for three runs, five hits and an error).

By 1920, the box score as we know it was tak-ing form. In addition to at-bats, runs scored and hits, box scores began adding put outs and assists to the individual player's line. Runs batted in were also noted in parentheses under the box score and above the line score. Errors were at times noted, also under the box score, and the time of the game and, when available, the attendance.

In 1957, the Associated Press, in order to make the box score thinner and thus better able

Early boxscore from 1867.

to fit in sports columns, dropped put outs and assists from the individual line score, leaving only at-bats, hits and runs, and adding runs batted in. There was an outcry from many purists, but the box score as they knew it was changing rapidly.

In 1958, the AP began adding the pitch-ing line, as many teams were using relievers. The pitching line included innings pitched, hits allowed, runs allowed, earned runs allowed, strikeouts and walks. The winning and losing pitchers were also designated with a "W" or "L."

In 1969, closers were recognized and given an "S" next to their name when they were credited with a save. This box score was used until 1989.

In 1990, Stats Inc. the statistics-oriented sports company, overhauled the box score, first for *USA Today* and gradually for all news organiza-tions. The Stats Inc. box scores included batters that grounded into double plays, runners left on base and relievers who "held" a lead for a closer. In addition, they noted how many players a team left on base, how many double plays a team turned and batters hit by pitches.

Stats Inc. also began listing the names of the umpires at the game and, in addition to the atten-dance, the capacity of the ballpark was listed to give fans a sense of how full the ballpark was.

In the past decade, further statistics have been added, in part to please fantasy players. These include two-out RBI for hitters, individual bases on balls, strikeouts and individual batting averages as well as sacrifice flies, the names of players who grounded into a double play and bat-ters who moved runners to the next base by meth-ods other than a base hit.

Pitch counts for each pitcher have also been added, as well as inherited runners who scored off the pitcher.

JOE MCCARTHY

HOW IT'S DONE
Leaders and Managers

JOE TORRE

There is simply no one way to be a manager. One can be a taskmaster, like Joe McCarthy or John McGraw; a talker, like Walter Alston or Casey Stengel; or a consensus builder, like Joe Torre. But the key is to be fair and to have the respect of one's players. And, by the way, you better win, or you're gone.

WALTER ALSTON

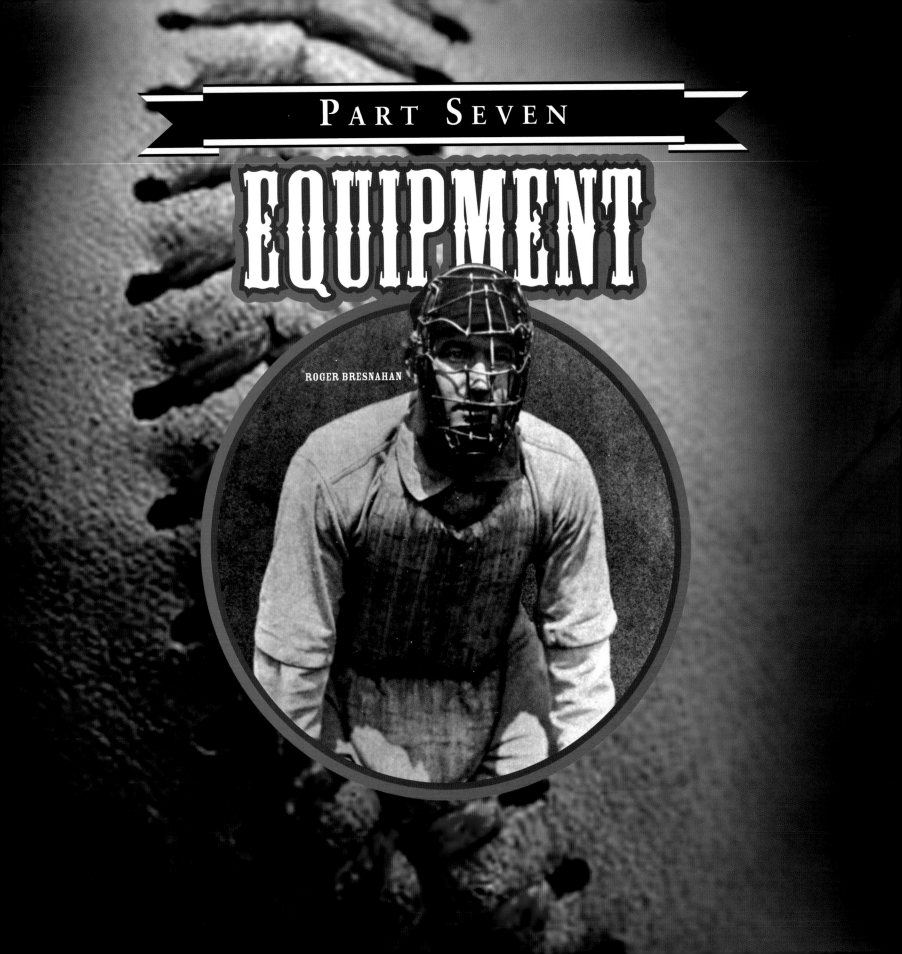

PART SEVEN

EQUIPMENT

ROGER BRESNAHAN

BATS

ABOVE: Willie Keeler used one of the heaviest bats with a compact swing to drive singles. RIGHT: Wood chips fly as a block of wood is turned into a Louisville Slugger. This photo was taken in 1964 at the Louisville Slugger Factory, in Louisville, Kentucky.

Up until the late 1800s, batters had to make their own bats, or have them custom made. Thus, ballplayers experimented with all kinds of shapes and lengths. In addition, many different types of wood were used, but the favorite kind of wood was willow (which led to the phrase "swinging the old willow"). Ash was also popular in the mid-19th century (leading to the phrase "swing the old ash"), as was basswood.

Hitters soon discovered that rounded bats seemed to work better than bats that were squared off. By 1857, a rule was passed that bats could no longer be more than 2.5 inches in diameter, but there was no restriction on their length. But in 1869, that rule was amended as well, and bat length was limited to 42 inches, a rule still in place today.

The National League and American Association made a rule in 1884 allowing bats to be flattened on one side. These flat-sided bats enabled hitters to bunt far more prolifically than previously, and observers saw a dramatic rise in bunting over the next few years. The rise was so dramatic, and the bunting became so overwhelmingly a part of the game, that both leagues banned flattened bats in 1892.

By 1891, the National League had also ruled that bats could no longer be sawed off, or flattened, at the ends. Thus, bats were rounded and the diameter was increased to 2.75 inches.

There have never been weight restrictions on bats, and how heavy or light they are depends on personal preference. The heaviest bats were often used by singles hitters like Bill Sweeney or Willie Keeler, who used compact swings to drive the ball between fielders.

That all changed in 1919, when Red Sox outfielder George Herman "Babe" Ruth began hitting home runs. Detroit star Ty Cobb once theorized that Ruth was able to experiment with a big swing because he was a pitcher, which is what Ruth did with the Red Sox when he was under less pressure to generate runs.

"I may be a pitcher," Ruth told sportswriter Grantland Rice in an interview in 1919, "but first off I'm a hitter. I copied my swing after [Shoeless] Joe Jackson's. His is the perfectest."

Unlike Jackson, however, Ruth told Rice that every time he swung at the ball, he swung hard. "Once my swing starts, though, I can't change or pull up. It's all or nothing at all," concluded Ruth.

Ruth's free-swinging style, and the results he generated, led to many imitators. But Ruth was Ruth, and even as Ruth was making home-run records, other hitting stars, such as Rogers Hornsby, suggested that using a lighter bat was better for sluggers, because it enabled them to generate more bat speed.

The bat-speed-versus-bat-weight controversy continued for several decades, but after Ruth's retirement and death, it was generally agreed that lighter bats, swung harder, caused more balls to go out of the park.

The first company to mass-produce bats was Albert Spalding's company, A.G. Spalding & Bros., in 1879. The company had been making individualized bats since opening in 1877, but the demand for a relatively cheap, durable bat was increasing from high school, college and minor and major leagues.

By 1887, Spalding was making more than 1 million bats a year at its plant in Hastings, Michigan. Spalding claims that his was the first company to attach a trademark

ABOVE: The Louisville Slugger is the most well-known bat in baseball history. LEFT: The Giants' Heinie Groh ordered a bat with a slim handle so he could get his fingers around it.

BATTING HELMETS

Negro League star Willie Wells (Negro League, 1924–50) appears to be one of the first players to use a batting helmet. In about 1937, Wells modified a construction worker's helmet to protect him from being hit by a baseball. Necessity was behind this innovation. Wells, a superior leadoff hitter, was often hit by pitchers when his Negro League team faced white squads.

In 1941, the Dodgers required all their players to wear a plastic helmet or protective headgear, as did the Washington Senators, at all times, even in the field. But many players complained that the plastic helmets were uncomfortable and, after a year, the use of the helmets, except in certain minor-league organizations, fell into disuse.

In 1952, the Pirates organization revived the custom, and the ballplayers were again required to don protective headgear, although only while at bat. There was, again, resistance, but by 1958, both leagues required batters to wear them.

Earflaps began in Little League long before they were required in the pros. But on May 3, 1960, according to *The Washington Post*, Senators outfielder Jim Lemon donned a helmet with an earflap. Lemon may have had good reason to wear the specialized helmet: he was hit by a pitch seven times that year, his career high. There was, as there always seems to be, some derision on the part of the Senators' opponents, but by 1974, batting helmets with earflaps became mandatory.

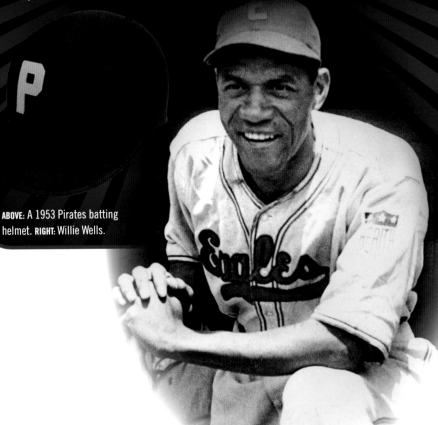

ABOVE: A 1953 Pirates batting helmet. **RIGHT:** Willie Wells.

to their bats, when it began in 1877. In 1884, woodworker John Andrew "Bud" Hillerich began making customized bats for individual players, and by 1894, the Louisville Slugger was born.

The most dramatic instance of customizing a bat was in 1913. That year, Giants infielder Henry "Heinie" Groh (Giants, Reds, Pirates, 1912–27) was struggling at the plate. Manager John McGraw suggested a bigger bat. Groh, at five-feet-eight and 130 pounds, told McGraw his hands were too small to grip a larger, heavier bat.

So, said Groh in Lawrence Ritter's *The Glory of Their Times*, he went to the Spalding factory. Groh and a Spalding worker took a slab of ash, whittled down the handle, and built up the head of the bat "so that it looked like some kind of crazy, upside-down bottle." And the bottle bat was born. Few of Groh's contemporaries actually tried to duplicate the bottle bat, which is somewhat strange, because his career average was .292.

Bats with cupped ends were made legal in 1975. They were popularized by St. Louis star Lou Brock, who claimed the slight reduction in weight gave him a little more bat speed.

Aluminum bats were first introduced in 1968, when Anthony Merola, who owned a company that manufactured aluminum pool cues, decided to branch out by marketing aluminum baseball bats. Worth Inc. teamed with Merola to manufacture the bats in 1970. In 1971, Little League Baseball entered into a contract with Worth to mass-produce the bats nationwide, which led to their popularity at the amateur level.

In 1993, Worth and another company, Easton, introduced the titanium bat, which is lighter and more durable than aluminum, and in 1995, the two companies introduced aluminum bats that are more durable still than the titanium models.

PINE TAR

Kansas City Royals outfielder George Brett was certainly not the first player to use pine tar on his bat. And let's not forget: the issue that day in 1983 against the New York Yankees wasn't that he used pine tar on his bat to improve the grip; that's legal. What Brett did was apply the pine tar past the legal distance from the bat handle, which is 18 inches.

In fact, the first player to be ejected from a game for using pine tar too far up the bat handle was Yankees catcher Thurman Munson, in 1975. That year Munson was batting against the Minnesota Twins and got a hit. But the Twins protested that the pine tar on Munson's bat was too far up the neck of the bat, and the protest was upheld. The hit was taken away.

Fast-forward eight years. The Yankees were playing the Kansas City Royals. The Royals' George Brett hit a home run to put his team ahead. But Yankees manager Billy Martin pointed out that, like Munson's bat, Brett's bat had pine tar on it that extended up the bat farther than the legal limit.

Brett's home run was disallowed (although American League president Lee MacPhail later re-allowed the dinger.)

Brett's reaction was interesting: he came charging out of the dugout like a wild man. One wonders what he would have done had some of his teammates and coaches not restrained him. He was certainly in the wrong. Maybe he believed that if he seemed angry enough, the ump would reconsider.

GEORGE BRETT

George Brett goes nutso against the Yankees in 1983. As one can see in the other photo (inset), there is quite a bit of tar on the old war club.

BASEBALLS

Until 1872, there were no specifications for making baseballs. Balls differed from league to league, state to state and often city to city. They were usually homemade. Sometimes a cobbler or a tanner made them. A story in the *Brooklyn Eagle* in 1884 described how, in the 1850s, some balls were made almost entirely of rubber. These balls were so lively, when a batter struck a base hit, the balls bounced all over the field.

But in 1872, baseball leagues and teams across the country realized the ball had to be as uniform in construction as possible. The circumference had to be between 9 and 9.25 inches, and the weight between 5 and 5.25 ounces, dimensions that remain to this day.

The initial requirement was for the core of the ball to be India rubber. The yarn that was wound around it would be wool. The cover would be horsehide.

These factors changed over the years. In 1910, A.G. Spalding & Bros. of Chicago, at the behest of both the American and National leagues, introduced a ball with a cork center. There are many theories about why the rubber center was replaced with cork. Cork-centered balls did appear to travel farther, and there was some speculation that this "livelier" ball was introduced to increase attendance. The reality was more simple: cork-centered balls were more durable, lasting nearly twice as long as balls with rubber centers.

There has often been confusion about exactly when these new baseballs were introduced. The fact is, Spalding trumpeted the new ball in many news stories at the time.

In 1925, Major League Baseball introduced a "cushioned" cork center, which was even more of an improvement on the old cork center. The cushioned center was merely a cork center with a film of vulcanized rubber around it to give the center even more durability.

Certainly the cork center made baseballs a little livelier, but the end of the Dead Ball Era didn't seem to actually arrive until 1919, or nine years after the cork-center ball was introduced.

So, what happened? Well, it wasn't the ball. A story in *Popular Mechanics* in 1924 explained that the principal reason baseballs were so lively was the umpires' practice of replacing baseballs much more frequently. Newer balls were livelier balls.

Woolen yarn has been used to wrap baseballs since 1872. In 1877, some manufacturers used cotton yarn, but the ball was harder than a woolen-wrapped baseball, and hard for fielders to catch.

The outer surface of the ball has traditionally been the most difficult part of the ball to manufacture. Initially, many manufacturers used leather covers, but they were difficult to sew together. In 1877, the National League decreed that horsehide would be the only acceptable cover (thus the old saying "He fired the old horsehide in"). Horsehide was durable and took considerable punishment. The decree lasted until 1974, when both leagues allowed baseballs to also be made of domestic cowhide, in large part because of a shortage of horses.

But the biggest problem was making sure it all held together. Several stitching designs were used, but they

IN CASE YOU DIDN'T KNOW

Early baseballs usually had rubber or cork cores. But in the Great Lakes region, some homemade baseballs had cores made of the eye of a sturgeon. A sturgeon's eye was the perfect size for a core, and had sufficient resiliency when hit.

tended to fray at the corners or edges. In 1858, according to a report by the Natick Historical Society, a Natick resident named Colonel William Cutler designed the figure-eight pattern now in use. Several other claimants to the figure-eight design have emerged since then.

The figure-eight design was perfect, as it had no outstanding corners or edges, and the design quickly caught on across the country.

There are 108 stitches in every baseball. Baseballs are threaded by straight needles, and the thread is waxed to prevent tangling.

Most baseball manufacturers in the mid- to late 19th century were based in and around New York City and eastern Massachusetts.

By the Numbers

600,000
THE NUMBER OF BASEBALLS
USED EVERY YEAR BY
MAJOR LEAGUE BASEBALL

7
THE MAXIMUM NUMBER OF PITCHES
A SINGLE BASEBALL REMAINS IN PLAY
BEFORE BEING THROWN OUT

GLOVES

According to the *Sporting News*, the first player to use a glove regularly was a catcher, Ben Delavergne, who caught for the old Albany Knickerbockers in the 1860s. The use of gloves in the early history of baseball was scoffed at as unmanly. But pitchers began throwing harder, and as catchers began moving closer to the plate, they began wearing for protection small leather gloves that were little more than what are known as golf gloves today. Some catchers opted to wear woolen mittens too.

Doug Allison, a catcher for the old Cincinnati Red Stockings, was another pioneer, using a small leather catching glove reportedly made for him by a saddle maker in 1869. Still, Allison and anyone else who tried to don a glove risked ridicule.

But that all changed in the 1870s, and there was one principal reason: Albert Spalding.

Spalding was one of the great early players in professional baseball, a dominating pitcher for Boston and later a great first baseman for Chicago. He did not smoke or drink and rarely used strong language. Where many players would ignore the fans after a game, Spalding often would stop and talk to them and sign autographs. He became a huge fan favorite.

In 1876, Spalding was preparing to retire. But unlike many other ballplayers, who generally spent their salaries almost as soon as they got them, Spalding actually had a postretirement business plan: sporting goods.

In February of that year, Spalding and his brother, J. Walter Spalding, opened a store in Chicago that sold bats, balls and a line of fielding gloves. So when the 1876 season opened, there was Al Spalding playing first base, with one of his patented black fielding gloves.

Previously, when ballplayers at the professional level had donned gloves, they were mocked. But this was Al Spalding, possibly the best player in baseball, wearing the glove. His fellow ballplayers figured there was something to it, so they began looking for gloves. And where was the best place to buy baseball gloves? Why, A.G. Spalding & Bros. Sporting Goods!

He took out advertisements in the local newspapers, noting, "No first baseman or catcher who suffers sore hands should be without" one of his gloves. Since virtually every first baseman and catcher in the National League suffered from that malady, the business took off like a rocket and, of course, is still around today.

By 1880, nearly every first baseman and catcher wore a glove. And these gloves were still little more than what we would consider today to be regular leather gloves: no padding and no "net" between the thumb and forefinger to assist in catching balls.

The rest of the infield caught on a little slower. Reportedly, shortstop Arthur "Doc" Irwin, who played in the National League between 1880 and 1894 for various teams, was the first infielder besides a first baseman to regularly wear a padded glove. This was in 1885, when he sustained an injury to his hand. Irwin, because of the injury, got a sort of dispensation from his fellow shortstops, who didn't ridicule him too much. But when the injury healed, Irwin discovered that using the padded glove to catch baseballs actually helped him control the ball. So he stuck with it.

Irwin, by 1885, was a veteran in his sixth year on a strong club, the Providence Grays, who had won the National League pennant the year before. There were probably other non–first basemen who donned gloves earlier than Irwin, but he was the player that made it acceptable.

Pitchers were the last players to don gloves. The first hurler to take the leap was, according to Cy Young, George "Nig" Cuppy, who pitched for the Cleveland Spiders, St. Louis Browns and Boston Braves from 1892 to 1901. Cuppy began wearing a glove in 1894.

Webbing was introduced in the early 20th century, not by players but by sporting-goods companies, who touted the "net" between the thumb and forefinger of a glove as an innovation that would improve a player's ability to catch a baseball. It caught on rather slowly, as many big leaguers considered webbing to be some sort of unfair advantage.

In 1920, Rawlings introduced a glove that had a rudimentary "pocket" or indentation in the palm of the glove to make catching a baseball easier.

With few restrictions on their size, gloves began to become larger in the 1950s. According to *Baseball Digest*, Wilson manufactured what is considered the forerunner of the modern-day glove in 1957: a baseball glove that was bigger than previous models, with a pronounced webbing.

As Craig Wright observed in his book, *The Diamond Appraised*, the introduction of a deeper pocket in fielders' gloves was another key innovation in 1959. But many old-timers decry the whole process, noting that the first ballplayers did fine without gloves.

IN CASE YOU DIDN'T KNOW

The last player to not wear a glove was probably pitcher Joe Yeager in 1902. Yeager was 6–12 that year with a 4.00 ERA for Detroit. It is not known if he broke down and wore a glove the next year, as he only appeared in one game for the Tigers, a losing effort in which he gave up 15 hits and 7 runs.

GLOVE SUPERSTITIONS

It's fair to say that a baseball glove is one of the most personal items a ballplayer has, with the possible exception of his bat. But there seem to be many more superstitions connected to gloves than bats.

Many players hate to part with their gloves and use them year after year, even as they fray into near uselessness. There is, in fact, a cottage industry for glove repairs.

Players like Phil Rizzuto, who played for the Yankees from 1941 to 1956, Shawon Dunston (Cubs, Giants, Pirates, Indians, Giants, Cardinals, 1985–2002), Amos Otis (Mets, Royals, Pirates, 1967–84) and Brady Anderson (Red Sox, Orioles, Indians, 1988–2002) all tried to hold on forever to the first glove they started out with as rookies.

Others weren't as picky about keeping an old glove, but they were protective. Former shortstop Royce Clayton (Giants, Cardinals, Rangers, White Sox, Brewers, Rockies, 1991–2005) was reported to have told the *St. Louis Post-Dispatch*, "I don't mess with your wife, so you don't touch my glove."

Many players name or otherwise personalize their gloves. Gold Glove first baseman George Scott (Red Sox, Brewers, Royals, Yankees, 1966–79) called his mitt Black Beauty. Mel Hall (Cubs, Indians, Yankees, Giants), dubbed his gloves Lucille. And Hall of Famer Kirby Puckett (Twins, 1984–95) didn't specifically name his gloves, but he called them "my babies."

As far as superstitions go, Nomar Garciaparra (Red Sox, Cubs, Dodgers, 1996–present) chews the laces of his glove during pitches. Zoilo Versalles (Senators, Expos, Twins, Dodgers, Indians, 1959–71) used to throw away his glove after every error; since he led the league in errors three times during his seven-year career with the Twins (a total of 221 in the span), that's a lot of gloves.

Casey Stengel (Dodgers, Pirates, Giants, Braves, 1912–25) was so attached to his glove that he reportedly got married wearing it. There's no record of Mrs. Stengel's reaction.

Phil Rizzuto would hold onto his glove until it literally fell apart. In 1949, he was playing a game and a ball was hit to him at shortstop. Rizzuto leapt to make the catch. The ball went right through the shabby lining of his glove.

Catchers' mitts developed differently from other fielders' gloves because they had to be more durable, flexible and offer more protection to catchers. This, of course, was because pitchers began throwing harder and faster, and the men behind the plate had to catch these offerings.

Some researchers, including Peter Morris in his book *A Game of Inches*, report that a player named Billy McGunnigle, a catcher for the Fall River, Massachusetts, club, was forced into using a bigger, more protective mitt because of injuries to his hands and was probably the first catcher to use a padded mitt. Prior to a game in 1877, he went to a hardware store and bought a pair of bricklayers' gloves, which had the advantage of being made of heavy leather.

But the problem was, catchers had to catch the ball in those days with both hands. So while a variety of gloves with heavier padding came on the market, the issue was finding a flexible, durable glove that would enable catchers to catch *and* throw while wearing it.

By 1884, catchers themselves solved the problem. The concept of catching the ball with one hand and throwing it with the opposite came into vogue. That meant a padded glove was only needed for the catching hand. Ted Kennedy, a right-handed pitcher who toiled briefly for the Cubs in the National League and a couple of teams in the old American Association from 1885 to 1886, devised a glove for his catchers that was, basically, a glove stitched to the back of a round pad.

It looked odd, and baseball players, never known for thinking too far outside the box, shunned it for a while.

Again, it was an established star, this time Buck Ewing, who introduced that style of mitt in the majors that year. Ewing (Troy, Giants, Reds, 1880–97) was the most respected man in the game at the time, and when he began wearing a mitt-style catcher's glove, other catchers deemed it appropriate.

In 1920, Rawlings, in addition to creating a smaller glove for fielders, also introduced a catchers' mitt with a small indentation or pocket in the mitt part of the glove, as well as webbing between the thumb and forefinger. It was still a small glove, but it was more flexible than previous mitts.

In 1930, Spalding introduced more padding, but according to former catcher Mickey Owen (Cardinals, Dodgers, Cubs, Red Sox, 1937–64), "[Catchers' mitts] were still pretty small, flat and had no shape when I came into the Big Leagues in 1937."

From 1940 to 1960, Rawlings was the leader in redesigning catchers' mitts, introducing several models that had deeper and more flexible pockets, and wider net-

ABOVE: Buck Ewing leaps to catch a throw in a pre-game warm-up in 1892. **RIGHT:** Mickey Owen, center, without his glove. Even though mitts were much larger in the 1940s than at the beginning of the century, they were still not the balloons they are in the 21st century.

ting or webbing between the thumb and forefinger. Gradually, catchers' mitts became larger.

The next big innovation was the oversize mitt, introduced in 1960 by Baltimore manager Paul Richards. Richards's catchers had difficulty catching pitcher Hoyt Wilhelm's knuckleball, so Richards had an extra-large mitt made for use when Wilhelm pitched. But this style eventually got out of hand, as catchers began wearing mitts that resembled beach umbrellas. By 1964, both the American and National leagues restricted the sizes of catchers' mitts to no more than 38 inches in circumference.

In the late 1960s, Reds catcher Johnny Bench (1967–83) and Cubs receiver Randy Hundley (Giants, Cubs, Twins, Padres, 1964–77) experimented with a "hinged" glove that was constructed to close around a baseball when it struck the pocket. Again, Bench, the best catcher in the National League, was the catalyst for this version's popularity. When his peers saw Johnny using it, they were more comfortable adopting the glove themselves.

Today's mitts have a long oval pocket and are nearly as flexible as fielders' gloves. Still, while the padding has taken most of the "sting" out of catching most pitches, some catchers still have to use tricks to reduce it even more. Many of the catchers who caught former flamethrower Nolan Ryan (Mets, Angels, Astros, Rangers, 1966–93) admit to sliding a piece of cardboard or foam padding in their gloves.

Harvard baseball captain Fred Thayer designed the first catchers' mask, basically using a fencing mask and reinforcing the front with thicker wire rather than mesh. Two of Thayer's teammates, Howard K. Thatcher, who played in 1876, and James Tyng, who played a year later in 1877, both claimed to be the first to use the mask.

Thatcher may have used the mask in 1876, but Tyng's use of it throughout the 1877 season drew attention to the concept and eventually popularized it.

As with many inventions in the early days of baseball, the use of a mask was considered unmanly, except by many catchers.

JOHNNY BENCH

Perhaps the best way to sell the new device was to do what Thayer did in 1878: upon visiting the clubhouse of the Boston Braves, he donned the mask and allowed players to throw at him. The mask easily deflected the pitches, and Boston manager Harry Wright was reportedly clearly impressed.

The catchers' mask evolved over the next several decades, but the most dramatic addition came in 1976: that was the year Dodger catcher Steve Yeager was standing in the on-deck circle and was accidentally struck in the throat by the splinter of a bat that had been shattered by a pitch. Yeager developed an attachment for the bottom of his mask that protected his throat from further injury. Today, the device is optional, and only a few catchers still use it, with most catchers at the big-league level eschewing it.

Another innovation came in 1996, when catcher Charlie O'Brien of the Toronto Blue Jays developed a hockey-style catchers' mask. O'Brien reported that he had attended a hockey game and became convinced that such masks, which cover the entire face, would provide

more protection than conventional masks. On September 13, 1996, he donned such a mask, which he had helped design. The new design has proven popular, and many catchers at all levels can be seen using the "hockey mask."

Charley Bennett's wife is credited with inventing the chest protector. Bennett was a fine catcher who played for Milwaukee, Worcester, Detroit and Boston in a stellar career that lasted from 1878 to 1893. Bennett led the National League in fielding percentage seven times in his career.

But his wife was worried about the punishment he absorbed. So, according to an interview with Bennett in a 1914 issue of the *Detroit Free Press*, prior to the 1883 season she stitched together a padded blanket made of strips of cork that would fit over Bennett's chest. Bennett, fortified with this shield, led the league in fielding six of the

BASEBALL SPIKES

Spikes on athletic shoes go all the way back to cricketers and footballers who wore them in England at the turn of the 19th century. They are the one basic piece of long-standing baseball equipment that probably predates baseball players. For many years, baseball spikes were fairly sharp, for the simple reason that most baseball shoes were custom made, and cobblers would actually sew metal nails, or spikes, into regular shoes.

When customized baseball shoes became more common in the latter part of the 19th century, the spikes were squared off and not as pointed. As Frank Grant and other second basemen would attest, these squared-off spikes were still dangerous for a defensive player when baserunners slid into him, but much less so.

But this didn't prevent some players, including Detroit Hall of Famer Ty Cobb, from sharpening his spikes. According to his autobiography, *Memoirs of 20 Years in Baseball*, Cobb would sharpen his spikes in the dugout before a game, in full view of the opposing team, in order to intimidate them. That may be a bit of hyperbole on Cobb's part, however; such antics would have been frowned upon by umpires. (Although, admittedly, there were not a lot of umpires who relished taking on Cobb in those days!)

next nine years. A year later, sporting-goods companies began making the protectors, which quickly caught on.

Shin guards were first worn by African American Hall of Famer Frank Grant in 1887. Grant was a second baseman, and he nailed together slats of wood to wear around his shins to protect him from racist opponents who would slide into him feetfirst. A second African American player of that era, John W. "Bud" Fowler, who also played second base in the white minor leagues, adopted Grant's idea the next year.

But the first catcher to wear shin protectors is a little harder to pinpoint. Harry Steinfeldt (Reds, Cubs, Braves, 1898–1911), the superb third baseman, had problems similar to Grant's, with opponents deliberately sliding into him, and reportedly experimented with shin protectors in the minor leagues. But by the time he was called up to the Reds in 1898, he'd discarded them.

At the dawn of the 20th century, it is clear that several catchers began donning shin guards, including Mike Kahoe, a teammate of Steinfeldt's on the Cubs in 1902. Kahoe was a backup for most of his 11-year career (1895, 1899–1905, 1907–09) in the majors, but was known as an excellent fielder and a gritty man behind the plate.

Hall of Famer Roger Bresnahan was recognized as the man who "invented" shin guards, but this is a minor glitch in the baseball history books. What Bresnahan did was, in 1906, dare to wear his shin guards outside his pants. Again, it took a star like Bresnahan (Cubs, Orioles, Giants, Browns, 1897–1915) to convince his fellow backstoppers that wearing shin guards was not the act of a coward, but a strategy that lengthened a ballplayer's career.

It did not hurt that Bresnahan's manager, John McGraw, endorsed the move, knowing it would keep his star catcher on the field more often.

ROGER BRESNAHAN

LEFT: Charlie O'Brien sits in the dugout with his hockey-style catcher's mask. RIGHT: Bresnahan poses in catcher's shin guards, which he allegedly invented.

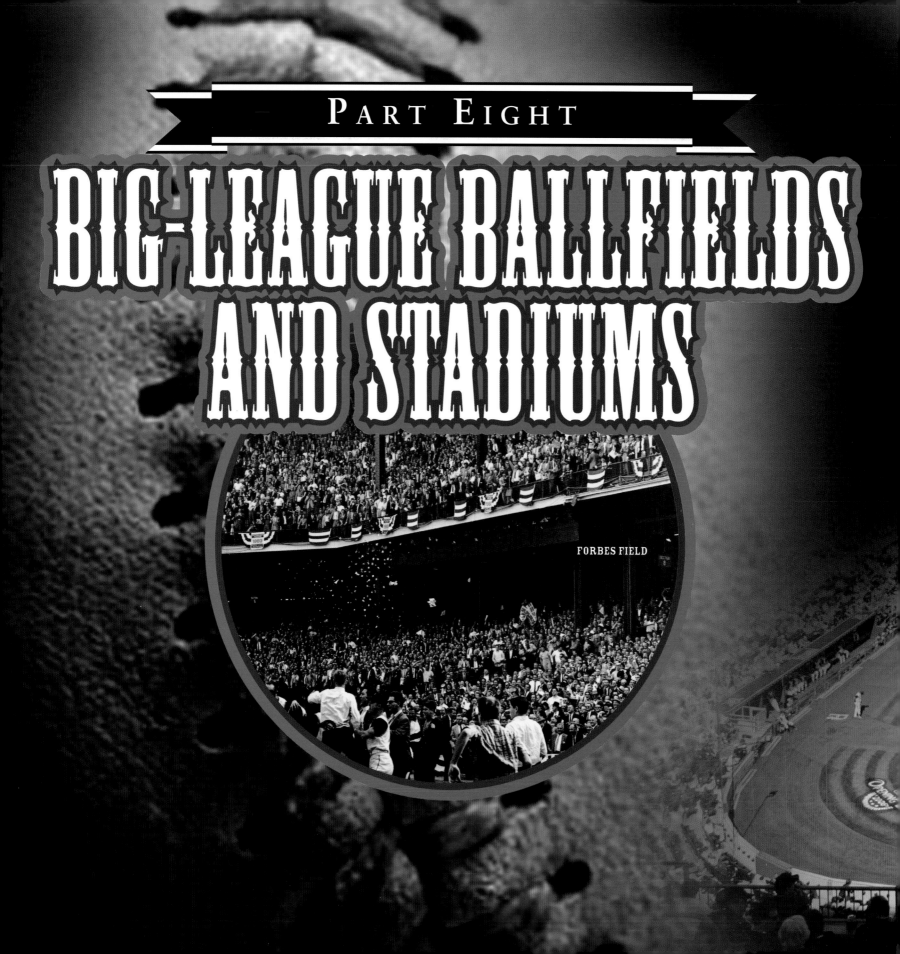

PART EIGHT

BIG-LEAGUE BALLFIELDS AND STADIUMS

FORBES FIELD

THE EVOLUTION OF THE BALLFIELD

The concept of enclosing ballfields to generate income is much older than the professional leagues of the late 19th century. Semipro clubs began to see the potential financial benefits by the early 1800s. In 1862, according to the *Sporting News*, the Union Grounds in Brooklyn became the first enclosed field used largely for baseball. Patrons were charged 25 cents to get in to see the game.

Many other cities followed suit over the next decade, but like the Union Grounds, these fields were often used for other activities, such as skating in the winter, when the fields were flooded and frozen.

All of these parks were constructed primarily of wood, which was a problem in an era in which cigars and cigarettes were smoked by most of the park's patrons—not to mention the practice of building fires in the stands on cold days! There were a rather large number of ballparks completely or partially destroyed by fire during this time. By far, the best known of these fires occurred in 1871.

The summer of that year had been unusually dry. So it was that on October 8, at about 9:00 p.m., flames began to whip through the cow barn of Patrick and Catherine O'Leary. Before the O'Learys—or anyone—could react, the fire had spread onto DeKoven Street, and soon half the town was in flames. About 17,000 structures were destroyed, including the Union Base-Ball Grounds, the ballpark constructed by the Chicago White Stockings a year earlier on Michigan Avenue.

The park had housed the equipment and uniforms of the White Stockings, and the team was forced to borrow equipment and uniforms, and play the rest of that season's games on the road; it then folded for two years until a new park could be built.

The ballfield in Chicago was only the most prominent example. Other wooden parks were also at risk. Washington Park in Brooklyn was destroyed by fire in 1889, and National League Park in Cleveland burned to the ground after being struck by lightning in 1890.

In 1900, John T. Brush, owner of the Cincinnati Reds, rebuilt League Park (which had also burned down) using iron and stone, although portions of the grandstand were still made of wood (and those portions, of course, burned down in 1901).

In 1905, the minor-league Columbus Senators built a park entirely of brick and steel. The Senators drew well, and the sturdiness of their park attracted the interest of major-league owners, who began to look into similar types of construction. In 1909, the Philadelphia Phillies debuted Shibe Park and the Pittsburgh Pirates opened Forbes Field, both brick-and-steel facilities. Over the next 15 years, 8 major-league teams would follow suit.

These facilities were not cheap: Forbes Field, for example, cost $2 million to build. But along with Shibe Park, Forbes reflected the growing popularity of baseball: both were larger and much sturdier than previous facilities, each holding more than 20,000 fans. Clearly, baseball was here to stay, and these newer facilities reflected that optimism.

Other classic ballparks sprang up quickly after that: Comiskey Park in 1910; Navin Field (Tiger Stadium) in Detroit; Crosley Field in Cincinnati and Fenway Park in Boston in 1912; Ebbets Field in Brooklyn in 1913; and Braves Field in Boston and Wrigley Field in Chicago in 1914.

These parks were better built, better looking and perhaps, most important, almost exclusively used for baseball. All were positioned in or near the center of the cities in which they were located, and some, like Fenway Park, were shaped by the urban factors around them. Fenway's Green Monster, for example, was necessitated by the presence of Lansdowne Street, which runs along the north end of the park. The owners of the street would not allow the Sox to annex that land and, thus, forced the owners to sort of chop off a portion of left

field and build first a fence there and then later a wall.

But the evolution of ballparks took a quantum leap in 1923. That was the year the New York Yankees built Yankee Stadium. The Yankees had begun their professional life as the New York Highlanders, a ragtag group of ballplayers run by a ragtag group of owners. Moved from Baltimore in 1903, the Highlanders threw together a ballpark in New York in six weeks. The offi-

OPPOSITE: At Camden Yards, the Baltimore Orioles organization is seeking to recapture the majesty of old ballparks like Forbes Field in Pittsburgh and the former Yankee Stadium in New York (both above). Many fans believe they have succeeded.

cial name of the ballfield was Hilltop Park, because it sat on one of the higher points in Manhattan. But after a while it was known to one and all as "The Rock," in reference to its stony infield and dusty outfield. Eventually, since the owners had no interest in refurbishing the field or the facility, the Highlanders, now called the Yankees, were forced to move, leasing space in the Polo Grounds from the New York Giants.

Thus, from 1913 to 1922, the Yankees were tenants of their archrivals, the Giants. The Giants didn't mind for a while, as they took most of the best attendance days for themselves, such as the Fourth of July and Labor Day, every year. But in 1915, the Yankees were purchased by beer mogul Colonel Jacob Ruppert and engineer Colonel Tillinghast Huston.

Both Huston and Ruppert set about improving their club, and their announced plans included a new ballfield for the Yankees—maybe not right away, but at some point. Their purchase of pitcher-outfielder George Herman "Babe" Ruth from the Red Sox was part of the upgrade plan.

The plan also moved the Giants to kick the Yankees out of the Polo Grounds. Ruth was a huge hit in New York, and the Yankees began outdrawing the Giants by a hefty margin, which did not make Giants manager John McGraw particularly happy. By 1920, the Giants were making it clear to the Yankees that it was time to look for another place to play.

Huston and Ruppert eventually settled in the Bronx. And when they began envisioning their plans for a new ballfield, they wanted to take the next step up in terms of baseball playing fields. Ruppert explained to a newsman that the new facility would be Yankee "Stadium," not Yankee Park and not Yankee Field. It would be bigger and sturdier than any stadium being used at the time.

It was. Yankee Stadium, when finished, had the largest capacity of any ballpark in baseball: 62,000. (Ruppert and Huston were fond of inflating attendance figures to tweak McGraw, so many of those early Yankee Stadium numbers in excess of 70,000 were something of a fib.) It had a beautiful scalloped frieze, a deep center field and a wonderfully short right-field "porch," into which Ruth gladly drilled many of his home runs for the team over his career. For a few months, the newsmen of the day worked over in their minds what to call this giant edifice. The most popular name, initially, was "The Colonels' Concrete Cashbox." Not bad, but in 1921, sportswriter Fred Lieb came up with a better name: "The House That Ruth Built." And so it has been ever since.

The evolution of ballfields slowed considerably over the next 30 years. In fact, from 1923 to 1953,

EARLY DOMES

The first domed baseball field was almost built in Pittsfield, Massachusetts, in 1947. The biggest problem with building any indoor stadium is maintaining the interior field, and artificial sunlamps were thought to be sufficient to keep grass growing (they weren't). Serious discussions of domed stadiums began after World War II.

Just after the war, the United States government was selling off a lot of its military equipment and materials. One of these was a huge airplane hangar in New Mexico. The government was having an understandably difficult time unloading the giant structure, until it came to the notice of the Pittsfield City Council in 1946. According to the *Berkshire Eagle*, an enterprising councilor suggested the city buy the hangar and lay out a baseball field inside. The idea generated some excitement for a few weeks, but the city eventually discarded the thought.

In 1952, according to the *New York Times*, Walter O'Malley of the Brooklyn Dodg-ers was seriously considering a domed field, with a retractable roof. Eventually, of course, the Dodgers moved west to Los Angeles.

There were several other false starts, mostly on the East Coast, where weather was more of an issue than in, say, the south or west, but in January of 1961, Houston voters approved funding for a domed stadium that would house the National League's Houston Colt .45s. The Astrodome was completed and opened on April 9, 1965, for an exhibition between the Colt .45s and the New York Yankees.

There was an initial problem: the ceiling lights were so bright that players could not pick up fly balls. That problem was eventually addressed by repainting the ceiling, but not after Houston received permission to use different-colored baseballs (including yellow, red and orange) to make fly balls easier to see.

Because it was indoors, the grass began to die after awhile, leading to another innovation: artificial turf—which was good for the groundskeepers but bad for the ballplayers.

ASTRODOME

only one park, Cleveland Stadium, was built, in 1932. And that was because Cleveland was bidding to host the Olympic Games that year. (They didn't win.)

But starting in 1953, major-league baseball saw a series of franchise shifts that would generate the need for a number of new ballparks. The migration began with the National League's Boston Braves moving to Milwaukee in 1953, the St. Louis Browns of the American League moving to Baltimore in 1954 and the Philadelphia Athletics moving to Kansas City in 1955. The Orioles actually moved to a reconfigured football stadium, while the Athletics expanded an existing facility.

In 1958, however, the Brooklyn Dodgers and New York Giants made the most dramatic shifts: they packed up and moved to the West Coast, to Los Angeles and San Francisco, respectively.

Both the Giants and the Dodgers needed bigger stadiums and, more important, room for more parking. Over the previous 50 years, the automobile had become a regular commodity for a vast majority of American families. The concept of taking the bus or trolley anywhere, including to a baseball game, was no longer popular. The two former New York–based teams needed parking, badly, and New York real estate was simply too scarce.

Dodger Stadium didn't actually open until 1962, and the Dodgers played in the Los Angeles Coliseum for a few years. But Dodger Stadium reflected owner Walter O'Malley's decision to create a more fan-friendly atmosphere, featuring field-level seats between the dugouts, two scoreboards beyond the outfield bleachers and wider, more comfortable seats.

Similarly, Candlestick Park was built in 1960 as the league's only heated, open-air stadium. That was actually a necessity, since the winds coming in from San Francisco Bay were often fierce. But the park was larger and roomier than the old Polo Grounds, and thus more fan friendly.

In 1964, the Houston Astros brought space-age technology to baseball. They debuted the gigantic Astrodome, an enclosed facility that also, by 1966, featured an artificial surface. Astros owner Roy Hofheinz crowed that rainouts would no longer curtail his schedule, and that ballplayers would not be forced to play in inclement conditions, such as windy or cold days. For a while, artificial surfaces were the rage in both professional baseball and football.

In 1966, the Cardinals relocated to Busch Stadium. In 1970, the Pirates moved into Three Rivers Stadium, the same year the Reds moved into Riverfront Stadium, while a year later, the Phillies moved to Veterans Stadium.

The stadiums were all bigger, with more fan amenities, such as a wider variety of food and more comfortable seats. But they were all large, near-circular stadiums with artificial turf. There was an aura of sameness that made some ballplayers uncomfortable. And the artificial turf, well, that eventually proved to generate major medical problems for some ballplayers because of its overall hardness.

"If a cow can't eat it, I don't want to play on it," was big leaguer Dick Allen's comment on phony turf. It was a cry that many pro athletes would eventually take up.

A dozen years after the Astrodome opened, Seattle unveiled another domed facility, the Kingdome. Five years later, the Hubert H. Humphrey Metrodome in Minneapolis opened, and after that came the SkyDome in Toronto in 1987 and Tropicana Field in Florida in 1998.

The domed stadiums reflected a desire on the part of owners to control the environment as best they could. Rainouts and other natural handicaps—handicaps that could postpone or cancel games—were no longer an issue. Later domes, such as Toronto's SkyDome, have retractable roofs that can let the sun in. (In fact, 10 years after the SkyDome was built, the Mariners and Astros both abandoned their dome stadiums for stadiums with retractable roofs.)

Purists, which included fans, players and sportswriters, weren't as comfortable with these kinds of changes. One of the more striking contrasts of new versus old was the 1975 World Series, played alternately in the Reds' antiseptic Riverfront Stadium and the Red Sox's venerable Fenway Park.

But the modern stadium era, which gives a nod to older parks, has been much more popular. In 1992,

the Orioles moved to Oriole Park at Camden Yards, a throwback to the legendary stadiums of the past.

Camden Yards features a brick façade and a view of the old B&O Warehouse beyond right field. The warehouse has been renovated and is used for the team offices. Between the ballpark and the warehouse is a walkway lined with souvenir and food stands. The ballpark is asymmetrical, with the left-field foul line only 333 feet and the right-field foul line 318 feet. The grandstand seats are closer to the action.

Camden Yards was a huge hit with fans, baseball officials and players, and over the next few years, several teams followed that path. Colorado's Coors Field opened in 1995. With its redbrick façade, hand-operated scoreboard, innovative video screens and fountain-and-rock display beyond the bullpen, Coors has been a huge fan favorite, regularly drawing well over 2 million annually.

Since then, several teams, including the Mariners, Diamondbacks, Tigers, Giants, Pirates, White Sox and Reds, have moved into newer fields with a more "retro" feel. Meanwhile, the Red Sox, who had pondered a move or an expansion, have gone in the other direction: realizing that the already legendary Fenway Park would be nearly impossible to replace, the Sox have renovated the place, a move that included adding seats above the legendary Green Monster. "Sitting on the Monster" is the new hip place for some Sox fans to be.

In Case You Didn't Know

The first electronic scoreboard was introduced in 1902, in Sportsman's Park in St. Louis. It was nothing like the electronic scoreboards fans see today, but that first board had lights that indicated the number of outs, the number of balls and strikes, the inning and the score. Initially, this scoreboard was battery powered.

"IF A COW CAN'T EAT IT, I DON'T WANT TO PLAY ON IT."

DICK ALLEN

NIGHT BASEBALL

Night baseball was an experiment that had its origins in a number of places. Minor-league teams in the 1800s tried out the concept of hanging lights around a field to illuminate it at night.

According to Preston D. Orem's *Baseball (1845–1881)*, the first night game was played on Nantasket Beach in Hull, Massachusetts, between two department-store teams. The Northern Electric Company of Boston provided the lights, which were situated on three 100-foot-high towers made of wood. The towers were 500 feet apart.

According to Orem's book, the towers were each mounted with 12 lamps. Each tower generated

COMERICA PARK

30,000 units of candlepower, for a total illumination of 90,000 candles.

The two teams, representing employees from Jordan Marsh & Company and R.H. White & Company, played to a 16–16 tie after nine innings. The game was called so the employees and their families could take the last Boston ferry home.

Reporters covering the game from the *Boston Transcript* and the *Boston Globe* deemed the experiment a failure. The light, according to one reporter, was inconsistent and resulted in many errors on both sides. Spectators apparently had trouble picking up the ball, and fielders often had to hesitate a split second in order to pick up the teammate to whom they were throwing the ball.

But a scribe from the *Boston Post* was less dismissive, indicating that night baseball had possibilities.

The experiments continued. On June 2, 1883, the Jenny Electric Light Company, owned by Charles Jenny, illuminated League Park in Fort Wayne, Indiana. A total of 17 large arc

lamps, generating 4,000 candlepower each, were installed. In the game, players from the Northwestern League in Quincy, Illinois, defeated a team from Methodist College 19–11 in seven innings.

Again, press reaction was less than enthusiastic. All three periodicals that covered the game, the *Gazette*, the *Fort Wayne News* and the *Sporting Life* were all unenthusiastic about the concept—although like the *Boston Post*, the *Sporting Life* opined that, with a better lighting system, night baseball could be successful.

But for several decades, the problem was generating enough wattage to light up the entire field. When a field was surrounded by lights in those days, there tended to be dark spots in unexpected areas.

For example, in 1896, the Union Street Grounds in Delaware hosted a tripleheader. The first two games were played in daylight, with the third contest played under the lights. The lights were barely adequate for players to see across the field, let alone the pitcher's mound or batter's box. Any ball hit into the outfield was usually lost in darkness. The game was declared a disaster by local reporters.

Illumination of football fields began in the early part of the 20th century, and this was far more successful, in part because a football is larger and darker, and therefore easier to pick up against a lighted backdrop. So while night baseball began in fits and starts, there was clearly a market for evening athletic contests.

The first entrepreneur to make night baseball pay off was J. L. Wilkinson, the founder and owner of the Kansas City Monarchs of the Negro League. In 1929, Wilkinson bought a portable generator and several banks

COORS FIELD

of lights. He mounted the lights on flatbed trucks and took the lights with his team on the road.

The trucks would ring the fields on which the Monarchs would play, and, according to most newspaper accounts, were an immediate hit—except with members of the Monarchs.

The problem, as far as Wilkinson's players were concerned, was not the lights. It was the fact that Wilkinson could now schedule a game in the morning, afternoon and evening, sometimes in three different towns. It made an already exhausting Negro League schedule even more enervating.

"With those lights, Mr. Wilkinson got in an awful lot of baseball," reported Wilkinson's star player, Satchel Paige, in his autobiography. Paige was ready and willing to pitch a complete game in the morning and come back and start another contest in the eve-

ning, usually going five or six innings and allowing a teammate to finish up. But one day in 1940, reported Satch, "we got into a little trouble."

That day, Paige had no problem winning the opener of a tripleheader against a club team in Indiana, but teammate Hilton Smith got shelled in the second contest, and Monarchs manager Newt Allen asked Paige to pitch the last three innings in relief. The Monarchs came back and won the second game, and Paige had a beer or two, massaged his arm and took the mound for the third game.

"That night, I pitched the whole ballgame and we won again," wrote Paige. "There ain't many that can say they won three games in one day. I know of some pitchers that don't win that many in a season."

But Wilkinson's success with his barnstorming team inspired many minor-league operations to

follow suit. By the end of 1929, more than 30 minor-league teams had installed or were planning to install lights on their fields or stadiums.

The installation of lights in the major leagues took a bit longer. The commissioner at the time, the always acerbic Kenesaw Mountain Landis, thought major-league baseball was fine the way it was, and installing lights in big-league stadiums was a bush-league maneuver.

But by 1935, financial issues were forcing major-league teams to think about night baseball. Cincinnati installed lights at Crosley Field and played a handful of night contests. Fans enjoyed the novelty, but it didn't appear that night baseball would really catch on.

Still, by the end of the decade, Cleveland and Philadelphia had added lights to their fields, and many other teams were quickly following. Teams discovered that midweek night games drew better than midweek day games, because people working during the day could attend games scheduled for the evening. By 1941, 12 of the 16 major-league teams played night games, and by 1948, every team but the Cubs offered night baseball.

The Cubs held out stubbornly until 1988.

In 1971, the first World Series night game was played between the Baltimore Orioles and the Pittsburgh Pirates. Within the next two decades, major-league baseball was playing most of its playoff games at night. Gradually, the league began scheduling the games later and later, to the point where many games now end well after midnight. Attendance at these games, particularly World Series tilts, has not suffered appreciably, but critics point out that the games now end so late, the next generation of baseball fans, younger children, are rarely awake to see the end of the contests.

CROSLEY FIELD

THE HOME-FIELD ADVANTAGE

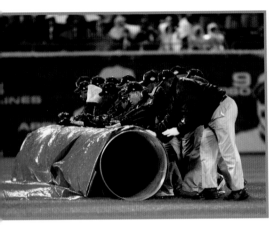

ABOVE: In major league baseball, a well-maintained field is a matter of pride. Workers hustle to get down the tarp. RIGHT: Fresh dirt is shoveled onto the infield to keep it dry.

In the mid-1800s, when semipro baseball began to flourish, the fields themselves were often facilities with poor drainage, rocky infields, uneven outfields and a host of other problems. The fields usually needed some kind of preliminary maintenance before ballplayers could perform on them.

But baseball in this era wasn't particularly lucrative, so groundskeepers for many teams at this time were hired on a part-time or as-needed basis. And when the money got tight, teams often went without a maintenance man, leaving the job to the manager and a spare player or two.

The arrival of the first pro league, the National Association in 1870, mandated that teams consistently keep their respective fields in relatively good shape.

During this span, most teams hired a groundskeeper, sometimes more than one, to maintain their fields.

By the 1880s, team owners in the National League began to be more proactive when it came to taking better care of their fields. Cincinnati was the first team, in 1888, to use a waterproof tarpaulin to cover their infield.

Owners, at this time, were also experimenting with reconfiguring certain aspects of their ballparks to give their teams an edge. The Baltimore Orioles and their groundskeeper, Thomas J. Murphy, were the best at this of the early lot.

Manager Ned Hanlon and Murphy hit on a way of contouring the first- and third-base lines ever so slightly to enable the bunts of Hanlon's Orioles to roll fair. Murphy also hit on the technique of raising or lowering the pitcher's mound to discombobulate pitchers, and of packing the infield clay to facilitate speedy Oriole runners.

Murphy's younger brother John was hired by the Giants a few years later. But John Murphy was better known for his artistic flourishes at the Polo Grounds, the Giants home field from 1883 to 1957.

The groundskeeper best known for tailoring a ballfield to its lineup was the legendary Emil Bossard, who worked the grounds for the Cleveland Indians from 1936 to 1960. Bossard would talk with the Indians pitchers and fielders at the beginning of the year and determine what kind of a field the team needed. Slower teams got slower infields, but when the Indians began running the bases more aggressively in the early 1950s, the infield clay got harder. For Cleveland teams with an unusual number of bunting players, Bossard would raise the dirt behind the first- and third-base foul lines ever so slightly, so a bunted ball would tend to stay fair.

Emil's contributions were so significant that in 1950, Indians manager Lou Boudreau called him "the 10th man in our lineup," and said, "I wouldn't be surprised if Emil was worth 10 wins a year for us." New York's Joe DiMaggio, in 1941, admitted that he "hated" playing in Cleveland, "because of the way the field was prepared for us."

Emil's son, Gene Bossard, was hired by the White Sox in 1940 and carried on the Bossard tradition in that city until his retirement in 1980. Gene

Allegations that the Twins' groundskeeping crew adjusted the ventilators to blow toward the outfield when the Twins were at bat have never been proven. That didn't prevent many managers from thinking it was true.

Bossard's most devious invention was "Bossard's swamp," a soft patch of turf right in front of home plate that the White Sox second baseman Nellie Fox credited with turning him into a first-class bunter.

Gene's son, Roger Bossard, began working for his father when he was 8 or 9 years old. He recalled in a 2008 interview in *Smithsonian* magazine that one weekend around that time, Gene simply asked him to come down and help him with some field maintenance. Roger jumped at the chance. He's been there for 41 years.

These days, Roger is also a consultant for other teams. He and a team of other design professionals helped design and build, among other facilities, the renovation of Busch Stadium in St. Louis, Safeco Field in Seattle, Bank One Ballpark in Arizona and Comerica Park in Detroit. Bossard now runs groundskeeping training camps in December. All this has earned him the title "The Sodfather."

The Bossard family does not hold a monopoly on molding fields to help their teams. (For the record, Roger has stated that, unlike his celebrated ancestors, he doesn't "doctor" fields…much.) During the 2007 World Series, the groundskeeping crew at Coors Field, home of National League Champions the Colorado Rockies, let the infield grass grow a little longer than the outfield grass to slow down ground balls and try to curtail the hot-hitting visiting Boston Red Sox.

The infield grass, according to a Fox Network report, was 1.625 inches high, or about 0.625 inches higher than usual. The outfield grass was 0.0875 inches high, which was the usual height of the grass.

This was a classic case, however, of groundskeeping shenanigans not working. The hot-hitting Red Sox continued their hot hitting, generating a .333 average for the World Series, which included scoring 14 runs in the 2 games they played at Coors. The Sox won both games at Coors Field, and swept Colorado out of the World Series.

There are other ways to affect the path of the ball. In the late 1980s and early 1990s, there were allegations that the grounds crew at the Hubert H. Humphrey Metrodome in Minneapolis would adjust the ventilation during a game to favor Twins hitters and hinder opponents.

In 2003, Dick Ericson, the former superintendent at the Metrodome from 1982 to 1995, told the Minneapolis *Star Tribune* that if the team was down a few runs, he'd adjust the ventilation system to blow outward; if the Twins were ahead, he'd adjust the ventilation system to blow air inward.

Ericson said the fans were blowing out when Twins star Kirby Puckett hit his dramatic 11th-inning home run in Game Six against the Atlanta Braves.

"I don't feel guilty," he said, "[…I]t's your home-field advantage. Every stadium has got one."

KIRBY PUCKETT

"I BECAME VERY SUSPICIOUS, MAYBE PARANOID. THEY HAD SUCH AN UNCANNY WAY OF WINNING."

BOBBY VALENTINE

Twins officials denied Ericson's actions and issued an official statement doubting that he actually did what he said.

Still, Bobby Valentine said that while he was managing the Texas Rangers in that span, his players told him they often noticed a breeze in their faces when they were in the field and then a breeze in their faces, again, when they were at bat.

"I became very suspicious, maybe paranoid," said Valentine. "They had such an uncanny way of winning."

HOW IT'S DONE
The Home-Field Advantage

There are a host of ways to doctor the field to a team's advantage. In his famous book, *Pitching in a Pinch*, the Giants' Christy Mathewson called it "doping the field." When Mathewson pitched against the Brooklyn Dodgers, the opposing groundskeeper would lower the mound on Mathewson, a noted control pitcher who was often discombobulated by the move. "I was," he noted ruefully, "throwing from a hollow instead of off a mound."

Mathewson insisted that the originators of "doping the field" were John McGraw's old Baltimore Oriole teams of the late 1890s. The Orioles' infield was packed with a particularly dense clay, "which made the basepaths hard as concrete," said Mathewson, and assisted Orioles runners in navigating the basepaths. In addition, to help their star hitter, Wee Willie Keeler, who often hit the ball to right field, the Orioles groundskeepers reportedly built right field at a slight downward angle, to better "cup" hits to that area.

"The Orioles," added Mathewson, "provided no topographical maps to visiting teams."

How to Doctor the Field

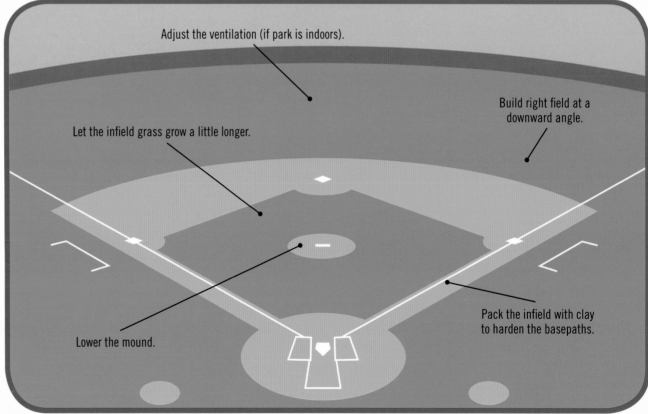

Adjust the ventilation (if park is indoors).

Build right field at a downward angle.

Let the infield grass grow a little longer.

Pack the infield with clay to harden the basepaths.

Lower the mound.

Thomas J. MURPHY

Baltimore Orioles, New York Giants 1894–1912

Murphy, in conjunction with Orioles manager Ned Hanlon, and later Giant skipper John McGraw, was among the first groundskeepers to deliberately alter the mound or the field for his team.

Emil "The Evil Genius" BOSSARD

Indians 1936–1960

Grandfather to Roger, Emil Bossard was recognized as the best-ever groundskeeper when it came to innovative ways of tailoring a ballpark to a specific team or player. Then Indians owner Bill Veeck called him "The Michelangelo of Groundskeepers."

Roger "The Sodfather" BOSSARD

Chicago White Sox, 1967–present

Bossard is the latest member of the Bossard clan, which includes his grandfather, Emil, and father, Gene, both of whom were groundskeepers for the Cleveland Indians and White Sox, respectively. Bossard himself has been a groundskeeper for 41 years and has designed and built many other ballparks in both the major and minor leagues. If Bossard doesn't know it, it's not worth knowing.

Hot Dogs and Other Refreshments

Chris Von der Ahe was born in Germany. In 1882, he knew almost nothing about baseball, but, being a beer distributor, he knew a lot about beer.

Von der Ahe also knew that baseball games drew lots of men. Men, he knew, liked to drink beer. So when Von der Ahe and three other Midwestern businessmen created the American Association (which was also called the Beer Ball League by some scoffers) to compete with the National League, he made sure there was a franchise in his town of St. Louis.

When his St. Louis Browns began operation, Von der Ahe was as concerned about the team's beer concession as he was about the team itself. He owned a saloon next to the Browns' ballpark and hired boys to haul buckets of beer to thirsty patrons. Soon after, he set up concessions in the park itself, and the Browns were one of the first franchises to send vendors into the stands.

In the 19th century, though, many cities and many owners were wary of selling beer. One of the reasons the old National Association (which ran from 1870 to 1876) folded was rowdiness in the stands. There was, for many years, controversy over the sale of the beverage, particularly on Sunday. But after Prohibition was repealed in 1930, the larger breweries began to forge relationships with the ball clubs. Baseball by then was as American as apple pie. Eventually, beer became a staple of the game.

These days, most teams stop the sale of beer after the seventh inning and limit the number of beers a fan can buy to two at a time, to try to control the flow to the fans. The last team to allow beer to be sold in ballparks was the Toronto Blue Jays. The province of Ontario refused to grant the team a liquor license, reportedly because the premier at the time, William Davis, had promised his mother he would not allow the sale of intoxicants at the park. When she died in 1982, however, Davis granted the license.

In 1880, another German entrepreneur from St. Louis, Antoine Feuchtwanger, began selling hot sausages in the streets. The problem was, people would burn their fingers trying to eat the sausages. Feuchtwanger provided white gloves for his patrons, but he soon began losing money, because the patrons were constantly walking off with the gloves. Eventually, his brother-in-law fabricated long soft rolls in which to put the sausages. Feuchtwanger was in business.

Several years later, in 1893, Von der Ahe reportedly heard about Feuchtwanger's "red hots" and introduced his own version at his ballpark. A few years later, New York concessionaire Harry M. Stevens, a vendor at the Polo Grounds, began selling sausages in specially made buns.

Ballparks had been selling peanuts to go with beer from probably around the time beer was actually introduced. It is difficult to trace when and where peanuts first appeared on the ballpark menu, but it was probably around 1885 or 1886. During that time, recogniz-

HARRY STEVENS

ing that young people also attended games, many parks also began selling soda pop.

At the turn of the century, sandwiches, tripe, onions, tobacco and pie were also offered in many parks.

Stevens was credited for actually naming hot dogs. Prior to 1902, they were called, believe it or not, "dachshund sausages." During an early April game in the Polo Grounds, sports cartoonist T. A. "Tad" Dorgan (1877–1929) was nearing his deadline and had still not found anything worth drawing.

But Dorgan heard the Stevens vendors shouting, "They're red hot! Get your red hot dachshund sausages here!" Dorgan quickly whipped up a picture of a sausage with four legs and a dachshund's head. Unsure how to spell dachshund, Dorgan captioned the picture, "Hot dog!" Stevens saw the drawing the next day, and "hot dogs" were born.

Cracker Jack, which is popcorn and peanuts covered with a caramel glaze, was introduced in 1893 at the World's Columbian Exposition, Chicago's first World's Fair, by candy maker F.W. Rueckheim and Brother. It was called at the time "candy popcorn."

The popcorn was popular, but the problem of how to keep the sticky caramel corn from bunching up into huge chunks was a considerable one. In 1896, Louis Rueckheim, F.W.'s brother, worked out a special oil to keep the popcorn separated. When he heard of the plan, an unnamed salesman with the firm said it was a "crackerjack idea." The Rueckheims trademarked the words that year.

Cracker Jack began showing up in major-league parks the next year, contained in a small cardboard box. They became hugely popular and, in 1908, Jack Norworth wrote "Take Me Out to the Ball Game." The third line, "Buy me some peanuts and Cracker Jack" immortalize the candy popcorn. In 1912, the company began putting little prizes inside the boxes.

Cracker Jack, by the way, has always been singular. At some point in its history, many people began calling the confection "Cracker Jacks."

This is a completely subjective list of the best food in various ballparks around the country, courtesy of a number of sportswriter and baseball fan friends and acquaintances.

HOT DOGS AND REFRESHMENTS

Boog's BARBEQUE

Oriole Park and Camden Yards, Baltimore

First baseman Boog Powell of the Orioles was a very good player. But his barbecued ribs and pulled pork are perhaps a greater contribution to the franchise than his hitting. Powell began this enterprise in 1993, and it remains one of the outstanding restaurants in big-league baseball. It doesn't hurt that Powell is often at the counter, ready and willing to dispense autographs with his barbecue.

Fenway FRANKS

Fenway Park, Boston

If you have to have a hot dog, you might as well travel to Boston. Yes, Nathan's Franks in New York are better known, and Los Angeles fans swear by their Dodger Dogs, but Fenway Park offers sweet, crisp hot dogs in a soft, chewy roll. The best, by the thinnest of margins.

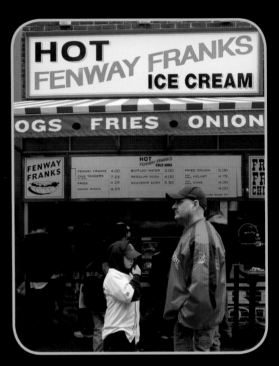

Rick's STEAKS

Citizens Bank Park, Philadelphia

Philly is the capital of the steak sandwich, so this is no surprise. But Rick's offers thick, juicy steak sandwiches that are the best in baseball.

Ivar's Grilled Salmon SANDWICH

Safeco Field, Seattle

This sandwich would be a delight in any five-star restaurant, so cheers to the Mariners organization for this offering. Lightly seared on the outside, fresh and pink on the inside. Perfect.

BRATWURST

Miller Park, Milwaukee

Milwaukee is the bratwurst capital of the world, so it's not shocking that the Brewers offer the best in the bigs. The Brewer brats are also festooned with the team's own secret sauce, a sweet-yet-biting concoction that makes the whole thing work.

HOW IT'S DONE
Hot Dogs and Refreshments

In the mid-1800s, ballparks that sold refreshments generally sold them from one spot near the entrance to the park. The term "hot dog stand" or any kind of a "stand" derives from the fact that patrons who purchased beer or hot dogs or peanuts in these areas had to stand by the counter and consume them. There were no benches or chairs for this purpose in the early ballparks.

Some teams, meanwhile, believed that a more proactive approach was needed to get refreshments into the hands of fans. As early as 1879, vendors were sent to traverse the stands with their wares, mostly beer and peanuts; hot dogs were introduced later. Nowadays, most ballparks have beer, soda, hot dogs and popcorn vendors, and also offer more exotic sandwiches, salads and drinks under the stands.

Vendors selling refreshments at Dodger Stadium (inset) and Yankee Stadium.

BIBLIOGRAPHY

Alexander, Charles C., "John McGraw", Penguin Books, New York, 1988.

Allen, Dick and Tim Whitaker, "Crash: The Life and Times of Dick Allen", Ticknor and Fields, New York, 1989.

Creamer, Robert W., "Babe, The Legend Comes to Life", Simon and Schuster, New York, 1974.

Frommer, Harvey, "Shoeless Joe and Ragtime Baseball", Taylor Publishing Co. Dallas, 1992.

Golenbock, Peter, "Red Sox Nation", Triumph, Chicago, 2005.

Golenbock, Peter, "Wrigleyville," St. Martin's, New York, 1996.

Hoyt, Waite, "Babe Ruth as I Knew Him, Dell Publishing, New York, 1948.

Halberstam, David, "The Summer of '49", William Morrow, New York, 1989.

James, Bill, "The New Bill James Historical Abstract," The Free Press, New York, 2001.

James, Bill and Neyer, Rob, "The Neyer/James Guide to Pitchers, Simon and Schuster, New York, 2004.

Kahn, Roger, "The Head Game", Harcourt, Inc., New York, 2000.

Lee, Bill and Dick Lally, "The Wrong Stuff," Viking Press, New York, 1984.

Leventhal, Josh, "Take Me Out to the Ballpark, Black Dog and Levanthal, New York, 2003.

Mack, Connie, "My 50 Years in Baseball", John C. Winston, Philadelphia, 1950.

Mathewson, Christy, "Pitching In A Pinch", Putnam, New York, 1912.

McGarigle, Bob, "Baseball's Great Tragedy: The Story of Carl Mays," Exposition Press, Jericho, NY, 1972.

Morris, Peter, "A Game of Inches: The Game on the Field", Ivan R. Dee, Chicago, 2006.

Morris, Peter, "A Game of Inches: The Game Behind the Scenes", Ivan R. Dee, Chicago, 2006.

Paige, Leroy, "Maybe I'll Pitch Forever," University of Nebraska Press, Lincoln, 1993.

Riley, James A. "The Biographical Encyclopedia of the Negro Leagues," Carroll and Graf, New York, 1994.

Ritter, Lawrence S., "The Glory of Their Times, William Morrow, New York, 1984.

Robinson, Ray "Iron Horse" W.W. Norton and Co., New York, 1990.

Ruth, Babe, with Bob Considine, "The Babe Ruth Story", Dutton, New York, 1948.

Shatzkin, Mike, "The Ballplayers," Idea Logical Press, New York, 1999.

The Sporting News, various editions, St. Louis, Missouri.

The Sporting News, Official Baseball Guides, various editions, St. Louis.

Sports Illustrated, various editions, Chicago, Ill.

Stout, Glenn and Johnson, Richard A., "Red Sox Century," Houghton Mifflin, New York, 2000.

Thomas, Henry W., "Walter Johnson, Baseball's Big Train", Phenom Press, Washington D.C., 1995.

Williams, Ted with John Underwood, "My Turn at Bat," Simon and Schuster, New York, 1969

Zumsteg, Derek, "The Cheater's Guide To Baseball", Houghton Mifflin, New York, 2007.

INDEX

Aaron, Henry "Hank," 108, 110, *110*, 187

Adams, Franklin P., 149

Alexander, Charles, C., 98

Alexander, Grover Cleveland, 32

Allen, Dick, 233

Alley, Gene, 151, *151*

Allison, Doug, 220

Alston, Walter, 209, *209, 210*

Altizer, Dave, 178

Andersen, Larry, 32

Anderson, Sparky, 206

Anson, Adrian "Cap," 10, 98, 102, 136, 154, 174

Ashford, Emmett, 202

Auker, Elden, 21

Babe (Creamer), 117

Bagwell, Jeff, *157*

ball(s)
    altering of, 79
    center of, 218
    hidden, 166–169
    history of, 218–224
    number of used, 219
    rubber, 180
    stitching on, figure-eight design, 219
    structure of, 218–219
    super, 182

Ball Four (Bouton), 66

ball, intentionally hit by, 170–179
    beginning history of, 170–172
    best of, 176–177
    body armor for, 170, 172
    mechanics of, 178
    records of players, 170
    statistics on, team, 173

ballfields, 226–245. *See also* stadiums
    artificial turf in, 232–233
    domed, 232
    environment of, controlled, 232–233
    evolution of, 228–233
    financial benefits from, 228
    fires and, 228
    multi-purpose of, 228
    stadium vs., 231

Baltimore Chop, 93

Barlow, Tom, 90, 166

Barnes, Clint, *62*, 126

Barnes, Ross, 93, 126, *126*, 127

Barr, George, 202

Barrett, Marty, 100, *100*, 168, *168*

Baseball (Orem), 234

baseballs. See ball(s)

baserunning, 124–145
    crashing into players and, 136–140
    home-run trot during, 140–145
    stealing bases and, 126–135

bat(s), 214–217
    aluminum, 216
    customized, 216
    equipment, 214–217
    evolution of, 214
    Heinie Groh, 215
    helmets, 216
    length of, 214–215
    Louisville Slugger, 215
    pine tar on, use of, 217
    shape of, 214–215
    titanium, 216
    width of, 215
    wood type for, 214

bat(s), corked, 180–185
    beginning history of, 180–183
    best of, 184
    hollowing out, 180
    materials used for, 185
    mechanics of, 185
    quality control for, 182

Baylor, Don, *89*, 170, 176, *176*

Beckert, Glen, 102

Beckett, Josh, 9, 18, *18*

Beckley, Jake, 128

Belanger, Mark, 150, *150*

Beltran,Carlos, *163*

Bench, Johnny, 223, *223*

Benitez, Armando, 17

Bennett, Eddie, 180

Biggio, Craig, 170, *171*, 177, *177*

Bird, Larry, 34

Blaeholder, George, 32

blazer. *See* fastball

Bloomberg, Ron, 107

Blyleven, Bert, 24, *24*, 29

body armor, 172

Bonaparte, Napoleon, 80

Bonds, Barry, *105*, 109, 111, *111*, 113, 129, 144, 187, 189, *189*, 192, *193*

Bonham, Ernest "Tiny," 44

Boozer, John, 74

Bossard, Emil "The Evil Genius," 241, *241*

Bossard, Gene, 239

Bossard, Roger "The Sodfather," 241, *241*

Boudreau, Lou, 178, 236

Bouton, Jim, 66

box score, 210

Brasnahan, Roger, 98, *225*

The Breaks of the Game (Halberstam), 19

Brett, George, *217*

Brock, Lou, *127*, 128, 130, *130*

Brown, Mordecai Centennial "Three Finger,"
    20, *20*, 26, *26*

Broxton, Jonathan, 17

Brush, John T., 71, 228

brushback. *See* knockdown

bunting, 90–98
    Baltimore Chop, 93
    beginning history of, 90–93
    best of, 94–96
    fair-foul in, 90
    mechanics of, 96
    sacrifice, 92
    trick hit, 90

Burdock, Jack, 166

Burkett, Jesse, 118, 119

Burnett, A.J., 17

Burns, Tommy, 92, *92*, 136, 148

Burr, Hartford, 27

Bush, "Bullet" Joe, 44, *45*

Cain, Matt, 97

Callaspo, Alberto, 166, *166*

Caminiti, Ken, *186*, 188, *188*

Candiotti, Tom, 66

Canseco, Jose, 186, 187, *187*, 188, *188*, 192

captains, 204

Carlton, Steve, 34, *34*

Cash, Norm, 184, *184*

catchers' equipment
    evolution of, 222–223
    flexibility of, 223
    mask's for, 223, 224
    padded blanket, 224
    protection from, 222–223
    shin guards, 225
    spikes, 225

catching, in outfield, 158–163
    basket catch, 162
    beginning history of, 158–159
    best of, 160–161
    fly balls, 158
    mechanics of, 163
    one-handed catch, 158
    reading batter and, 163
    snap catch, 162

Chadwick, Henry, 126, 204

Chamberlain, Joba, 17, *17*

Chance, Frank, 149, 170

changeup, 38–43
    beginning history of, 38–39
    best of, 40–41
    circle change and, 38
    eephus, 39
    mechanics of, 42
    slowball, 38

Chapman, Raymond, 56, *57*

Charleston, Oscar "The Hoosier Comet," 94,
    94

The Cheaters Guide to Baseball (Zumsteg), 182

Chesbro, Jack, 70, *70*, 76, *76*

Chylak, Nestor, *196*, 201, *201*

Cicotte, Eddie, 6, 64

Clemens, Roger, *11*, 13, 191, *191*, 192, *192*

Clemente, Roberto, *159*, 160, *160*, 162

clothing, protective. *See* body armor

coaches, college of, 102, 207

coaching. *See* managers

Cobb, Ty, *58*, 59, *94*, 95, 101, 119, 120, *120*,
    121, *123*, 126, 127, 130, *130*, *136*, 137,
    138, *138*, 215

Collins, Eddie, 95, *95*

Collins, Jimmy, 80

Combs, Earle, 93, 94, *94*

Comerica Park, *234*

Comiskey, Charlie, 126

Conlan, John "Jocko," 58, 201, *201*

Connolly, Tommy, 200, *200*

Coors Field, *234*

Corcoran, Larry, 10, *10*, 28

corked bats. *See* bat(s), corked

Corridon, Frank, 70, 72

Coughlin, Bill, *164*, 166, 168, *168*

Coveleski, Stan, 77, *77*, 79

Craig, Roger, 50, 52, *52*, 55

Crandall, James Otis "Doc," 80

crashing, into players, 136–140
    beginning history of, 136–137
    best of, 138
    holding onto ball and, 136
    mechanics of, 139
    running into baseballs, 137

Crawford, Sam, 101, *101*, 119, 126, 127, 128

Creamer, Robert, 93, 117

Crosley Field, 235, *235*

Cummings, Aurthur "Candy," 6, 22, *22*, 27, 28

Cuppy, George "Nig," 221

Curtis, Chad, 187

curveball, 22–31
    beginning history of, 22
    best of, 24–26
    fadeaway, 23
    invention of, 6
    knuckle, 64
    mechanics of, 27, 31
    nicknames for, 29, 31

cut fastball, 13

Cuthbert, Eddie, 126, 132

Cy Young Award, 35, 45, 86, 192

Daley, Arthur, 13

Dalkowski, Steve, 13, *13*

Damon, Johnny, 135

Dandridge, Ray, 100, *100*

Darling, Ron, *50*, 53, *53*

Davis, Harry, 155

Davis, William, 242

defensive shifts, 178

Delahanty, "Big Ed," 118, *118*, 119

Delavergne, Ben, 220

designated hitter, 107

Devore, Josh, 56

The Diamond Appraised (Wright), 221

Dibble, Rob, 17

Dickey, R.A., *65*

Dierker, Larry, 12

DiMaggio, Joe, 82, 134, 135, *135*, 141, *146*, 160, *160*, 163, 236

Dodger Stadium, *245*

domes
    astrodome, 232
    early history of, 232

double play, 3-6-3, 148

double play, 6-4-3, 148–153
    beginning history of, 148
    best of, 150–151
    mechanics of, 152
    19th century, 148
    20th century, 148

double steal, delayed, 126

drugs, performance-enhancing, 16, 109, 187.
    See also steroids

Drysdale, Don, 61, *61*, 63, 115, 172

Duffy, Hugh, 118, 119

Durocher, Leo, 74, 102

Earnshaw, George, *64*

Eckersley, Dennis, 29, 83

eephus, 39

Elston, Don, 207

equipment, 212–225
    baseballs, 79, 166–169, 170–179, 180, 182, 218–224
    bats, 214–217
    catchers', 222–225
    gloves, 220–221

Ericson, Dick, 239

Evans, Billy, *198*, 202

Evers, Johnny, 132, 148, 149, 158, *158*

Ewing, Buck, *222*

Faber, Urban "Red," 77, *77*

Face, Elroy, 47, *47*, 48

fadeaway curveball, 23

Fainaru-Wade, Mark, 187

Farnsworth, Kyle, 17

fastball, 10–21. *See also* split-finger fastball
    beginning history of, 10–12
    best of, 14–15
    cut, 13
    Dalkowski's, 13
    four-seam, 19
    live, 12
    sinker, 20
    speed of, 16–17
    submarine delivery, 21

Feller, Bob, *8*, 12, 13, 14, *14*, 28, 32, 34, *34*, 36

Fenway Park, *229*

Ferguson, Bob, *27*, *102*

Ferrell, Wes, 114, 115

fielding, 146–163
    catching in outfield, 158–163
    double play, 6-4-3, 148–153
    stretch, 154–157

Finch, Hayden "Sidd," 73

Fingers, Rollie, 83, *83*

Finley, Charles O., 133

Fisk, Carlton, 142, *142*

fly balls, 158

Ford, Edward "Whitey," 41, *41*, 77, *77*

forkball
    beginning history of, 44–45
    best of, 46–47
    mechanics of, 48

Fosse, Ray, *139*

four-seam fastball, 19

Fox, Nellie, 239

Foxx, Jimmie, 23, 108

Francona, Terry, 83, *206*, 207

Froemming, Bruce, 201, *201*

Gagne, Eric, 17

A Game of Inches (Morris), 38

Game of Shadows (Williams & Fainaru-Wade), 187

Garman, Mike, 50

Gehrig, Lou "Biscuit Pants," 21, 23, 88, 106, *106*, *140*, *154*, 155, 205

Gehringer, Charlie, 162

Giambi, Jason, *193*

Gibson, Bob, 34, 35, *35*, 60, *60*

Gibson, Josh, 107

Gibson, Kirk, 143, *143*

The Glory of Their Times (Ritter), 119, 127, 128, 172

gloves, 220–221
    evolution of, 220
    pockets in, 221
    protection by, 220
    superstitions, 221

Goldsmith, Fred, 27, 28

Golenbock, Peter, 50, 102, 136, 174

Gonzalez, Juan, 187, 190, *190*, 192

Gooden, Dwight "Doc," 25, *25*, 29, 31, *31*

Gordon, Joe, 150, *150*

Gore, George, 98

Gossage, Richard "Goose," 12, *12*, 83, *83*, 84, *84*

Gould, Stephen Jay, 122

Grant, Frank, 132, *132*, 225

Greenberg, Hank, 106, 108

Greenwood, Bill, 137

Grich, Bobby, 150, *150*

Grimes, Burleigh, 60, *60*, 73, 78

Gross, Kevin, 75

Grounds, Polo, 56

Grove, Lefty, 12, 14

Guidry, Ron "Louisiana Lightning," 32, 34, *34*, 37, *37*

Gullett, Don, 45, 47, *47*

Haefner, "Itsy Bitsy," *65*

Haeger, Charlie, 66

Haines, Jesse "Pop," 68, *68*

Halberstam, David, 19, 82, 206

Hall, Bert, 44

Hall, George, 112

Hamilton, Steve, 39

Hampton, Mike, 115

Hanlon, Ned, 236

Harris, Bucky, 82

Harvey, Doug, 200, *200*, 202

helmets, batting, 216

Henderson, Ricky, 99, *125*, 131, *131*, 141, 162, *162*

Herman, Billy, 151, *151*

Hernandez, Keith, *147*, 156, *156*

Herzog, Whitey, 178

hidden-ball trick, 166–169
  beginning history of, 166
  best of, 168
  mechanics of, 169
  records of, 166

Hildebrand, George, 70

Hillerich, John Andrew "Bud," 216

hit and run, 98–103
  best of, 100
  history of, 98
  invention of, 98
  managers role, 205
  mechanics of, 103
  pitchout, 98
  switch-hitting, 102

hitting, 88–123
  bunting, 90–98
  designated hitter, 107
  hit and run, 98–103
  hitting .400, 118–123
  home run, 104–117

hitting .400, 118–123
  average, 122
  beginning history of, 118–119, 122
  best of, 120–121
  mechanics of, 123
  19th-century and, 119
  20th-century and, 122

Hoffman, Trevor, 38, 39, *39*, 40, *40*, 85, *85*, 86

Hofheinz, Roy, 232

home run, 104–117
  beginning history of, 104–109
  best of, 110–111
  mechanics of, 117
  pitchers' numbers, 114–115
  power game, 106
  records, 112–113
  Yankee Stadium, 107

home-field advantage, 236–241
  beginning history of, 236–239
  best of, 241
  field's manipulations with, 239, 240
  mechanics of, 240
  molding fields and, 239

home-run trot, 140–145
  best of, 142–143
  cap tip, 140
  dance, 140
  low key, 140
  mechanics of, 145
  Piersall's reverse, 144
  showboat era, 141

hook slide, 134

Hooten, Bert, *64*

Hornsby, Rogers, *104*, 106, 118, 119, 120, *120*

hot dogs. *See* refreshments

Hough, Charlie, 66

House, Tom, 15

"How Good was Tinker to Evers to Chance?" (Adams), 149

Howard, Elston, *75*

Hoyt, Waite, 81, 104

Hrabosky, Al, 83, *83*

Hubbard, Cal, 74

Hubbell, Carl, 23, *23*

Hudson, Tim, 20

Hunt, Ron, 170, 176, *176*

Hurst, Tim, 128

Huston, Tillinghast, 230, 231

Jackson, Joe, 121, *121*, 123, 126

Jackson, Reggie, 107, *137*, 141

James, Bill, 10, 32, 44, 65, 80, 98

Jenkins, Ferguson, 12

Jenks, Bobby, 17, *17*

Jennings, Hughie, 93, 98, 170, 176, *176*

Jeter, Derek, *58*, 90, *91*, *103*, *169*

Johnson, Randy, 15, *15*, 17, 19, *19*, 32, 33, *33*

Johnson, Walter "The Big Train," 11, *12*, 14, *14*, 19

Johnstone, Jim, 202

Jones, Charley, 112

Juiced (Canseco), 187
Jurges, Billy, 151, *151*

Kahn, Roger, 40
Kaline, Al, 107
Keefe, Tim, 71
Keeler, Wee Willie, 93, *93*, 98, 101, *101*, *214*, 240
Kelly, Mike "King," 92, *92*, 98, *98*, 101, *101*, 128, 134, 136, 198
kelly slide. *See* hook slide
kelly spread. *See* hook slide
Kennedy, Ted, 222
Klem, Bill, 200, *200*, 202
knockdown, 56–63
    beginning history of, 56–59
    best of, 60–61
    mechanics of, 63
Knowles, Darold, 50
knuckle curve, 64
knuckleball
    beginning history of, 64–66
    best of, 68–69
    how to catch, 66
    invention of, 6, 64
    knuckle curve, 64
    mechanics of, 67
Koenig, Mark, 93
Koufax, Sandy, *28*, 28–29
Kraczyk, Jack, 42

Lajoie, Napoleon, 121, *121*, 122
LaRoche, Dave, 39
LaRussa, Tony, 204, *205*
Latham, Arlie "The Freshest Man on Earth," 90, 94, *94*, 126, *128*, 129
Leach, Tommy, *104*
Lee, Bill, 39, 155

Legree, Simon, 73
Lemon, Bob, *114*
Leonard, Dutch, 65
Leonard, Jeffrey, 144
Lewis, Alan, 132
Lieb, Fred, 231
Lindstrom, Matt, 17
live fastball, 12
Lowe, Derek, 20
Lowell, Mike, *165*, 166, *167*, 168, *168*, 169
lubricant(s), hidden location of, 79
Lugo, Julio, 148, *153*, 166
Lyle, Albert W. "Sparky," 32, 35, *35*, 83, 86, *86*

Mack, Connie, 132, 204, 208, *208*
Madden, Bill, 192
Maddux, Greg, 40, *40*
Maglie, Sal "The Barber," 25, *25*, 28, 59, 61, *61*, *63*
managers, 204–211
    beginning history of, 204–207
    best of, 208–209
    mechanics of, 211
    relief pitching and, 205
    role of, 204
    strategy of, 205
    taskmaster, 211
Mantle, Mickey, 107, 108
Manush, Heinie, 197
Maranville, Rabbit, 158
Marberry, Frederick "Firpo," 80, 81
Maris, Roger, 108, 109, 113
Marshall, Mike, 133
Martin, Alphonse "Phonney," 38
Martin, Billy, 102, 206
Martin, Fred, 50, *50*
Martin, Phonney, 27, 28
Martinez, Edgar, 107

Mathews, Bobby, 28, 71, *74*
Mathewson, Christy, 23, *23*, 56, 205, 240
Mattingly, Don, 156, *156*
Mays, Carl, 21
    deadly pitch of, *57*, *57*
    submarine "inside" pitch of, 56
Mays, Willie, 59, 110, *110*, 158, 159, 161, *161*
Mazeroski, Bill, 151, *151*
McCarthy, Joe, 27, *206*, 208, *208*, 210
McCarthy, Tommy, 98, 134
McCarver, Tim, 38
McClung, Seth, 17
McDaniel, Lindy, 82
McGinnity, Joe "Iron Man," 56, *56*, 60, *60*
McGraw, John, 56, 71, 80, 93, 98, 101, 133, *171*, 205, 208, *208*, 225, 231
McGwire, Mark, 108, *108*, 109, 113, 129, 186, 190, *190*
McLean, Billy, 196
McPhail, Larry, 82
Me and the Spitter (Perry), 75
Merriwell, Frank, 73
Mexican League, 50
Minoso, Minnie, 172
Mirabelli, Doug, 66
Mitchell, George, 192
Morgan, Joe, 16
Morris, Jack, 53, *53*
Morris, Peter, 38, 222
Mota, Guillermo, 17
Moyer, Jamie, 42, *42*
Munson, Thurman, 137
Murphy, Johnny, *81*, *82*, 98
Murphy, Thomas, J., 241, *241*
Myers, George, 137

National Association, 148
The National Game (Spink), 134

Negro Leagues, 12, 75, 107, 132

Nettles, Graig, *181*, 184, *184*

Newcombe, Don, *115*

Newsome, Bobo, 74

Neyer, Rob, 10, 32, 44

The Neyer/James Guide to Pitching (James & Neyer), 10

Nicol, Hugh, 126

Niekro, Phil "Knucksie," 66, 67, 69, *69*, 75

Niggeling, Johnny, *65*

night baseball, 234–235

Nomo, Hideo, 47, *47*, 48, *48*, *49*

O'Doul, Lefty, 119

Okajima, Hideki, 83

O'Leary, Catherine, 228

O'Leary, Patrick, 228

Oliva, Tony, 107

O'Loughlin, "Silk," 202

O'Malley, Walter, 232

O'Neill, Tip, 126, *174*

Orem, Preston D., 234

Orioles, Ned Hanlon, 93

Orth, Al "The Curveless Wonder," 21, 29, *29*

Ortiz, David "Big Papi," 107, 144, *145*, 172, *179*

Orwell, George, 192

Otis, Amos, 180, *181*

Overmyer, Jim, 132

Owen, Mickey, 222

Page, Joe, 82

Paige, Leroy "Satchel," 12, 41, *41*, 235

Palmeiro, Rafael, 187, 189, *189*, 192

Papelbon, Jonathan, 83, 86

Pascual, Camilo "Little Potato," 24, *24*, 28

Patten, Gilbert, 73

Pearce, Dickey, 90

Pedroia, Dustin, 148

Pena, Tony, 17

Pennock, Herbie, 81

Perez, Tony, 174

Perry, Gaylord, *71*, 74, 75, 76, *76*

Petrocelli, Rico, 155

Pettitte, Andy, 191, *191*, 192

Pfeffer, Fred, 148

Phillipe, Deacon, 21

Piersall, Jimmy, 144, *145*

Piez, Charles "Sandy," 133

pinch runners, 133

Piniella, Lou, 137

Pipp, Wally, 57

pitching. *See also* ball, intentionally hit by

    changeup, 38–43

    curveball, 22–31

    eephus, 39

    18th-century, 71

    fadeaway, 23

    fastball, 10–21

    forkball, 44–49

    four-seam fastball, 19

    home run numbers for, 114, 115

    knockdown, 56–63

    knuckleball, 64–69

    mythical, 73

    pitchout, 98

    relief, 80–87

    sinker, 20

    slider, 32–37

    spitball, 70–79

    split-finger fast ball, 50–55

    World War II, techniques popular during, 65

Pitching in a Pinch (Mathewson), 23, 56, 240

Podres, Johnny, 38

Potter, Nelson "Nels," 74

Povich, Shirley, 12

Puckett, Kirby, *239*

Pujols, Albert, *154*, 155

Quinn, Jack, 81

Quisenberry, Dan, 21, *21*, 86

Radcliffe, Ted "Double Duty," 75

Ramirez, Manny, *140*, 144

Ramsey, Jack, 19

Ramsey, Thomas A. "Toad," 64

Reardon, Jeff, 83, *83*

refreshments, 242–245

    beginning history of, 242–243

    best of, 244

    mechanics of, 244

relief pitching, 80–87

    beginning history of, 80–83

    best of, 84–85

    facial hair and, 83

    managers role and, 205

    mechanics of, 86

Reyes, Jose, 144

Richard, J.R., 17

Rickey, Branch, 132

Ritter, Lawrence S., 127, 172

Rivera, Mariano, *81*, 83, 84, *84*

Rizzuto, Phil, *95*, *95*, 150, *150*, 152

Robays, Maurice Van, 39

Robinson, Frank, 138, *138*

Robinson, Jackie, 58, 128, *129*, 130, *130*

Rodriguez, Alex, *145*

Rodriguez, Francisco, 86, *87*

Rodriguez, Ivan, 187, 190, *190*

Rodriguez, Javy, 83

Roe, Edwin Charles "Preacher," 38, 40, *40*

Rolen, Scott, 144

Rommel, Edward, *65*

Rose, Pete, 138, *138*, *139*

Rucker, George "Nap," 6, 64

Ruffing, Red, 114

Ruppert, Jacob, 230, 231

Russell, Bill, 137

Ruth, George Herman "Babe," 23, 73, 93, 102, 104, 106, 107, 108, 111, *111*, 112, 113, 117, *117*, 128, 140, 143, *143*, 180, 205, 215, 230, 231

Ryan, Nolan, 15, *15*, 17

Sallee, "Slim," *56*

Santana, Johan, 43, *43*

Score, Herb, 28, *28*

Scott, George "The Boomer," 155, 156, *156*

Scott, Mike, *52, 52*

screwball. *See* fadeaway curveball

Segar, Elzie Crisler, 73

Sewell, Luke, 180

Sewell, Truett Banks "Rip," 39, *39*

Sheckard, Jimmy, 104

Sheffield, Gary, 62, 189, *189*

Shocker, Urban, 26, *26*

Simmons, Curt, 20

sinker fastball, 20

Sisler, George, 119, 121, *124*

Sizemore, Ted, *163*

Slagle, Jimmy, 166

Sleeper Cars and Flannel Uniforms (Auker), 21

slider, 32–37

    beginning history of, 32

    best of, 34–35

    invention of, 32

    mechanics of, 36

sliding feetfirst, 132

slowball, 38

Smith, Lee, 85, *85*

Snider, Duke, 61, 144

Snodgrass, Fred, 172

Society for American Baseball Research, 93

Sosa, Sammy, 108, *108*, 109, *144*, 182, *183*, 184, *184*, 186

Spahn, Warren, 38, 114

Spalding, Albert, 38, 220, *220*

Speaker, Tris, 159, 160, *160*

Spink, Alfred, 134

spitball, 70–79

    beginning history of, 70–75

    best of, 76–77

    family of, 75

    invention of, 70

    mechanics of, 79

spliter. *See* split-finger fastball

split-finger fastball, 50–55

    beginning history of, 50

    best of, 52–53

    mechanics of, 55

stadiums, 226–245. *See also* ballfields

    ballpark vs., 231

    indoor, 232

stealing bases, 126–135

    beginning history of, 126–129

    best of, 130–131

    delay, 126

    "delayed double steal," 126

    hook slide, 134

    mechanics of, 135

    pinch runners and, 133

    skip play, 128

    sliding feetfirst, 132

Steinfeldt, Harry, 149

Stengel, Casey, 135, 206, 209, *209*

steroids, 109, 186–194

    allegations of, 186

    anabolic, 186

    best of, 188–191

    mechanics of, 193

    medicinal uses of, 192

    Olympic Games and, 186

    teenage use of, 192

    testosterone-based, 186

Stevens, Harry M., 242

Stewart, Dave, 45, 46, 48, *48*

Stovey, Harry, 111, *111*, 112

Strawberry, Darryl, 141

stretch, 154–157

Stricklett, Elmer, 70

submarine fastball, 21

The Summer of '49 (Halberstam), 82, 206

Summers, Ed, *64, 65*

Sutter, Bruce, 50, 51, *51*, 52, *52*, 55, *55*, 85, *85*

Swisher, Nick, *157*

switch-hitting, 102

Taylor, Luther "Dummy," 56

Tebeau, Patsy, 174

Tejada, Miguel, 191, *191*

Tekulve, Kent, 21, *21*

Tenace, Gene, *175*

Tenney, Fred, 148, 154, 156, *156*

Terry, Bill, 118, 119, *122*

testosterone-based steroids, 186

Thayer, Fred, 223

Thomas, Roy, 178

Thorpe, Jim, 28

Timlin, Mike, 83

Tinker, Joe, 149

Torre, Joe, 209, *209, 210*

Trachsel, Steve, 109

Trucks, Virgil "Fire," 24, *24*

Tucker, Tommy, 170

Tyng, James, 223

Uhle, George, 32

umpires, 194–203

beginning history of, 196–199
best of, 200–201
ejection's for mistreating, 197
hand signals, 203
mechanics of, 203
schooling for, 202
strike zones and, 199
two-umpire system, 198
uniforms, 198
Updike, John, 141, 228

Valentine, Bobby, 239
Varitek, Jason, 144
Verlander, Justin, 17
Von der Ahe, Chris, 242, *242*

Wagner, Billy, 17
Wagner, Honus, 127
Wakefield, Tim, 66, 68, *68*, 86
walks, intentional, 174–175
Wang, Chien-Ming, 20, *20*, 45, *45*
Ward, John J., 32
Warhop, Jack, 21
Washington, Herb, 133, *133*
Weaver, Earl, 180, 206
Webb, Brandon, 20
Welch, Curt, 137, 170
White, Sol, 132
Wilhelm, Hoyt, 69, *69*, 82, 223
Wilkinson, J.L., 234
Williams, Lance, 187
Williams, Matt, 166
Williams, Ted, 39, 118, 119, 120, *120*, 122, 123, *123*, 140, 141, 143, *143*
Williamson, Edward "Ned," 98, 112, 132, 148
Wills, Maury, 128, 131, *131*
Wilson, Earl, 114, 115, *115*
Wilson, Hack, *106*, 108

Wiltse, Hooks, 56, 80
Wohlers, Mark, 16
Wolff, Roger, 65
Wood, Wilbur, 66, 68, *68*
World War II, 65
Wright, George, 136, 180, *180*, 221
Wright, Harry, 38, *38*, 204, *204*, 208, *208*
Wrigley, P.K., 207, *207*
Wrigleyville (Golenbock), 102, 136, 174
The Wrong Stuff (Scott), 155

Yankee Stadium, 107, 228, 231, *245*
Yastrzemski, Carl, 59, 107
Youkilis, Kevin, 148
Young, Denton True "Cy," *10*, 11, 14, *14*, 80, *80*, 221
Young, Lemuel "Pep," 19

Zambrano, Carlos "The Big Z," 54, *54*, 55
Zito, Barry, 30, *30*
Zumaya, Joel, 16, *16*
Zumsteg, Derek, 182